ENTS

Introduction 5

Jane AUSTEN 7
J. G. BALLARD 12
Alan BENNETT 20
Maeve BINCHY 25
Charlotte BRONTË 32
Emily BRONTË 39
Dan BROWN 45
Bill BRYSON 50
Anthony BURGESS 56
John le CARRÉ 64
Lewis CARROLL 70
Raymond CHANDLER 76
Tracy CHEVALIER 82
Lee CHILD 89
Agatha CHRISTIE 95
Harlan COBEN 100
Roald DAHL 106
James ELLROY 114
J. G. FARRELL 122
Helen FIELDING 128
Ian FLEMING 134
Ford Madox FORD 140
Kenneth GRAHAME 147
Graham GREENE 152

John GRISHAM   157
Thomas HARDY   164
Robert HARRIS   169
Ernest HEMINGWAY   175
James HERBERT   181
James HERRIOT   187
Aldous HUXLEY   194
Howard JACOBSON   199
Stephen KING   205
Harper LEE   210
Elmore LEONARD   217
Hilary MANTEL   224
Andy McNAB   229
Michael MORPURGO   235
George ORWELL   241
Beatrix POTTER   247
Ian RANKIN   254
Ruth RENDELL   261
J. K. ROWLING   266
Salman RUSHDIE   273
C. J. SANSOM   279
Dr SEUSS   286
Georges SIMENON   292
Martin Cruz SMITH   297
Robert Louis STEVENSON   304
Evelyn WAUGH   310

Bibliography of Primary Sources   316
Acknowledgements   320

INTRODUCTION

Who hasn't dreamt of writing a bestseller?

For most of us, it will remain just a dream. Yet it is possible – even if you are an unknown author – to write a bestseller. The odds may be against it, but it has been done in the past and someone will do it in the future. Why not you?

There's no magic formula that guarantees success. No two authors work in exactly the same way or have the same views about writing. The learning points with which each chapter of this book concludes are different – and occasionally contradictory. What works for one author does not necessarily work for another. Writing is a personal, individual thing and we all have to find our own way of doing it. That usually means trial and error and lots of rewriting.

J. K. Rowling may be the UK's most successful living author, with sales in excess of £238 million, but her first Harry Potter book was rejected by no fewer than 12 publishers. When it comes to spotting the next bestseller, publishers have an abysmal track record; persistence in the face of repeated rejections is vital. Self-publishing is an option if you have the time and the skills to edit and market your book effectively. Whichever route to publication you choose, this book will improve your chances of success.

There is no shortage of how-to writing books. Some even claim to tell you how to write a bestseller, with chapters devoted to plotting, characterisation, dialogue and so on. This book is different. It doesn't tell you how to do it; it shows you how others have done it. Imitating the methods – rather than the content – of a favourite writer is an excellent apprenticeship for anyone who wants to master the craft of writing. It's how many of the most successful authors began.

Learning from an author you admire can help you to develop your own individual style.

For anyone who wants to write a bestseller, this book is the perfect starting point. But whatever your motivation for reading, enjoy the journey of discovery through 50 of the world's bestselling authors and the techniques that made them famous.

JANE AUSTEN

(1775–1817)

What does *Pride and Prejudice* mean to you? Does it evoke one of the best-known opening sentences in English literature? Or Colin Firth in a wet shirt?

Jane Austen is known as much from film and television adaptations of her novels as from the books themselves. She wrote six famous novels (*Sense and Sensibility*, *Pride and Prejudice*, *Mansfield Park*, *Emma*, *Northanger Abbey* and *Persuasion*) and is widely regarded as the originator of romantic comedy. Here I'll focus mainly on *Pride and Prejudice*, a book seen as the inspiration behind works as diverse as *Eugene Onegin* and *Bridget Jones's Diary*.

Today Jane Austen's novels are read all over the world. But soon after her death in 1817 they were out of print, and for the next 50 years she was largely ignored. Perhaps her restrained Regency romances (avoiding extravagant language, heightened emotions, dramatic situations and any but the sparest description) seemed old-fashioned compared with the novels of Dickens and Thackeray, then selling in their hundreds of thousands. It's a salutary reminder of how literary taste and fashion can change. They were reprinted in 1833, but for more than 30 years sales were negligible, with no more than 1,000 copies of each title being sold every eight years or so.

All that changed in 1870, when the first biography was published. This resulted in the first huge surge of interest in Austen's novels; the second huge surge was to come over a hundred years later with the burst of film and television adaptations in the 1990s.

Continuous improvement

Today Jane Austen is a towering figure of English literature, but she achieved popular success only posthumously. Her six famous novels were the result not of instinctive brilliance, but of trial and error and constant rewriting over a long period of time. A common error of novice authors is to submit work too soon. So it's worthwhile taking as much time as you need to review, revise and improve your manuscript before you expose it to the outside world. Be hard on yourself: make sure it's as good as you can possibly make it. Once you have sent it out, that's it; you won't be able to retrieve it and revise it.

Plotting

All six of Austen's famous novels revolve around what she described as 'three or four families in a country village', and the plots focus almost exclusively on courtship, marriage and money – and how young women (from the country gentry class of society) deal with the choices involved. Austen was the first popular English novelist to show how young women really think and behave.

With *Pride and Prejudice* Austen hit upon the archetypal romantic plot, used today by countless writers of romantic fiction. An independent-minded young woman meets an arrogant man and conceives an instant loathing for him. He is attracted, but refuses to acknowledge this even to himself. However, he can't help thinking about her. Eventually he shows, usually by some act of unselfishness or tenderness, that for all his strength and self-sufficiency, he has succumbed. The plot is simple but potent. It works in *Pride and Prejudice* because the heroine and the hero are sufficiently complex and capable of change to engage our interest and to make the vacillations between them convincing. Austen makes the eventual coming together of Elizabeth Bennet and Mr Darcy seem as inevitable as it once seemed unthinkable.

Characterisation

At the heart of *Pride and Prejudice* is the convincing characterisation of Elizabeth and Mr Darcy. They are presented very differently. While we are often inside Elizabeth's head, Mr Darcy remains on the periphery of our vision. He is aloof and difficult for anyone to know – and this heightens his appeal and our interest in him. Elizabeth laughs at the follies she sees around her, but she has inner strength and submits neither to an unsuitable suitor like Mr Collins nor to a powerful figure like Darcy's aunt Lady Catherine de Bourgh. She is determined to live a good and moral life. Of all Austen's heroines, Elizabeth is the one whose character is thought to be closest to that of the author.

Pride and Prejudice also has a raft of memorable comic characters, notably Mr Collins, Lady Catherine, and Elizabeth's parents Mr and Mrs Bennet. Mr Collins and Lady Catherine complement one another in their folly and stupidity. With his 'mixture of pride and obsequiousness, self-importance and humility' and his absurd eulogies of Lady Catherine, Mr Collins condemns himself out of his own mouth. His character is further exposed by the rapid switching of his attentions from Jane Bennet to Elizabeth, his farcical proposal to Elizabeth, and then his prompt shift from Elizabeth to her friend Charlotte Lucas.

Mr and Mrs Bennet also complement one another, as Mrs Bennet is too slow-witted to understand her husband's verbal wit and sarcasm masquerading as politeness. She is full of 'follies and nonsense, whims and inconsistencies', but she is motivated by a genuine concern for her daughters' future.

With *Emma*, Austen shows that a heroine does not need to be likeable to be compelling. Emma may be solicitous for the well-being of her father, but she is vain, snobbish and manipulative, as shown by her disastrous attempts to find her new friend Harriet a husband above her station in life.

Emma's disregard for the feelings of others is shown during the excursion to Box Hill, where Frank Churchill invents a game in which everyone has to make either one very clever, two moderately clever, or three dull remarks. When the garrulous but good-natured Miss Bates says, 'I shall be sure to say three dull things as soon as ever I open my mouth,' Emma can't resist interjecting, 'Ah! ma'am, but there may be a difficulty. Pardon me – but you will be limited as to number – only three at once.' When the meaning of this sinks in, Miss Bates is plainly hurt.

Irony

Jane Austen is famous for her irony, and that much-quoted opening sentence of *Pride and Prejudice* is an excellent example: 'It is a truth universally acknowledged, that a single man in possession of a good fortune, must be in want of a wife.' As we read on, it soon becomes clear that Austen means the precise opposite of this: it is single women without fortune (or their mothers) who are desperately looking for rich husbands. This gives us one definition of irony – stating the opposite of what is meant. Another, slightly different definition is a statement which has a double audience: when what is said means more than meets the ear, and one person hears and does not understand, while the other both understands what is meant and is aware of the other person's incomprehension.

Austen's irony comes in various disguises: sarcasm, wit, parody, ambivalence, caricature, hyperbole and understatement. She uses ironic humour to expose her characters' foibles – for example, when Miss Bates says, 'My mother's deafness is very trifling you see – just nothing at all. By only raising my voice, and saying anything two or three times over, she is sure to hear.' But the major irony in *Emma* is that the heroine is so busy trying to match-make that she doesn't realise she is in love herself. Only when she thinks that Harriet is to marry Mr Knightley does she realise that he is the man for her.

Sometimes the irony depends upon a disparity between appearance and substance, as seen in the characters of Willoughby (*Sense and Sensibility*), Wickham (*Pride and Prejudice*) and Mr Elliot (*Persuasion*). Willoughby's 'person and air' are 'equal to what [Marianne's] fancy had ever drawn for the hero of a favourite story', but he behaves like a cad. Disparity between what someone seems to be and what they really are is commonplace in today's fiction, but was less so in Austen's time and may have made her readers question their assumptions about what a hero should look like.

Moral values and social attitudes

By mocking some characters' assumptions and beliefs, Austen implicitly questions the social norms that fostered those assumptions and beliefs. She depicts a society where breeding and manners are all-important, and women are under monetary pressure to marry. In *Pride and Prejudice* she draws attention to inheritance laws involving the entailing of property along gendered lines, but she also pokes fun at the institutions of marriage and the family.

Critics and academics have given Austen different political labels: conservative, radical, feminist. Whatever her attitudes towards society, her novels are underpinned by a gentle, undogmatic morality – encapsulated in Mr Knightley's question to Emma: 'Does not everything serve to prove more and more the beauty of truth and sincerity in our dealings with each other?'

How Austen wrote

Writing poems and stories from an early age, Austen worked in a corner of the sitting room, subject to all kinds of casual interruptions. She wrote on small sheets of paper, which could be covered with a piece of blotting paper, and a creaking door alerted her when anyone was coming. The six famous novels were published between 1811 and 1818 (the last two posthumously), but she had been working on them for many years.

Completing initial drafts of the first two (which were to become *Sense and Sensibility* and *Pride and Prejudice*) some 15 years before publication, she was a constant rewriter. She lived with and developed her characters for most of her adult life. Her writing style, known as 'free indirect', combines third-person narrative with a character's inner voice.

The only drafts of any of Austen's novels to have survived are two manuscript chapters of *Persuasion*. Comparing these with the finalised, published chapters, it is clear that her writing was neither instinctive nor unerring. She improved her work through trial and error, and the wholesale changes made both to the story and the style show how much effort she was prepared to put into this.

Learning points

- Living with your fictional characters over a long period of time can help you to make them believable and distinctive.
- Irony in all its forms is a powerful ingredient of romantic comedy.
- Treat a first draft as raw material that needs to be worked on, possibly over many years. Be prepared to rewrite and rewrite and rewrite again.
- Use trial and error to find the right voice for your story.

J. G. BALLARD
(1930–2009)

Empire of the Sun (1984) was the international bestseller that catapulted J. G. Ballard to fame. It won the *Guardian* Fiction Prize, was shortlisted for the Man Booker and was later adapted by Tom

Stoppard for the film made by Steven Spielberg. Known initially for his science fiction, Ballard proved to be one of the world's most original and imaginative writers, producing genre-crossing work that mixed action adventure with science, psychiatry with surrealism and postmodernism with popular fiction.

Empire of the Sun

Ballard's bestseller is a semi-autobiographical novel based on the two and a half years he spent as a child in a Japanese internment camp outside Shanghai during World War Two. The book received glowing reviews. 'May well be that great British novel about the last war for which we've had to wait forty-odd years,' said the novelist Angela Carter. 'Significantly enough, there are no heroics – scarcely any combatants, in fact. Only a British schoolboy lost in Shanghai when the Japanese invade, a vast company of the doomed...' 'Horror and humanity are blended into a unique and unforgettable fiction,' said *The Sunday Times*.

Ballard had grown up in quasi-colonial style in a large upper middle-class house in Shanghai, tended by Chinese servants and Russian governesses. When the Japanese invaded in 1937, his family, like most European expatriates, were able to carry on their normal existence, despite occasional shelling around their house in the International Settlement. But in 1943 all 'enemy civilians' were interned and Ballard's family were put in the camp at Lunghua.

There are powerful descriptions of the violence and brutality of everyday life in 1930s Shanghai, where thousands of destitute Chinese had no social security of any kind and it was not uncommon to see dead bodies piled up in the street. But the most chilling passages are those depicting the cruelty of the war:

> The Japanese soldiers, Jim knew, would take ten minutes to kill the coolie... The whole display, like their lack of weapons, was intended

to show the British prisoners that the Japanese despised them, first for being prisoners, and then for not daring to move an inch to save this Chinese coolie.

Ballard said that for the purposes of his narrative he had reshaped incidents from his life, but that the general picture of Lunghua in *Empire of the Sun* is as he remembered it. Paradoxically, his time in the internment camp set him free. 'My upbringing was so middle class and repressed,' he said. 'It wasn't until I was placed in Lunghua that I met anyone from any other social strata. When I did I found them colossally vital.' He was especially struck by the optimism and free-and-easy ways (with 'no stiffness or class-consciousness') of a group of American merchant seamen interned in the camp.

Empire of the Sun ends with the hero, Jim, reunited with his parents and returning to their house in Amherst Avenue. But his time in the camp has changed him for ever:

> To his surprise he felt a moment of regret, of sadness that his quest for his mother and father would soon be over. As long as he searched for them he was prepared to be hungry and ill, but now that the search had ended he felt saddened by the memory of all he had been through, and of how much he had changed. He was closer now to the ruined battlefields and this fly-infested truck, to the nine sweet potatoes in the sack below the driver's seat, even in a sense to the detention centre, than he would ever be again to his house in Amherst Avenue.

How he began writing

In 1946 Ballard was repatriated to England. The change from a world of warfare, death and political upheaval to one of bourgeois comfort was a culture shock. He attended the Leys School in Cambridge and then studied medicine at King's College, Cambridge with a view to becoming a psychiatrist. He discovered 'modernist' writers such as Hemingway, Joyce, Dostoyevsky, Kafka and Camus. He developed an early interest in psychoanalysis and surrealism, and came to believe that these 'were a key to the truth about existence and the human personality and also a key to myself'.

After two years studying medicine, he realised that what he really wanted to do was to write. He then read English at Queen Mary College, University of London, but he left after the first year and started to earn a living with short-term jobs – Covent Garden flower market porter, advertising copywriter, door-to-door encyclopaedia salesman – and began to submit stories – unsuccessfully – to literary magazines. Obsessed since childhood with aircraft and flying, he then spent a year as a trainee pilot with the RAF, much of it at a frozen airfield in Canada. Here he discovered American science-fiction magazines. These made a lasting impression and proved to be a turning point in his development as a writer.

Science fiction

In 1955, awaiting discharge from the RAF, he wrote his first science-fiction story, 'Passport to Eternity' (eventually published in 1962), in emulation of US writer Jack Vance. His first science-fiction success was 'Prima Belladonna', published in *Science Fantasy* (1956). In the late 1950s/early 1960s he worked as a librarian and as a scriptwriter for a scientific film company before becoming assistant editor of a weekly science journal, *Chemistry and Industry*. In 1959 *Naked Lunch* by William S. Burroughs was published, mixing science fiction with experimental fiction, and this was an important influence. Ballard had more than 20 short stories published in science-fiction magazines including, in 1960, 'The Voices of Time', a story set in desert landscapes in a near-future world situated in a larger, declining universe. His first novel, *The Wind from Nowhere,* was published in 1961, whereupon he gave up his job at *Chemistry and Industry* to write full time. Written in ten days, he later dismissed it as 'a piece of hack work' and preferred to regard *The Drowned World*, published in 1962 to wide acclaim, as his first novel.

Ballard's science fiction has none of the spaceships or aliens often associated with the genre. His first four novels each depict the destruction of civilisation by some elemental disaster – respectively Water, Air, Fire and Earth. *The Drowned World* gives us a remarkable foretaste of the possible effects of global warming, as the ice caps melt in the wake of a solar storm, which heats up the planet, and cities are flooded. Plant and animal life change as they adapt to the watery environment:

> In response to the rises in temperature, humidity and radiation levels the flora and fauna of this planet are beginning to assume once again the forms they displayed the last time such conditions were present – roughly speaking, the Triassic period. Everywhere … countless mutations completely transforming the organisms to adapt them for survival in the new environment.

The main characters in these early science-fiction novels are usually scientists, who often live in abandoned hotels, ignore danger and prefer the destroyed civilisations to the living cities in which they grew up.

Surrealism

Ballard was heavily influenced by surrealist painters such as Max Ernst, Salvador Dalí and Paul Delvaux. 'The surrealists have been a tremendous influence on me,' he said in 1984. 'They've certainly played a very large part in my life, far more so than any other writer I know. Sometimes I think that all my writing is nothing more than the compensatory work of a frustrated painter.'

His most famous (some would say infamous) novel of the 1970s was *Crash* (1973), a highly controversial book which has been categorised as transgressive fiction (i.e. going beyond accepted limits). It was based on the extraordinary theory that only through car crashes can humans achieve true eroticism. The publisher's reader who first saw the manuscript famously commented, 'This author is beyond psychiatric help. Do not publish!'

Diverse influences

From his early interest in psychoanalysis to his fascination with surrealism, Ballard believed his writing owed more to these than to any literary influence. Consider how your own interests and enthusiasms can stimulate your writing. For example, if you enjoy cooking exotic meals, perhaps the origins of the ingredients will get your creative juices flowing and feed into your writing. If you're in need of inspiration, don't limit yourself to the books you've read. Be open to all kinds of influences and experiences.

Miracles of Life

The autobiography *Miracles of Life* (2008) was written after Ballard was diagnosed as suffering from advanced prostate cancer. 'If there's a better memoir by a contemporary English writer, I don't know it,' said *The Daily Telegraph*'s reviewer, while the *Financial Times* described it as 'exquisitely written' and 'Ballard's crowning achievement'. It's fascinating to compare this non-fiction account of his life with the fictionalised versions in *Empire of the Sun* and its sequel *The Kindness of Women* (1991). As *The Observer* put it, 'A particular delight of this lyrical autobiography lies in spotting the landscapes and events that appear, subtly reconfigured, in Ballard's fiction.'

Writing routine

For almost 50 years Ballard wrote on an old dining-room table against the wall of a downstairs room in his semi-detached house in Shepperton, Surrey. He wrote every day, five days a week, two hours in the late morning and another two in the early afternoon, usually working to a target of 700 words a day. He then went for a walk, when he would think about the next day's writing.

Everything Ballard wrote was always well-prepared in his mind beforehand. He usually began by writing a sheaf or two of notes, covering everything from the main themes to the details of the setting, the principal characters, and so on. He then wrote a synopsis. For short stories this was quite brief – not much more than a page. The purpose was to find out whether or not the story worked as a dramatic narrative. Would it grip the reader's imagination? In the case of novels, the synopsis was much longer and more detailed. For *High-Rise* (1975) it ran to some 25,000 words (he later thought it better than the completed novel, and regretted having destroyed it). It usually took him between a year and 18 months to write a novel.

He wrote a complete first draft in longhand, keeping to the structure of his detailed synopsis, before doing any revising or editing. He then went back to the beginning and started work on 'a very careful longhand revision of the text'. This involved cutting superfluous phrases and paragraphs (and occasionally pages). He then typed out a final manuscript.

After Ballard's wife died suddenly in 1964, he single-handedly brought up his three children. In *Miracles of Life* (2008) he says that this helped rather than hindered his writing:

> My children were at the centre of my life, circled at a distance by my writing. I kept up a steady output of novels and short story collections, largely because I spent most of my time at home. A short

story, or a chapter of a novel, would be written in the time between ironing a school tie, serving up the sausage and mash, and watching *Blue Peter*. I am certain that my fiction is all the better for that.

Ballardian

Ballard's characters have typically abandoned themselves to personal obsessions, and the stories are played out against a backdrop of dark, surreal landscapes and recurring images: drained swimming pools, flooded or burned cities, billboard hoardings, infested swamps and jungles, abandoned hotels and hospitals, crashed cars, buried aeroplanes, high-rise apartment blocks.

The distinctiveness of his work has given rise to the adjective Ballardian, defined in *Collins English Dictionary* as 'resembling or suggestive of the conditions described in Ballard's novels and stories, especially dystopian modernity, bleak manmade landscapes, and the psychological effects of technological, social, or environmental developments'.

I'll conclude with Ballard's own words: 'My novels offer an extreme hypothesis which future events may disprove – or confirm. They're in the nature of long-range weather forecasts.'

Learning points

- Go over what you plan to write in your own mind before you put pen to paper or fingers to keyboard.
- Establish a regular writing routine that fits in with family or other commitments.
- Draw on your own life experiences, interests and enthusiasms.
- Writing a synopsis before you embark on a story can enable you to see whether or not it will work.
- Improve your manuscript by cutting superfluous phrases, paragraphs and even pages.

ALAN BENNETT

(1934–)

A spoof Anglican sermon got Alan Bennett started. Put together in half an hour, it earned him his place, alongside Peter Cook, Dudley Moore and Jonathan Miller, in *Beyond the Fringe*, the satirical revue, first performed at the 1960 Edinburgh Festival, which ran for three and a half years in the West End and New York.

Beyond the Fringe showed that Bennett could write material that made people laugh. But he wanted to develop a more nuanced skill – the ability to make the audience laugh one minute and cry the next. That is what he succeeded in doing with his first play, *Forty Years On* (1968), in which a headmaster who is about to retire attends his public school's end-of-year entertainment. This turns out to be a satirical look at England's 'progress' during the first 40 years of the twentieth century and provokes an outraged reaction from the headmaster who sees everything he has believed in being mocked. This play within a play is a parody, but it also shows the misunderstanding of one generation by another and nostalgia for a more peaceful age.

Affection and scepticism

Forty Years On is clever, funny and poignant – three words that can be applied to almost everything Bennett has written; its combination of affection and scepticism epitomises his attitude to England and its institutions. For more than 50 years this has been a recurrent theme of his writing.

Alan Bennett is not only one of our best-loved writers; he is also one of the most versatile: sketch-writer, playwright, screenwriter, diarist, short-story writer, essayist, reviewer, lecturer, broadcaster, humorist (to say nothing of Bennett the actor). Frequently dubbed a 'national treasure' (an epithet he is said to dislike), he seems the most English of writers. So what is it about his writing that strikes a chord with so many people?

Tone and dialogue

Part of the explanation may lie in Bennett's self-deprecating tone. Here's a nice example: 'I'm sent a copy of Waterstones' Literary Diary which records the birthdays of various contemporary figures… Here is Dennis Potter on 17 May, Michael Frayn on 8 September, Edna O'Brien on 15 December, and so naturally I turn to my own birthday. May 9 is blank except for the note: "The first British self-service launderette is opened on Queensway, London, 1949".'

From an early age Bennett felt that life ('that awkward gap between the cradle and the grave') 'is generally something that happens elsewhere'. In 2003 he notes in his diary, 'I walk back through the streets of Oxford and as always I have a sense of being shut out and that there is something going on here that I'm not a part of; not that I was part of it, even when I was part of it.' This feeling of being an outsider ('an impostor in the literary world') translates into characters in his plays who are often the overlooked or the downtrodden – people the English, with their instinctive sympathy for the underdog, can recognise and to whom they can relate.

He has an ear for authentic dialogue – and especially for the speech rhythms of the north, where in Bennett's experience 'women did most of the talking'. As one critic has said, 'He writes the way people talk. When you see his plays you think "Oh I know her. She lives down the street".' Or, as another put it:

> Bennett's ear for the way people reveal themselves through the words they utter is mercilessly exact, and yet, having exposed them so precisely for what they are, he accepts them with understanding and generosity at exactly that valuation.

One of Bennett's techniques is to juxtapose the mundane with the tragic or the comic in a way that seems to reflect – and at the same time gently to mock – real life: 'I am having supper at The Odeon [in New York] when word goes round the tables that John Lennon has been shot. "This country of ours," sighs the waiter. "May I tell you the specials for this evening?"'

Perhaps Bennett's ability to make his audience laugh one minute and cry the next is seen at its best in his *Talking Heads* monologues written for BBC television in 1987 (a second series appeared in 1998). These are rooted in reality, with character traits and occurrences that are often based on people and events in Bennett's own life.

> **Real talk**
>
> Bennett's ear for the way people really speak was honed early on by copying down phrases he heard as he made his trolleybus journey to school. If you want to write authentic dialogue, get into the habit of carrying a notebook (or an iPad) and making a note of interesting snippets of conversation you overhear. Listening not just to the words but also to the speech patterns and turns of phrase of people from different parts of the country, different professions and different social classes will help you to make your characters sound like real, believable human beings.

Making mountains out of molehills

'A writer has to use whatever is to hand in the way of experience,' says Bennett. 'He or she is in the business of making mountains out of molehills.' He puts a lot of his own life into his writing, sometimes giving characters in his plays lines he heard spoken by his parents. 'By, you've had some script out of me,' his mother once said. His life is mined most explicitly in his three collections of prose, *Writing Home* (1994), *Untold Stories* (2005) and *Keeping On Keeping On* (2016) – treasure troves for anyone who is interested in autobiographical non-fiction.

Some of the same material was used in his monologue *Hymn* (2002) and the short play *Cocktail Sticks*, which opened to great acclaim at the National Theatre in 2012. The latest collection, *Keeping On Keeping On*, is full of witty, finely observed anecdotes and breathtaking turns of phrase, such as his description of 'fairy rings of polyps, innocent enough but ruthlessly lassoed and garrotted by the radiographer'. It shows that Bennett's ability to entertain and surprise his readers is undiminished.

It's a bit of a surprise when Bennett says: 'You don't put yourself into what you write. You find yourself there.' He goes on to explain: 'A writer does not always know what he or she knows, and writing is a way of finding out.' So it's the actual process of writing – the hard slog of putting one word after another down on paper or on to your computer screen – that helps you to discover yourself.

The Lady in the Van

In 1974 Bennett allowed an eccentric old lady who was living in a van parked in his street in Camden Town to move the van into his front garden. It was to remain there until she died in 1989. He did not always feel generous: 'One seldom was able to do her a good turn without some thoughts of strangulation.' Allowing such an intrusion into his life seems the epitome of English accommodation, but 'allow isn't quite the word', says Bennett. 'I was just faced with her – it was like Eleanor Roosevelt moving in! I just got used to it. I know this sounds odiously modest, but I don't think it needed much goodness. It's more laziness. Just as you can do harm by being lazy, you can do some good as well.'

Some years after Miss Shepherd's death Bennett wrote his play *The Lady in the Van* (1999), in which two Alan Bennetts, played by different actors, reflect his own conflicting attitudes:

There was one bit of me (often irritated and resentful) that had to deal with this unwelcome guest camped literally on my doorstep, but there was another bit of me that was amused by how cross this eccentric lodger made me and that took pleasure in Miss Shepherd's absurdities and her outrageous demands.

By dividing the character into two parts, Bennett shows the clash between the private person and the writer. When the two Bennetts fear that Miss Shepherd has died, the private Alan Bennett hangs back: 'Give over. This could be really sad.' But Bennett the writer elbows him out of the way: 'I know. I can't wait!' It is the writer who holds sway.

Writing regime

Bennett began writing by furtively copying down phrases he overheard into a notebook, and he served his apprenticeship by writing sketches. 'I still write in three-minute bursts so that beneath the most elevated stretch of dialogue or description lie buried the breeze blocks of revue.' He writes, usually from about 10.30 a.m. until 5 p.m., at a table in his front room overlooking the street. He has no computer or word processor, just a manual typewriter. His diary is written in longhand on loose-leaf sheets: 'A year's entries make a pretty untidy bundle. The writing is often untidy too; immediacy in my case doesn't make for vivid reporting, which is why I've not had any scruples about improving and editing, though I've never altered the tone or the sentiments of what I've written at the time.'

Bennett's play *The Habit of Art* is about an imagined meeting between W. H. Auden and Benjamin Britten. It opened in November 2009 at the National Theatre, original venue for Bennett's plays *The Madness of George III* (1991) and *The History Boys* (2004). In the latter Hector, the eccentric schoolmaster, tells his sixth-formers:

The best moments in reading are when you come across something
– a thought, a feeling, a way of looking at things – which you had

thought special and particular to you. Now here it is, set down by someone else, a person you have never met, someone even who is long dead. And it's as if a hand has come out and taken yours.

If you've had that experience, you'll know that it's a lovely feeling.

Learning points

- A writer has to use whatever experience is to hand.
- Writers are in the business of making mountains out of molehills.
- Don't wait for perfectly formed ideas before you put pen to paper or fingers to keyboard. The process of writing itself can help you to discover yourself and to find out what you know.
- Try to find the tragic or the comic in the mundane content of everyday life.

MAEVE BINCHY
(1939–2012)

'The queen of Irish popular fiction' was how one obituarist described Maeve Binchy. Her debut novel, *Light a Penny Candle* (1982), sold for £52,000, the highest sum ever paid for a first novel. Her books have sold more than 40 million copies worldwide and have been translated into 37 languages, outselling those of such eminent Irish writers as James Joyce, Seamus Heaney, Edna O'Brien and Roddy Doyle. In a poll for Britain's favourite authors, carried out for World Book Day in 2000, she finished ahead of Stephen King, Charles Dickens and Jane Austen.

Binchy wrote 16 novels. They are notable for their easy readability – short sentences, lots of dialogue and compulsive storytelling that keeps the reader turning the pages. There are sympathetic portrayals of the everyday lives of ordinary people, with strong characterisation, convincing depiction of women's friendships and evocative settings, often involving Irish village life. She was also a journalist, playwright and short-story writer.

How she began

As a child she was surrounded by books, and her parents encouraged her to read widely. She was educated at Holy Child Convent in Killiney and University College Dublin, where she obtained a BA in history. She went into teaching and taught history, French and Latin at various girls' schools. One holiday she went to Israel and worked for a short time in a kibbutz. From there she wrote regularly to her parents, telling them about life in the kibbutz. Her father was so taken with these letters that he cut off the 'Dear Daddy' bits and sent them to an Irish newspaper, which accepted them for publication.

This led to regular travel writing for newspapers and five years later she gave up her job as a teacher to become a full-time freelance journalist. In 1968 she was offered a job on *The Irish Times* as columnist and editor of its first Women's Page; she subsequently became the paper's London editor. Her report in 1973 of the wedding of Princess Anne and Captain Mark Phillips lacked the reverence of conventional accounts: 'The bride looked as edgy as if it were the Badminton Horse Trials and she was waiting for the bell to gallop off.'

After she became a famous novelist many of her Irish contemporaries still saw her first and foremost as the irreverent *Irish Times* columnist, with her amusing take on Irish life and her endearing habit of 'puncturing pomposity'. On *Desert Island Discs* in 1990 she said that the thousands of people who read *The Irish Times* were more important to her than the millions who read her novels.

Binchy's first book, published in 1970, was a compilation of her newspaper articles, entitled *My First Book*. She began to write fiction in spare moments and got into the habit of staying on in her London office to write from 6 p.m. to 8 p.m. after everyone else had gone home. Her first successes were two books of short stories, *Central Line* (1978) and *Victoria Line* (1980).

Light a Penny Candle

Her first novel, *Light a Penny Candle*, written when she was in her early 40s, was rejected by five publishers before the sixth one she approached took it on. She later described her five rejections as 'a slap in the face', but she recognised that they had taught her the importance of perseverance.

As with all her novels, there is a page-turning story with sympathetic characters and a strong sense of place. We meet many of the character types that populate her subsequent books, such as the capable wife, the feckless charmer, the village gossip and the good but blundering father. We are also introduced to some of Binchy's favourite themes, such as the parent–child relationship, the illusion of romance and the problems of conflicting cultures and lifestyles.

The novel, set in small-town Ireland and war-weary England during and after World War Two, is the story of a friendship between Aisling, a bold and outgoing Irish Catholic, and Elizabeth, a quiet English evacuee. The two girls form a bond that endures long after the war is over. We follow them over a period of some 20 years through love affairs and failed marriages, as two different worlds collide and their lives remain intertwined.

Circle of Friends

Circle of Friends (1990), regarded by some critics as Binchy's best novel, is about the lives and loves of three women coming of age at University College Dublin. The plot revolves around the friendship between Benny, an overweight, big-hearted girl who needs to break away from her small-town parents, and Eve, brought up by nuns after her disgraced mother's upper-class family rejects her. Again two worlds are juxtaposed: professional, upper middle-class Dublin and a small country town. The strength of the novel lies partly in the convincing portrayal of Benny, who loses in love but grows as an individual and learns that she can be a person in her own right.

Tara Road

Tara Road (1998) is the interlocking story of two women who have virtually nothing in common. Ria lives in a fashionable part of Dublin in a large house which is always full of family and friends; Marilyn is a self-contained academic from New England who keeps herself to herself. With each of them facing a crisis in their personal life, they both need a place to escape to, and they agree to swap homes for the summer. The experience has a profound effect on both of them, with each woman's life opening a window on to the other's. It's hard to imagine two more unlikely friends, but by the time they eventually meet that's exactly what they have become.

How she wrote

While working in London Maeve Binchy met Gordon Snell, a BBC producer, and they married in 1977. The couple encouraged each other's writing and Snell went on to become a children's author. When they moved back to Ireland they wrote on twin typewriters next to one another in the same room. 'The discipline of another writer sitting beside you makes you work,' said Binchy. At the end of each session they showed each other their work. The rule was that they had to tell the absolute truth. Then there would be what they called 'sulking time': ten minutes for each of them to decide whether the other's criticism would be taken on board or the original justified and retained.

Binchy was a consummate, highly organised planner. Each novel had its own file, notebooks, timelines, headings and lists. First she would sit down and write an outline of the story, usually running to some six or seven pages. The purpose was to be clear in her own mind about exactly where the story was going. The outline was sent off and as soon as she heard that the publisher liked it, she set to work.

She wrote details of each character, beginning with the birthday, on a large cardboard sheet. 'I try to make my characters kind of ordinary, somebody that anybody could be,' she said. 'Because we've all had loves, perhaps love and loss, people can relate to my characters… Sometimes they say to me, "I felt just like that."' She saw her characters as real people and did not hesitate to put the same one into a second novel if she felt this would help the story. She often drew a map of the location where the action was to take place. As soon as a character was introduced they would be given a house on the map, marked with the character's name. Hotels, pubs, shops would go on it too, as the whole village (or other locality) took shape. Finally she prepared time charts logging the duration of the writing and the number of words she needed to write each day. Between 800 and 1,600 words was the norm.

Write as you speak

'Always write as if you are talking to someone' was the advice Binchy would give to aspiring writers. 'It works,' she said.

> Don't put on any fancy phrases or accents or things you wouldn't say in real life… I write exactly as I speak. I don't say I was 'proceeding down a thoroughfare', I say I 'walked down the road'. I don't say I 'passed a hallowed institute of learning', I say I 'passed a school'. You're much more believable if you talk in your own voice.

A colleague who worked with her on *The Irish Times* in London in the 1970s said: 'I would find her typing at speed and handing the first draft to the telex operator before heading off for one of her long lunches. She dared not re-read the copy, she said, or she would spend the day rewriting it... Her natural talent for storytelling was such that she wrote just the way she spoke.' As the author Marian Keyes put it, she 'wrote books that read as fluidly as a conversation with an old friend who had lots of news.'

Binchy explained in the *Irish Independent* why the Irish were often thought of as natural writers: 'We don't like pauses and silences, we prefer talk and information and conversations that go on and on. So that means we are halfway there.' Like James Joyce and Charles Dickens – the two writers whose work she loved and who influenced her most – she was interested in ordinary people and the minutiae of their everyday lives. She eavesdropped on conversations in restaurants and on buses, and even learned to lip-read.

Everyday life

Careful observation of the habits of the people you come across in your daily life can help you to create believable characters the reader can relate to – especially if you write in the kind of informal, spontaneous way in which you would talk to a friend. We are always interested in seeing how other people live. However mundane it may seem, the routine of other people's everyday lives can be extraordinarily interesting.

Themes

It's probably a mistake to categorise Binchy as a romantic novelist. In her books the heroine does not usually end up with her Prince Charming.

Neither does she become rich. Typically she learns to live without her prince and to take control of her own life. As she put it herself:

> There are no makeovers in my books. The ugly duckling does not become a beautiful swan. She becomes a confident duck able to take charge of her own life and problems.

Her novels address issues such as child–parent relationships, betrayal, tensions between rural and urban life, and transformations in Irish cultural and religious life. There are faithless lovers, straying husbands, alcoholism, drug addiction, unwanted pregnancies and occasional violence.

She left sex to the reader's imagination. 'There's a huge interest in sex and writing about it very graphically,' she told the *Daily Mail* in 2007. 'But I am not going to do it – not because I'm a Holy Joe, far from it. Not because I'm very moral, far from that. But because I'm afraid I'll get it wrong.' She added, 'You see, I've never been at an orgy and I wouldn't know where legs should be and arms should be.'

Learning points

- Don't let rejections discourage you from writing.
- Begin by writing an outline of the novel you intend to write.
- Write the way you speak.
- Eavesdrop on conversations in restaurants, buses and other public places.
- Create ordinary characters the reader can relate to.

CHARLOTTE BRONTË
(1816–1855)

Published in 1847, *Jane Eyre* was a literary sensation. Despite its orthodox romantic structure (attraction, impediment, final marital resolution), it was a revolutionary novel. How did this quiet parson's daughter, whose social circle centred almost exclusively on her father's profession, come to produce one of England's greatest works of fiction? She completed four novels (*The Professor, Jane Eyre, Shirley* and *Villette*), but I'll concentrate on the one that made her famous, *Jane Eyre*.

Beginnings

In 1820, at the age of four, Charlotte, the third of six children, moved with her parents and siblings from Thornton, near Bradford, to Haworth, where her father had been appointed perpetual curate. Four years later she was sent, with her sisters Maria, Elizabeth and Emily, to the Clergy Daughters' School at Cowan Bridge in Kirkby Lonsdale, Lancashire. After less than a year there both Maria and Elizabeth died of tuberculosis, and Patrick Brontë removed Charlotte and Emily from the school.

It was after her return from Cowan Bridge that Charlotte and her surviving siblings, Branwell, Emily and Anne, began to create their imaginary fictional worlds. Branwell and Charlotte wrote episodic sagas about the inhabitants of their imagined kingdom of Angria, while Emily and Anne wrote articles and poems about Gondal. These provided Charlotte and her siblings with an obsessive interest that sustained them throughout their childhood and early adolescence. This was their writing apprenticeship. Some of the tiny manuscripts they produced can be seen in the Brontë Parsonage Museum in Haworth. Amazingly, the total length of this Brontë juvenilia – and Charlotte was the principal author – exceeds that of their published works.

In 1831 Charlotte continued her education at Roe Head School in Mirfield, Yorkshire, where she worked hard and made some good friends (something which, like her sisters, she never found easy). A year later she returned home, becoming, at 16 years old, the first superintendent of the Sunday School established by her father. Although at this time her ambition was to become an artist (the drawings which have survived demonstrate a high level of technical skill), she wrote prodigiously during the three years after her return from Roe Head. She often discussed her writing with Emily and Anne, though she rarely changed what she had first written.

She then returned to Roe Head as a teacher, and worked there for three years while Emily attended the school as a student. In 1839 she left Roe Head to take up the first of several governess posts in Yorkshire, all of which she found uncongenial. 'A private governess has no existence,' she wrote to Emily, 'is not considered as a living and rational being except as connected with the wearisome duties she has to fulfil... If she steals a moment for herself she is a nuisance.' Years later, one of her employers remembered her 'sitting apart from the rest of the family, in a corner of the room, poring, in her short-sighted way, over a book'.

Brussels

In 1842 Charlotte and Emily travelled to Brussels to enrol in the school run by Constantin Héger and his wife Zoë. In return for board and tuition, Charlotte taught English while Emily taught music. Charlotte returned to the school alone the following year, but this was an unhappy time. She suffered from homesickness and fell in love with Constantin Héger. On returning to England, she wrote to him – wrenching examples of unsolicited, unrequited love, revealing feelings which he did not reciprocate.

Charlotte's time in Brussels was not, however, wasted. She later transferred the passion, yearning and heartbreak revealed in her letters to Héger into her novels. She also developed her writing technique: up until then, she had generally written whatever came into her head, rarely revising or reshaping it. Héger's rigid discipline – (1) rough copy, (2) fair copy, (3) corrected copy – was new to her. With this experience behind her, she always wrote two or three different beginnings to her novels before deciding which one to use as her starting point.

She made extensive use of her Brussels experience in two of her novels, *Villette* (1853) and *The Professor* (published posthumously in 1857). *Villette*, which she began shortly after the deaths of Branwell and Emily (1848) and Anne (1849), is the most autobiographical of all her novels, with many of its characters, settings and incidents taken directly from her own experience. Paul Emanuel is Constantin Héger, and the novel reflects Charlotte's own emotional turmoil. She asked her publisher George Smith for his opinion of *Villette*, saying that with the deaths of her sisters she 'desponded and almost despaired because there was no-one to whom to read a line – or of whom to ask a counsel'. A fragment in one of her notebooks suggests that the first elements of what was to become *Jane Eyre* may also have been hatched in Brussels during the summer of 1843 when, with the school closed for two months, Charlotte was there alone.

Personal life

The personal turmoil Charlotte went through during and after her second stay in Brussels was reflected in the emotions and feelings she gave to both Jane Eyre and Lucy Snowe (heroine of *Villette*). Can difficulties or disappointments in your own personal life become material for your writing? If you have suffered some personal trauma, such as the loss of a lover or the death of someone close to you, transferring your own feelings to a fictional character may help you to come to terms with it – and result in a heartfelt piece of writing to which others who have experienced similar traumas will relate.

Rejection

In May 1846, Charlotte, Emily and Anne self-financed the publication of a joint collection of poems. Averse to personal publicity, and also conscious of the risk of prejudice against female authors, they used the assumed names of Currer, Ellis and Acton Bell. They sold just two copies. This did not, however, deter them from persevering with the novels they were working on. Charlotte completed her first novel, *The Professor,* in June 1846 and wrote to publishers proposing its publication together with Emily's *Wuthering Heights* and Anne's *Agnes Grey.* Her sisters' books were accepted, but *The Professor* was rejected. Charlotte made several further attempts to get it published, all of them unsuccessful (*The Professor* was published only after her death). However, publisher George Smith told her that the manuscript showed 'great literary power' and had convinced him that she could produce a publishable novel. She thereupon resolved to write 'something more imaginative and poetical – something more consonant with a highly wrought fancy, with a native taste for pathos – with sentiments more tender – elevated – unworldly'.

Jane Eyre

Following the rejection of *The Professor*, Charlotte set to work and wrote the bulk of *Jane Eyre* between August 1846 and August 1847, probably incorporating some earlier material. In seeking pathos, she drew on her own childhood, with the early deaths of her mother and two elder sisters; her unhappy days at Cowan Bridge; and her time as an unappreciated, overlooked governess.

Within a few days of its submission in August 1847, *Jane Eyre* was accepted for publication. Charlotte was, however, advised to tone down the early chapters about Jane's harsh treatment both at the hands of her aunt and at Lowood Institution, and the death of Helen Burns. The latter was closely based on the death of her own sister, Maria, whom Charlotte described as 'superhuman in goodness and cleverness'. After their mother's early death Maria became the children's emotional lynchpin – 'a little mother among the rest', in Charlotte's words. Charlotte told her publisher that she had already softened the truth on which these episodes were based and could do nothing more without damaging the book's integrity. She added that the book had been revised twice already and that the harsher parts 'may suit the public taste better than you anticipate'. In this she was proved right. Published in October 1847, the book was an immediate success; by April 1848 it was into its third edition.

A revolutionary novel

Jane Eyre was a bestseller, but it was regarded by many of its Victorian readers as 'a naughty book'. Rochester's casual discussion of former mistresses with his daughter's teenage governess, his improper behaviour during their courtship (when he kisses Jane repeatedly) and his intention to proceed with a bigamous marriage – these were the elements that led its detractors to accuse the author of 'a great coarseness of taste'.

The novel's revolutionary credentials, however, have a different basis: an unconventional heroine who is small, plain, poor and obscure; a first-person child narrator (the first ever); a defiantly feminist perspective; and characters created with more psychological insight than anything previously seen in an English novel.

The vivid characterisation of Jane derives from Charlotte's personal sorrows, her unhappy experiences as a governess and her identification with a heroine who represents all underlings – especially women:

> … women feel just as men feel; they need exercise for their faculties… they suffer from too rigid a restraint… and it is narrow-minded… to say they ought to confine themselves to making puddings and knitting stockings, to playing on the piano and embroidering bags.

Jane's outward appearance is that of a meek, retiring governess; but inwardly, she's resolute with a 'soul made of fire'. When Rochester asks her if she thinks him handsome, she responds crisply, 'No, sir!' 'Never was anything so frail and so indomitable,' says Rochester. Charlotte created a Victorian governess with the soul of a modern emancipated woman – the first in English fiction.

Rochester is an extraordinary creation: proud, witty, intelligent, cynical, domineering, vulnerable, ugly. He may have been based in part on one of her principal Angrian characters, the Duke of Zamorna. The novel's minor characters are deftly drawn, reflecting the complexity of real life with its mixture of good and bad: Adèle, silly but loving; Mrs Fairfax, good and simple, with a limited view of life; St John Rivers, noble, pious and impossibly stuffy. Rivers was based on Henry Nussey, brother of Charlotte's lifelong friend Ellen; he wrote to Charlotte in 1839 proposing marriage, but was rejected. Diana and Mary Rivers are veiled portraits of Emily and Anne.

Origins and style

In July 1845 Charlotte was holidaying in the Peak District with her friend Ellen Nussey when she visited a small battlemented Elizabethan house near Hathersage. Its owner, a widow called Mary Eyre, told her how a former mistress of the house had gone mad and been kept on the top floor, where she died in a fire that damaged the house. In the nearby parish church Charlotte saw ancient brasses of the Eyres as well as the tomb of one Damer de Rochester.

Jane Eyre may have an orthodox romantic structure, but it is also a gripping suspense novel, with plenty of unanswered questions to keep the reader hooked. Who exactly is Grace Poole? Why is Rochester protecting her? Who is Mason? What hold does he have over Rochester, his social superior? Why has Mason been attacked? Why does Rochester want to conceal the attempted arson attack on himself and the assault on Mason? Gothic features – dark stairways, unexplained noises, fire and madness – combine to create a mysterious, threatening aura that is in stark contrast to Jane's practical common sense.

Nature, landscape and weather often have a strong symbolic significance in the novel. When the chestnut tree at Thornfield is struck by lightning and severed into two, it foreshadows the course of Jane's relationship with Rochester, their parting and their eventual reunion:

> The cloven halves were not broken from each other, for the firm base and strong roots kept them unsundered below… 'You did right to hold fast to each other,' I said: as if the monster-splinters were living things, and could hear me. 'I think, scathed as you look, and charred and scorched, there must be a little sense of life in you yet.'

The novel is written in the past tense, but now and again Charlotte slips adroitly into the present for half a page or so, drawing us into the action and into Jane's thoughts. The story derives its power both from the melodramatic plot and – perhaps even more – from the intimate exposure of the narrator. The writing style is plain, strong and precise.

It has been said that Charlotte Brontë had no sense of humour, but she certainly had a sense of irony. After Jane had rejected his proposal of marriage (to accompany him as a missionary to India), St John Rivers addressed her with scrupulous politeness. 'No doubt he had invoked the Holy Spirit to subdue the anger I had roused in him…' says Jane.

She dedicated the second edition of *Jane Eyre* to one of her great literary heroes, Thackeray. When, as a now celebrated writer herself, she met him in London, she did not hesitate to speak her mind, pointing out what she perceived as errors in his works. Speaking about this later, Thackeray said that her predominant characteristic was 'an impetuous honesty'.

> **Learning points**
>
> - The orthodox structure of a romantic novel is: (1) attraction; (2) impediment or rejection; (3) coming together or resolution.
> - Use unanswered questions to maintain suspense and keep the reader hooked.
> - Descriptions of nature, landscape and weather can create atmosphere and can be given symbolic significance (for example, foreshadowing a future event).
> - Use your own feelings and experiences to create vivid, believable characters.
> - Experiment with more than one beginning to your novel.

EMILY BRONTË
(1818–1848)

'A compound of vulgar depravity and unnatural horrors.' That was how one early critic described *Wuthering Heights*. 'Powerfully written records of wickedness,' said another; and a third went even further: 'Read *Jane Eyre*,' he advised, 'but burn *Wuthering Heights*.' The novel was published in 1847 and these Victorian critics were shocked by its violence and its amorality. Nevertheless, they recognised its power – a word that recurs over and over again in those early reviews.

I rarely read a book more than once (too many unread books to get around to), but *Wuthering Heights* is an exception. Time and again I've been drawn back to it, and I'm not alone: in 2007 Emily Brontë's novel came top in a readers' poll for the greatest love story of all time, beating Jane Austen and Shakespeare into second and third places respectively. For an explanation of its enduring popularity we need look no further than the extraordinary power of the story. So as writers we must ask ourselves why it is so powerful. What are the ingredients that make it one of the masterpieces of English literature?

Themes

Wuthering Heights has two great themes – love and revenge. The story is told through two principal narrators, Lockwood (the London gentleman who is Heathcliff's tenant at Thrushcross Grange) and the servant Nelly Dean. Heathcliff's love for Catherine (unlike that of her husband Edgar Linton) is absolute and all-consuming – as is hers for him:

> Whatever our souls are made of, his and mine are the same; and Linton's is as different as a moonbeam from lightning, or frost from fire… I *am* Heathcliff! He's always, always in my mind: not as a pleasure, any more than I am always a pleasure to myself, but as my own being.

Heathcliff's love for Catherine is no less intense. 'He [Edgar] couldn't love as much in eighty years as I could in a day,' he says. Catherine dies halfway through the story, and Heathcliff is obsessed and haunted by her for the rest of his life. Towards the end of the novel we have the growing love between the young Cathy and Hareton – convincingly portrayed, but tame stuff compared with the Heathcliff/Catherine story.

Revenge is the second great theme. The catalyst is Mr Earnshaw's return home from Liverpool with his foundling, Heathcliff. Earnshaw's young son, Hindley, resents Heathcliff's arrival and the way in which his sister, Catherine, befriends and becomes close to him. When his father dies and Hindley becomes master of Wuthering Heights, he gets his own back by degrading Heathcliff and treating him as a servant.

This treatment at the hands of Hindley gives Heathcliff an iron resolve to get his own revenge, and it is this which provides the driving force for much of the novel. 'I'm trying to settle how I shall pay Hindley back,' he tells Nelly. 'I don't care how long I wait, if I can only do it at last.' Years later he achieves his goal. By encouraging Hindley's drunkenness and gambling he gains control both of Wuthering Heights and of Hindley. Heathcliff's desire for vengeance extends to Hindley's son, Hareton, whom he seeks to corrupt and degrade. 'Now, my bonny lad, you are *mine*!' he says after Hindley's death. 'And we'll see if one tree won't grow as crooked as another, with the same wind to twist it!'

It's a great irony that when, at the very end of the story, Heathcliff is in a position to get his final revenge – to achieve what he has been working towards for so long – he finds that he has lost the will to do it: 'My old enemies [Hindley and Edgar] have not beaten me,' he tells Nelly. 'Now would be the precise time to revenge myself on their representatives [Hareton and Cathy]: I could do it; and none could hinder me. But where is the use?... I have lost the faculty of enjoying their destruction, and I am too idle to destroy for nothing.' *Wuthering Heights* can be read as a bleak story of evil, dominated by Heathcliff's desire for revenge. But by depriving Heathcliff at the very last of his desire for revenge, Emily shows its futility.

Intertwined with love and revenge are other powerful themes: hatred, jealousy, suffering, the outsider fighting against the established order, death (its anticipation and its inevitability) and the continuum of life.

Characters

Heathcliff is an extraordinary creation. The mystery about his origins, his three unexplained years of absence from Wuthering Heights, and his transformation from degraded underling into a 'tall, athletic, well-formed man' with a dignified manner, only increase our interest and our fascination. Brutal, pitiless, ruthless, calculating, vengeful, unforgiving: Heathcliff is all of these. 'Had I been born where laws are less strict and tastes less dainty, I should treat myself to a slow vivisection of those two [Linton, his son, and Cathy], as an evening's amusement,' he says.

Heathcliff leaps off the page. We may despise his character, but we can't ignore him. We are forced to admire his death-defying love for Catherine and his virtues (all associated with strength and power) of energy, endurance, resolution and courage. Antecedents for Heathcliff can be found in some Byronic figures, and Walter Scott's Rob Roy may have been a particular inspiration. Catherine, too, is a memorable creation: passionate, self-centred, selfish, headstrong and feisty – traits replicated, in a more moderated form, in the young Cathy. Emily gives us a supporting cast of vivid characters, some of them (Hindley, Joseph, Nelly) probably based on people she knew.

Setting and symbolism

Wuthering Heights is set in the harsh, desolate landscape of the Yorkshire moors, and the four miles of wild open country that separate Wuthering Heights from Thrushcross Grange play a crucial role in the story. The sense of place is reinforced by the Yorkshire dialect of the sanctimonious and curmudgeonly old farm worker, Joseph. Emily rarely gives us minute descriptions of nature, but her writing is suffused with the natural elements of weather, times of day, seasons, clouds, winds, sunlight, grey stones and heather. The moors are a menacing presence, full of mystery and mysticism, but for the young Heathcliff and Catherine they represent freedom – a liberating and exhilarating escape from Wuthering Heights. And when Catherine dies her grave is 'dug on a green slope in a corner of the kirkyard where the wall is so low that heath and bilberry plants have climbed over it from the moor; and peat mould almost buries it'. So even in death Catherine is on the moors.

The conflict between wild nature and civilisation is symbolised by the contrast between Wuthering Heights, an ancient farmhouse set high up on a remote hillside, and Thrushcross Grange, down in the valley, with its well-appointed rooms and lush gardens. Wuthering Heights can also be seen as a prison. When Lockwood first visits it he is faced with vicious dogs, locked gates and a forbidding landlord. On his final visit, at the end of the story, he finds the doors and windows thrown open.

> ### Sense of place
>
> Emily's love of wild nature and of the Yorkshire moors permeates *Wuthering Heights*, and the surrounding landscape and local dialect reinforce the novel's geographical setting. By giving your story a setting which you know intimately, and which stimulates your imagination, you can create a strong sense of place, adding depth and texture to your writing. It may even (as in *Wuthering Heights*) play a crucial role in your story.

Gothic fiction

Wuthering Heights contains elements of horror, romance, melodrama and the supernatural – all characteristics of Gothic fiction (forerunner of today's horror genre). On his first visit to Wuthering Heights Lockwood notices the grotesque carvings and griffins above the entrance. These Gothic images set the scene for what is to follow, and the novel has other features typical of Gothic fiction: stormy weather, nightmares, extreme landscapes, melancholy figures, moonlight and candles, dark stairways, imprisonment, torture and cruelty, and communication between the living and the dead. 'I have a strong faith in ghosts: I have a conviction that they can, and do, exist among us!' says Heathcliff, and for 18 years after Catherine's death he is haunted by her.

The phantom of Catherine's hand grabbing Lockwood through the broken window is perhaps the most memorable ghost scene in all literature. The oak-panelled bed (also the setting for the discovery of Heathcliff's rain-soaked corpse) is the symbolic centre of *Wuthering Heights*. At the end of the story we have a shepherd boy's sighting of the ghostly image of Heathcliff and Catherine wandering on the moors. The success of both these scenes depends on their ambivalence. Are they real or imagined?

Resolution

In the novel's famous last paragraph Lockwood visits the graves of Heathcliff and Catherine:

> I lingered round them, under that benign sky; watched the moths fluttering among the heath and hare-bells; listened to the soft wind breathing through the grass; and wondered how anyone could ever imagine unquiet slumbers for the sleepers in that quiet earth.

After all the conflict that has gone before, Emily ends with this serene, subtly crafted image, and has her narrator interpreting closure. The reader, however, may prefer a more ambivalent interpretation.

Wuthering Heights has strong themes, unforgettable characters, a dramatic setting that permeates the novel from beginning to end, and a haunting ambivalence. Those are the ingredients that make it one of the most powerful stories ever written.

Learning points

- Choose a strong central theme.
- Strong characters need to be a mixture of good and bad – to have both positive and negative traits.
- Leaving gaps in what we know about a character can make him or her all the more intriguing and interesting.
- Ambivalent images (Catherine's hand grabbing Lockwood through the broken window, the shepherd boy's sighting of Heathcliff and Catherine) can leave a lasting impression – and stimulate the reader's imagination.

DAN BROWN
(1964–)

You don't have to write brilliant prose to be a bestselling author. Dan Brown has proved that. 'A book by someone who doesn't know how to write for people who don't much like reading' was how one critic described *The Da Vinci Code*.

Nevertheless, as a reader of *Writing Magazine* pointed out, 'Dan Brown is a writer, regardless of opinions as to the quality of his work... out of those millions [who have read the book] there will be some who have never read a novel in their lives and if Mr Brown's ill-written tosh means that even a few of those new readers are inspired to read another book, then surely that's a result.'

It's a fair point. There have always been authors who would never be regarded as great writers but have fulfilled the vital function of introducing people to the reading habit (Enid Blyton is one who springs to mind).

Some 90 million people around the world have read *The Da Vinci Code*, and Brown is the only novelist in the twenty-first century to challenge the sales of J. K. Rowling's *Harry Potter* books. Brown had written three little-noticed thrillers before he hit the jackpot with his fourth, *The Da Vinci Code*. It was followed by *The Lost Symbol* (2009) and *Inferno* (2013), but I'll concentrate on the book that made his name. How can we explain its phenomenal success? If we examine its main elements, we can see that the book reflects some contemporary trends in the publishing industry and also ticks some of the boxes required for a bestselling thriller.

Brainteaser puzzles

Look in any magazine or bookshop these days and you'll see whole sections devoted to books and magazines containing puzzles and word games. Brainteaser books, such as those with sudoku puzzles, have become enormously popular. Many people get great pleasure from pitting their wits against all kinds of head-scratching conundrums: riddles, word games, cryptic crosswords, anagrams and so on. *The Da Vinci Code*, with its string of hidden clues based on some of Leonardo's best-known paintings, and a succession of cryptic codes which need to be cracked in order to solve the puzzle, is a treasure trove of brainteasers.

Early interests

Brown's interest in secrets and puzzles stems from childhood. At Christmas he and his siblings had to follow a treasure hunt with codes and clues in order to find their presents. Codes and ciphers were the lynchpin tying together the mathematics, music, and languages with which his parents worked. These early influences led to a consuming interest in codes and puzzles which has informed and sustained his fiction. Try revisiting your own early interests and obsessions. Could one of them provide the spark that becomes the starting point for a book? The most mundane – or the most obscure – subject can be turned into a publishable book if you can write about it in an accessible and interesting way.

Telling you something you didn't know

Many boys and young men prefer factual books to fiction. The market for popular non-fiction has grown hugely, and there has been an explosion of interest in reader-friendly factual books, often based on popular science, containing arcane information. *Why Don't Penguins' Feet Freeze?* is just one example among many.

This trend may have created a market for fiction that gives the reader some new knowledge. *The Da Vinci Code* gives the reader a lot of interesting information about art history, the early Christian church, religious symbolism, medieval history and much more – information generally delivered in smallish, digestible doses, alongside the fast-paced plot. That many of the book's 'facts' have been hotly disputed does not diminish the attractiveness of fiction that tells you things you did not know.

If you write fiction, you're in the business of make-believe and invention. When an author takes liberties with facts and draws debatable conclusions, we just need to retain a healthy scepticism and to remember that what we're reading is a novel – not non-fiction.

A big, controversial theme

Themes don't come much bigger than this. At the centre of *The Da Vinci Code* is the suggestion that for 2,000 years the Catholic Church has covered up the union of Jesus Christ and Mary Magdalene and their resultant child, and that their bloodline, which is the real Holy Grail, is still with us.

For any Christian, that's a stunning, shocking proposition. Predictably, the book gave rise to a great deal of controversy. US Catholic bishops launched a website refuting the novel's key claims. Scores of articles and website features were written rebutting Brown's version of early Christianity and experts took issue with the book's art history, including the suggestion that Leonardo's famous painting *The Last Supper* depicts Mary Magdalene at the right hand of Jesus. When the film of *The Da Vinci Code* was released in 2006 a Vatican archbishop called for it to be boycotted on the grounds that it was 'full of calumnies, offences, and historical and theological errors'. Other Christian groups, such as the Anglican Church in Australia, challenged the film's claims but sought to use it as a tool for evangelism.

The Da Vinci Code's publishers must have been delighted with all this noise and fury, which gave the book an enormous amount of free publicity. There's nothing like controversy for boosting sales.

A fast-paced treasure hunt

The plot of *The Da Vinci Code* boils down to a treasure hunt conducted within a 24-hour timeframe. It's a modern variant of one of the very oldest, instantly recognisable, storytelling plots – the quest. Some of the most celebrated stories ever written, from Homer's *Odyssey* to Bunyan's *Pilgrim's Progress*, have been based on this plot. More recent examples include Tolkien's *The Lord of the Rings* and Richard Adams's *Watership Down*. In all these stories there is some far-away, priceless goal, worth any effort to secure. For the hero of the story, achieving this goal becomes the most important thing in the world. In *The Da Vinci Code* it is the Holy Grail.

Publication in 2003, some 18 months after the 9/11 terrorist attack on New York, may also have chimed with heightened interest in conspiracy theories and religious extremism. Put all these elements together and we have a bestselling formula.

Bad writing

For all its blockbusting merits, it's impossible to get away from the fact that *The Da Vinci Code* is poorly written. The narrative is marred by clunking prose, hackneyed description and wooden dialogue. The book begins with a sentence that reads like some stage instruction for a school play ('Renowned curator Jacques Saunière staggered through the vaulted archway of the museum's Grand Gallery') and then gets progressively less literate.

We can learn from bad writing as well as from good. Here's just one example of Brown's over-the-top description:

> Captain Bezu Fache carried himself like an angry ox, with his wide shoulders thrown back and his chin tucked hard into his chest. His dark hair was slicked back with oil, accentuating an arrow-like widow's peak that divided his jutting brow and preceded him like

the prow of a battleship. As he advanced, his dark eyes seemed to scorch the earth before him, radiating a fiery clarity that forecast his reputation for unblinking severity in all matters.

In the space of three sentences, Fache is an ox, a battleship and a blowtorch. We can question Brown's extravagant vocabulary and his overblown and unconvincing similes, but for me the main lesson is a very simple one: less is more.

Brown's dialogue, too, is often unconvincing: 'Help yourself to tea and savoury snacks,' says Sir Leigh Teabing (the wealthy historian and Holy Grail expert who turns out to be the principal villain). *The Da Vinci Code* is a plot-driven book, and the characterisation is sketchy and stereotypical. For those carried along by the pace of the narrative and the short chapters, often with cliffhanger endings, that may not be important. To my mind neither the hero, Harvard symbologist Robert Langdon, nor the heroine, Parisian cryptographer Sophie Neveu, are well-developed, rounded characters. I found it difficult to care very much about either of them.

Despite the many flaws in his writing Brown succeeded because he came up with a big, attention-grabbing theme and other key elements – brainteasers, interesting information, a treasure hunt – that appealed to a mass readership. Despite his leaden prose, Brown has an undeniable knack for storytelling, with a plot that grips the reader from the first page. That's one essential ingredient of a bestselling novel. Others, most would agree, are convincing, well-developed characters; authentic dialogue; and vivid descriptive detail, with fresh imagery and carefully chosen words that are both specific and appropriate.

> **Learning points**
>
> - Take account of market trends (Brown's brainteaser puzzles and use of interesting factual information).
> - Choose a big central theme.
> - Keep readers turning the pages with short chapters and cliffhanger endings.
> - Avoid leaden prose, clichés, hackneyed description and wooden dialogue: remember that less is more.

BILL BRYSON

(1951–)

'I come from Des Moines. Somebody had to.'

The opening words of Bill Bryson's first bestseller, *The Lost Continent: Travels in Small-Town America* (1989), make us smile. Right away we know this is one travel book that won't be hard-going. Bryson's tone is conversational: 'Well, honestly', 'You see my point'; it's almost as if he is talking to a friend.

Bryson hit the bestselling jackpot with *Notes from a Small Island* (1995), which topped a poll of BBC Radio 4 listeners to find the book that best represented England. Bryson makes an amiable travel companion because it's easy for us to identify with the way he reacts. We can empathise with his air of bewildered curiosity and the way he responds to setbacks as someone who is thoroughly resigned to his fate. And he does not take himself too seriously: 'She was… looking with undisguised interest at all the men in the room, except of course me. (I am invisible to everyone but dogs and Jehovah's Witnesses.)' (from *Neither Here Nor There* (1991), his account of a journey around Europe). He puts as much of himself into his books as he does of the places and people he is describing.

Twenty years after *Notes from a Small Island*, he took another trip around Britain. *The Road to Little Dribbling: More Notes from a Small Island* (2015) is a little grumpier in tone, as he complains about litter, ugly housing, traffic jams, the internet and much else. But his self-deprecating, caustic humour is as spot on as ever. Twenty years after his first *Notes*, he said: 'One of the finest qualities of the British is they'll let you take the mickey out of them as long as you're being affectionate. And I am.' He enjoys poking fun at the British, but what permeates the book, above all, is his obvious affection for the country and its people.

Self-deprecating humour and easy-going prose make Bryson's books an easy read. My guess – and I'd stake money on this – is that writing that is this easy to read has involved a lot of nose-to-the-grindstone graft and plenty of rewriting. So let's take a look at the techniques he uses.

Satire

Bryson's stock-in-trade is to satirise and poke fun: that's what he does. His subjects are many and various: landladies, restaurant menus, town planners, litter, the excesses of free enterprise, shopping, advertisements, hotels, airlines, bureaucracy, trains, pubs, 1960s architecture... you name it. Here's a sample of his humour:

> On the British aristocracy: 'It isn't every day after all that the British aristocracy produces someone of W. J. C. Scott-Bentinck's rare and extraordinary mental loopiness, though in fairness it must be said they give it their best shot.'
>
> On the Chinese: 'Am I alone in thinking it odd that a people... who have a noble history extending back 3,000 years haven't yet worked out that a pair of knitting needles is no way to capture food.'
>
> On Turkish music: 'If you can imagine a man having a vasectomy without anaesthetic to a background accompaniment of frantic

sitar-playing, you will have some idea of what popular Turkish music is like.'

This is just light-hearted mickey-taking to raise a smile; when he gets serious (as he does, for example, about architects and town planners) his barbs are delivered with a dry wit.

Exaggeration and invention

Exaggeration is a staple of most humorous writers and Bryson is no exception. Here's how he describes an evening of over-eating: 'Buttons popped off my shirt. My trousers burst open... Food began to leak from my ears... I ate the gross national product of Lesotho that night.' In New York he observes that, 'People [here] go to Calcutta to get some relief from begging.' Sometimes exaggeration tips over into invention: 'Outside town there is a big sign that says WELCOME TO DES MOINES. THIS IS WHAT DEATH IS LIKE.'

Here's Bryson making fun of his father's ability, when driving, to get lost, and then to go off in search of someone who could give directions. He returns only after a very, very long time, saying, 'Darnedest thing. Guy in there collects false teeth. He's got over 700 sets down in his basement. He was so pleased to have someone to show them to that I just couldn't say no.' No doubt those 700 sets of false teeth are pure invention, but it's obviously based on the *kind* of thing that his father did.

In *Notes from a Big Country* (1998), his collection of journalistic pieces about life in the US, he describes his father's first experiment with an electric carving knife:

Perhaps my memory is playing tricks on me, but I have a clear impression of him donning goggles and heavy rubber gloves before plugging it in... the blade struck the plate with a shower of blue sparks and the whole thing flew... out of the room, like a creature from a *Gremlins* movie. I don't believe we ever saw it again, though we used to sometimes hear it thumping against table legs late at night.

He describes a garage attendant allowing petrol to slosh out of the nozzle down the side of his car and then trying to light a cigarette.

All I could think of was a television newsreader saying, 'And in West Barnstaple today a tourist from Iowa suffered third degree burns over ninety-eight per cent of his body in an explosion at a gas station. Fire officials said he looked like a piece of toast that had been left under the grill too long.'

Probably the petrol sloshing down the side of the car and the cigarette-happy attendant are based on a real incident, while the newsreader's quotation was clearly invented by Bryson tapping away at his computer.

If poetry is (as Wordsworth said) 'emotion recollected in tranquillity', perhaps humorous writing is some incident you remember and then embellish with lots of exaggeration and a little invention.

Irony

Most Americans don't appreciate irony, but Bryson assuredly does. It's often applied with a light touch:

They were having a festival of litter when I arrived. Citizens had taken time off from their busy activities to add crisp packets, empty cigarette packets and carrier-bags to the otherwise bland and neglected landscape. They fluttered gaily in the bushes and brought colour and texture to pavements and gutters.

On the other hand it can be deadly serious: 'I fully accept Dr Waldheim's explanation that when he saw 40,000 Jews being loaded onto cattle trucks at Salonica, he genuinely believed they were being sent to the seaside for a holiday.'

Facts and attitudes

Interspersed with all the humour, Bryson gives us facts, figures and some telling nuggets of information: in *Notes from a Small Island* we learn that UK spending on rail infrastructure, per person per year, is a small fraction of that of France, Germany and Belgium; and that 'Between 1945 and 1985 England lost 96,000 miles of hedgerow – enough to girdle the earth four times.'

Bryson puts a lot of his own experiences and attitudes into his books (and notably, of course, into his account of growing up in Iowa, *The Life and Times of the Thunderbolt Kid* (2006)). One thing I like – and it may help to explain why he is so popular with British readers – is his characteristic siding with the underdog. In *Notes from a Big Country* he praises the Dartmouth College basketball team for its tolerance of a 7 ft giant named Chris who 'had all the attributes of greatness except, alas, an ability to play basketball'. Now *that* I can relate to: I used to play village cricket and for many years we had as an indispensable member of our team a chap called Basil who was almost certainly the worst cricketer the world has ever seen. Our Saturday afternoons would not have been the same without him.

Making the dull interesting

Bryson does not just write humorous travel tales. Among his other books are a short biography of Shakespeare and *Mother Tongue* (1990), an informative and hugely entertaining romp through the English language. Perhaps most impressive of all is his layman's guide to science, *A Short History of Nearly Everything* (2003), which has sold more than

2 million copies. Here the basic facts of physics, chemistry, biology, botany, climatology and geology are presented with exceptional clarity, enlivened with details of quirky personalities and biographical trivia. Did you know that Albert Einstein failed his first college entrance exam? The amount of research which must have been involved is mind-boggling. The book has won both the prestigious Aventis prize for the best general science book and the EU's Descartes prize for science communication. 'Science was not presented in an interesting way at school,' Bryson has said. 'I do enjoy... taking subjects that are generally dull and trying to make them interesting.'

At Home: A Short History of Private Life (2010) is a fascinating survey of everyday life over the past 150 or so years, based on a tour of Bryson's house (a former vicarage in Norfolk) which he conducts as the most amiable and curious of guides. In *One Summer: America 1927* (2013) Bryson uses that summer's key events as a prism through which to examine Americans' daily life and popular culture.

Accessible writing

Subjects that seem intrinsically dull or incomprehensible can be made interesting and comprehensible in the hands of a skilled writer. First, take the time to make sure – really sure – that you thoroughly understand the subject. Then put yourself in the shoes of the reader – someone who is not an expert. Finally, write in a way the reader will understand. That usually means using plain English – short everyday words, short sentences and the active voice. A little humour can also help.

Writing tips

Bryson's advice to the budding writer is straightforward and down to earth:

I think the main thing is just to write. There are an awful lot of people that just talk about a book they are going to write, but they never get round to writing it… Also don't be afraid of rejection. There are all kinds of reasons why articles and books don't get accepted. You shouldn't take it personally.

Bill Bryson, from Des Moines, Iowa, has become a British national treasure: recipient of an honorary OBE, Honorary Fellow of the Royal Society, former chancellor of Durham University and past president of the Campaign to Protect Rural England. It's an impressive CV, but at its core is just one thing: the writing of books that make us smile.

Learning points

- Get as much mileage as you can out of your own life experiences.
- Creativity and inventiveness can be as important in non-fiction as they are in fiction.
- A conversational style – writing as if you are talking to a friend – makes easy reading.
- Use self-deprecating humour, satire, irony and exaggeration to make the reader smile.
- Make the dull interesting by writing in an accessible way – and perhaps adding a little humour.

ANTHONY BURGESS
(1917–1993)

'I wish people would think of me as a musician who writes novels, instead of a novelist who writes music on the side,' he once said. His fondest dream was recognition as a composer – an ambition realised posthumously with his inclusion in *The New Grove Dictionary of Music and Musicians*.

Anthony Burgess was almost 40 when he wrote his first novel, but once he got going there was no stopping him. His prolific output included more than 30 novels, 25 works of non-fiction and two volumes of autobiography. He was also a respected and prolific critic, as well as a playwright, screenwriter, essayist, travel writer and translator (to say nothing of his substantial output as a composer). But he's remembered, above all, for his dystopian novel *A Clockwork Orange* (1962).

How he began

John Anthony Burgess Wilson was born into a Catholic family in Manchester. He wanted to study music, but his application to the music department of the Victoria University of Manchester was turned down because of poor grades in physics. Instead, he studied English language and literature. In 1942 he joined the Army Education Corps. Stationed in Gibraltar, he was a lecturer in speech and drama – work he continued when he left the Army in 1946. He then taught for four years at Banbury Grammar School before joining the Colonial Service as an education officer and teacher. Posted to Malaya in 1954, he began to devote some of his free time to creative writing. This resulted in the publication of his first novels, *Time for a Tiger* (1956), *The Enemy in the Blanket* (1958) and *Beds in the East* (1959). These became known as the Malayan Trilogy and were later published in one volume as *The Long Day Wanes*. Burgess's life was always one of the main sources of his fiction.

He was invalided home in 1959, diagnosed with a brain tumour and given only a year to live. Cushioned financially by savings during his time in the East and by a sum of money his wife had inherited, he decided to become a full-time writer. Talking about this in an interview for *The Paris Review* years later, he said:

I got on with the task of turning myself into a professional writer… it meant then, as it still does, the pursuit of a trade or calling to the end of paying the rent and buying liquor. I leave the myth of inspiration and agonised creative inaction to the amateurs. The practice of a profession entails discipline, which for me meant the production of two thousand words of fair copy every day, weekends included. Two thousand words a day means a yearly total of 730,000.

During that 'terminal year', he wrote – believe it or not – five and a half novels. 'It was just a matter of working hard every day,' he said. 'Working very hard every day – and *all* day – including the evenings.' The brain tumour diagnosis proved to be inaccurate, as Burgess had suspected. However, the habit of hard work, acquired when he was determined to make the most of whatever time he had left, remained with him for the rest of his life.

Disciplined writing

Burgess did not buy into the romantic myth of a writer's life. Once he had decided to turn himself into a full-time writer, he adopted a highly disciplined approach. He looked upon writing as a trade or profession. His consistent output of 2,000 words every day will be beyond the scope of most aspiring writers (it is certainly beyond this author's), but the principle of setting a target and working steadily and conscientiously to meet it is one adopted by many professional scribes. If you want your writing to be more than a pleasant hobby, discipline is essential.

A Clockwork Orange

Inspiration for Burgess's best-known novel came from several sources. In London during World War Two his wife Lynne was assaulted and raped one night in the blackout by four deserters from the US Army. In Gibraltar, Burgess found himself working alongside a language teacher who had a strong communist ideology. When he returned to Britain after his time in the Far East, he was struck – and dismayed – by the youth culture of coffee bars, pop music and teenage gangs.

The immediate stimulus for the novel was a visit he made in 1961 to Leningrad, where he experienced the repressive atmosphere of a centrally controlled state. One night he was eating dinner at a restaurant when a gang of bizarrely dressed teenagers pounded on the door. Burgess thought they were targeting him as a westerner, but they stepped aside when he left. *A Clockwork Orange* was written in Hove after he returned from Leningrad. He later described it as 'a *jeu d'esprit* knocked off for money in three weeks'.

The novel is the first-person account of a juvenile delinquent, Alex, who has a passion for classical music and a love of violence. He and his three friends commit random acts of brutality, including rape and murder. When he is caught, he undergoes state-controlled aversion therapy – psychological rehabilitation which conditions him to find acts of violence repellent. This seems to cure his aberrant behaviour, but it removes both his capacity to enjoy classical music and his ability to act freely – to choose between good and evil. To that extent, the novel is in the tradition of George Orwell's *Nineteen Eighty-Four*, in which people are conditioned by state-imposed fear, and Aldous Huxley's *Brave New World*, where they are conditioned by state-imposed drugs.

A Clockwork Orange is Burgess's most original, as well as his most widely read, novel – thanks in part to the invented teenage slang, Nadsat, based largely on Russian. The book's opening sentences give the flavour:

'What's it going to be then, eh?' There was me, that is Alex, and my three droogs, that is Pete, Georgie, and Dim, Dim being really dim, and we sat in the Korova Milkbar making up rassoodocks what to do with the evening, a flip dark chill winter bastard though dry. The Korova Milkbar was a milk-plus mesto, and you may, O my brothers, have forgotten what these mestos were like, things changing so skorry these days, and everybody very quick to forget, newspapers not being read much neither.

Here Burgess seamlessly incorporates four Russian words, and the reader is unlikely to have much difficulty understanding *droog* (friend), *rassoodock* (mind), *mesto* (place) and *skorry* (quickly).

With its negative portrayal of a government that seeks to solve social problems by removing freedom of choice, *A Clockwork Orange* has been seen in part as an attack on communism. But the dystopian world of the novel owes just as much to those elements of British and American society (such as pop music) that Burgess detested.

In the final chapter of the book Alex grows up and realises that ultraviolence is a bit of a bore, and it's time he had a wife and a *malenky googoogooing malchickiwick* (little goo-gooing baby boy). However, this last chapter was cut from the American edition of the book – and it was this which was adapted into the controversial 1971 film made by Stanley Kubrick. Burgess agreed to the omission of the final chapter because, with his agent reluctant to promote it, he thought the publisher was 'being charitable in accepting the work at all' and he wanted to make some money out of the book.

A good many critics found the final, twenty-first chapter of the book anticlimactic. They preferred the American version, and Burgess came to think that perhaps they knew best. But in 1985 he wrote:

The book I am best known for, or only known for, is a novel I am prepared to repudiate: it became known as the raw material for a film which seemed to glorify sex and violence. The film made it easy for readers of the book to misunderstand what it was about, and the misunderstanding will pursue me until I die.

The American version of the novel became a cult classic among college students, and Burgess acknowledged that it was Kubrick's film that made the book a bestseller: 'Films help the novels they're based on, which I both resent and am grateful for. My *Clockwork Orange* paperback has sold over a million in America, thanks to dear Stanley.'

Other writing

Working in the tradition of Rudyard Kipling in India, Joseph Conrad and W. Somerset Maugham in Southeast Asia and George Orwell in Burma, it was Burgess's ambition to become 'the true fictional expert on Malaya'. He followed his Malayan Trilogy with *Devil of a State* (1961) set in a fictionalised version of Brunei. Of his numerous other novels, perhaps the most noteworthy are his comic Enderby quartet, begun in 1963 with *Inside Mr Enderby* (1963), and *Earthly Powers* (1980).

Earthly Powers was shortlisted for the Man Booker Prize and is regarded by many critics as Burgess's best novel. It's a parody of a blockbuster novel – a panoramic saga of twentieth-century life as told by an 81-year-old man (believed to have been based loosely on Maugham). According to Malcolm Bradbury, it 'summed up the literary, social and moral history of the century with comic richness as well as encyclopaedic knowingness'.

Burgess's two acclaimed volumes of memoirs, *Little Wilson and Big God* (1987) and *You've Had Your Time* (1990), were described by one critic as 'his best novels, his masterpieces'. In these it's not easy to distinguish fact from fiction – to work out where real life ends and art takes over. Some of the people (former teachers, army colleagues) depicted in these volumes were put out by Burgess's fictional embellishments.

He wrote critical studies of James Joyce, William Shakespeare, Ernest Hemingway and D. H. Lawrence. Last but by no means least, Burgess was a prodigious and highly regarded literary journalist, writing more than 400 reviews and other pieces for *The Guardian* and *The Observer*, and reviewing more than 350 novels in a two-year spell for *The Yorkshire Post*.

How he wrote

For over 30 years Burgess wrote 2,000 words every day. He was driven by a need to put as many words down on paper as his lifetime would allow; he did not believe in wasting time. He would often write more than one book at a time and then compose music in the evenings to relax.

In Malaya he acquired the habit of writing in the afternoon, after he had finished work. Once he was a full-time writer he worked both morning and afternoon. He believed that the morning was a writer's conscious time, but that in the afternoon, when the body was quiescent, the unconscious mind could assert itself.

As a literary critic Burgess was renowned for his speed and punctuality in submitting copy. 'Good journalistic manners tend to lead to a kind of self-discipline in creative work,' he said in an interview for *The Paris Review*. 'It's important that a novel be approached with some urgency. Spend too long on it, or have great gaps between writing sessions, and the unity of the work tends to be lost.'

Although he charted each novel a little in advance, often with a synopsis and a list of names, he believed that over-planning was fatal to creativity. He considered that his unconscious mind and the act of writing itself were the indispensable props. He liked to run through a scene in his mind before writing it down, seeing everything happen and hearing some of the dialogue.

His method of writing was to get one page finished to his complete satisfaction before moving on to the next page. He revised and corrected as he went along: 'I don't write drafts,' he said. 'I do page one many, many times and move on to page two. I pile up sheet after sheet, each in its final state, and at length I have a novel that doesn't – in my view – need any revision.'

He did a great deal of reviewing. 'It's good for a writer to review books he is not supposed to know anything about or be interested in,' he said.

> Doing reviewing for magazines like *Country Life*... means doing a fine heterogeneous batch, which often does open up areas of some value in one's creative work. Reviewing [Claude] Lévi-Strauss's little lecture on anthropology (which nobody else wanted to review) was the beginning of the process which led me to write the novel *MF*. I had to review books on stable management, embroidery, car engines – very useful solid stuff, the very stuff of novels.

Learning points

- Establish a disciplined writing regime – ideally, producing so many words every day.
- Reading books on subjects you know nothing about can open the door to new areas of interest that you may be able to use in your own writing.
- Writing with a sense of urgency helps to preserve the unity of your work.
- Avoid over-planning.

JOHN LE CARRÉ
(1931–)

'The best spy story I have ever read.' That's how Graham Greene described *The Spy Who Came in from the Cold*. Published in 1963, it became an international bestseller and established le Carré's reputation. A gripping story of loyalty and betrayal, it is widely regarded as one of the best novels of the twentieth century.

John le Carré (aka David Cornwell) writes books that transcend the spy genre. They are more than exciting stories. They explore the moral problems and ambiguities of patriotism, espionage, ends versus means, and tension between the individual and the state. They have psychological depth, and there is no easy split between the good guys and the bad guys.

Characters

The hero of *The Spy Who Came in from the Cold*, burnt-out British Intelligence agent Alec Leamas, came to le Carré when he was sitting in the bar of an airport departure lounge:

> An Englishman of about 40 with a drained, travelled face appeared beside me and ordered himself a large Scotch, neat, no ice. Spotty fawn raincoat, scuffed suede shoes, a bronzed, beat-up face, dog tired, dark Celtic eyes... He dug a hand in his raincoat pocket, slammed a bunch of loose change on the counter, and barked 'help yourself' like a challenge at the barman. The coins were in half-a-dozen different European currencies... The barman thought of quarrelling, then changed his mind, in my opinion wisely, and set to work quietly sorting his way through the coins... By the time he'd finished, my sharer had drunk off his Scotch in a couple of gulps and without a word swung away, leaving the change on the counter. And

for all I shall ever know, he was just a weary travelling salesman down on his luck. But for me he was Alec Leamas.

George Smiley, le Carré's most famous creation, made his first appearance in his debut novel, *Call for the Dead* (1961). A central character in some novels, including *Tinker Tailor Soldier Spy* (1974), he has a minor role in several others. Short and fat, wearing expensive but badly fitting clothes, he looks nothing like the popular image of a spy. Diffident and mild-mannered, he wears thick spectacles and has a habit of cleaning the lenses on the thick end of his tie. 'Small, podgy and at best middle-aged, [George Smiley] was by appearance one of London's meek who do not inherit the earth.'

In the 1990s le Carré identified Lord Clanmorris, his one-time boss at MI5, and more especially the Reverend Vivian Green, chaplain at Sherborne (the Dorset public school) and subsequently his tutor at Lincoln College, Oxford, as inspirations for the character of Smiley. Le Carré gave him Green's short-sightedness, his quiet disposition, his 'ability to disappear into the crowd like a shrimp in sand... his powers of observing and remembering... the strength of his intellect and spirit'.

The characters of le Carré's spy novels are unheroic figures, with thwarted hopes and conflicting emotions, who are aware of the moral ambiguity of their work. They are a world away from the flamboyant, amoral lifestyle and slick gadgetry of James Bond. Their only violent actions are those necessary to propel the plot, and the conflicts they are engaged in are more psychological than physical.

Creating convincing characters

Convincing characterisation is at the heart of le Carré's writing. George Smiley had real-life inspirations. The hero of *The Spy Who Came in from the Cold* was inspired by a man le Carré spotted in the bar of an airport departure lounge. Careful observation of people you meet or see can be the starting point for creating a fictional character of a similar appearance – and then adding whatever personality traits suit your purpose. While some writers see plot development as the first priority, many others put characters first. If you can create arresting characters, you are halfway there. After all, more often than not it is the characters, rather than the plot details, that make the strongest impression and stick in the mind.

Grab the reader by the ear

'I think the first thing you've got to do is grab the reader by the ear, and make him sit down and listen,' says le Carré. The first line or two of *The Constant Gardener* (2001) is a good example: 'The news hit the British High Commission in Nairobi at nine-thirty on a Monday morning. Sandy Woodrow took it like a bullet...' Immediately we are asking: What news? Who is Sandy Woodrow? Why did this news have such a devastating effect on him? We are compelled to read on in order to find out. 'We all want to be entertained at a very high level,' says le Carré.

> Most people like to read about intrigue and spies. I hope to provide a metaphor for the average reader's daily life. Most of us live in a slightly conspiratorial relationship with our employer and perhaps with our marriage.

He does not plot before he starts writing – he just establishes the characters and 'lets them do the rest'. Astonishingly, *The Spy Who Came in from the Cold*, written while he was still working for MI6, was completed in just six weeks. He lives mainly in Cornwall and works in a study with one small monastic window overlooking the sea. In his autobiography, *The Pigeon Tunnel: Stories from My Life* (2016), he says, 'I love writing on the hoof, in notebooks on walks, in trains and cafes, then scurrying home to pick over my booty.' He writes by hand, saying, 'I prefer to remain with the centuries-old tradition of unmechanised writing. The lapsed graphic artist in me actually enjoys drawing the words.'

He often scribbles fragments of text on scraps of paper, which his wife Jane then types up. He cuts these up into strips, rearranges them and staples them onto a fresh sheet, making handwritten alterations and additions. His wife then types up a fair copy, and he again splatters the pages with spidery corrections and revisions. This process is repeated through a succession of drafts – often half a dozen, and sometimes many more. He carries on revising the manuscript until he is satisfied, and does not hesitate to jettison dozens of pages if he thinks them unsatisfactory. He prides himself on doing his own research – for example, travelling to Rwanda and Congo for *The Mission Song* (2006).

An alienated childhood

Le Carré believes that all writers feel alienated: 'Most of us go back to an alienated childhood in some way or another. I know that I do... People who've had very unhappy childhoods are pretty good at inventing themselves. If nobody invents you for yourself, nothing is left but to invent yourself for others... We lie to one another every day, in the sweetest way, often unconsciously. We dress ourselves and compose ourselves in order to present ourselves to one another.'

He has said that the need for solitude, even perhaps the secret life, flows from his father who had a shady business outfit in Mayfair. He had scores of registered companies and shuffled deals and moneys between them. He was, le Carré has said, 'manipulative, powerful, charismatic, clever, untrustworthy.' When he was at boarding school one weekend his father simply failed to turn up to take him home: he was in prison.

According to biographer Lynndianne Beene, he was 'an epic con man of little education, immense charm, extravagant tastes, but no social values.' He appears in various guises in his books – most especially in *A Perfect Spy* (1986), the author's most autobiographic espionage novel. Writing this book, he has said, was 'probably what a very wise shrink would have advised.'

An unglamorous world

The world of espionage which le Carré depicts is seedy and down-at-heel. The M16 headquarters at Cambridge Circus are shabby and warren-like, and the descriptions of day-to-day life at the Circus focus on mundane office procedures and routines with which anyone working in a large organisation will be familiar. It's a world of recorded documents and filing systems, attendance records, financial controls, travel authorisations, weekly meetings, and a top floor where the boss and his senior management team sit. There is little glamour, but plenty of intrigue and rivalry.

In *Tinker Tailor Soldier Spy* a change in leadership (following the death of Control) has resulted in a change in the organisation's structure: geographical regions are out and 'lateralism' is in. In this novel and its two sequels, *The Honourable Schoolboy* (1977) and *Smiley's People* (1979), le Carré constructs a whole new vocabulary to describe the technical details of intelligence operations. 'Scalp-hunters' handle assassination, blackmail, burglary and kidnap, while 'lamplighters' provide surveillance and couriers. 'Wranglers' are radio-signal analysts and cryptographers, and 'ferrets' find and remove hidden microphones and cameras. 'Pavement artists' are experts at following people inconspicuously. 'Nuts and Bolts' are engineers who develop and manufacture espionage devices, while 'shoemakers' produce forged passports and suchlike. 'Housekeepers' are the Circus's internal auditors and financial disciplinarians. The 'mothers' are the secretaries and trusted typists who serve the senior officers. 'Janitors' are the headquarters operations staff, and 'babysitters' are bodyguards. The 'inquisitors' debrief Circus intelligence officers and defectors. Some of these words have passed into the jargon of real-life intelligence agencies.

Recent writing

Le Carré made his name with his Cold War spy stories, but the more recent of his 24 novels focus on contemporary themes and preoccupations. *A Most Wanted Man* (2008) deals with the War on Terror, illegal immigration and extraordinary rendition, while *Our Kind of Traitor* (2010) is about a larger-than-life Russian mafia boss who made his millions laundering drugs money in the 1990s. Both books highlight the imperfections of Western democracy and question the moral superiority of the West. It's a nice irony that whereas le Carré's Cold War stories are based on threats to Britain by Soviet communism, the threat in *Our Kind of Traitor* comes from Russian capitalism. *A Delicate Truth* (2013), which focuses on a covert British/American mission in Gibraltar, has been described by le Carré as his most British novel. It also has significant autobiographical elements, with two of the book's characters based on le Carré himself: Toby Bell is an ambitious 30-something British diplomat and Sir Christopher Probyn a retired Foreign Office civil servant living in Cornwall.

John le Carré was named among the 13 finalists for the 2011 Man Booker International Prize (disliking the idea of writers judging other writers, he asked for his name to be withdrawn). His writing has narrative power, and the prose is straightforward and unaffected. There is realistic descriptive detail, snappy dialogue and Byzantine elaboration of plot. His work is rooted in character and it's the subtle and convincing characterisation, above all, that makes him one of our finest writers.

> **Learning points**
>
> - Grab the reader's attention with your first sentence.
> - Carry on revising, writing draft after draft after draft, until you are satisfied.
> - Establish convincing, psychologically rounded characters and let the story grow out of them.
> - Consider whether any odd or unusual people you have come across could provide the basis for your fictional characters.
> - Realistic descriptive detail (for example, MI6's seedy office with its mundane bureaucratic procedures with which anyone who has worked in an office will be familiar) adds authenticity to a story.

LEWIS CARROLL
(1832–1898)

'Curiouser and curiouser!' The words are probably as familiar to us today as they were to Lewis Carroll's Victorian readers.

Alice's Adventures in Wonderland is full of words and phrases – puns, witticisms, nonsense poetry – that have stood the test of time. With one-liners like 'No wise fish would go anywhere without a porpoise' and 'We called him Tortoise because he taught us', Carroll's wordplay can still make us smile.

On 4 July 1862 Lewis Carroll (aka Charles Lutwidge Dodgson, a mathematics lecturer at Christ Church College, Oxford) took a friend and the three daughters of Henry Liddell (Dean of Christ Church) on a rowing-boat trip up the Thames. When they reached Godstow they stopped for a picnic and Carroll amused the girls by telling them the story of 'Alice's Adventures Under Ground' (the title he originally gave it).

It was a fairy tale invented on the spur of the moment, without any thought of publication. The handwritten version which he was later persuaded to produce (and which he illustrated himself) was intended for one person, Alice Liddell. This came to about 15,500 words, but in preparing it for publication Carroll expanded it to 27,500, most notably adding chapters about the Cheshire Cat and the Mad Tea-Party (to my mind, two of the most memorable episodes). He also realised that he needed a professional illustrator.

Oral storytelling

A story told to a child on the spur of the moment, perhaps at bedtime, could be the beginning of a writing career. It might be a story based on your own life or pure invention. In either case, test it out on different children. You might even be able to organise a reading in your local school or library. Watch the children's body language and ask them what they think about your story. They are more likely than adults to give you an honest opinion. Chances are, if they find it boring or baffling, they'll tell you.

Why *Alice* is still read and enjoyed today

Published in 1865, *Alice's Adventures in Wonderland* was an immediate, sensational success. Queen Victoria and the young Oscar Wilde were among its first, avid readers. Most of the nonsense verse and songs are parodies of well-known Victorian poems, and it is easy to see why the book, with its memorable illustrations – integral to the text – by the *Punch* political cartoonist John Tenniel, was such a hit with the Victorian public, children and adults alike. But few of today's readers can have any knowledge of the Victorian originals that Carroll satirised. So why, some 150 years later, is *Alice* still read and enjoyed?

Perhaps the Cheshire Cat gives us the answer when he tells Alice: 'We're all mad here.' In a world which often seems to have gone mad, that's a sentiment to which many of us can relate. 'You don't have to be mad to work here, but it helps,' says the notice displayed above the water cooler in many workplaces today. The surreal world of Wonderland, with its nonsensical people and creatures, its illogicalities and its ridiculous goings-on, strikes a chord with us because it evokes the absurdities of modern life. Twentieth-century examples of surreal humour, such as the 1950s radio programme *The Goon Show* and television's *Monty Python's Flying Circus* (1969–1974), have their origins in the mad-cap world invented by Lewis Carroll.

Surreal humour that tells us something about the modern world helps to explain the continuing popularity of *Alice's Adventures in Wonderland*. But Lewis Carroll's masterpiece has many other compelling ingredients. It's a unique mixture of fantasy, whimsy, wordplay, satire, nonsense and wit. All of this is held together by the dry, ingenuous tone of Carroll's narration.

Nonsense poems

Like Tenniel's illustrations, the nonsense poems are an integral part of *Alice's Adventures in Wonderland* and of its sequel, *Through the Looking-Glass, and What Alice Found There* (1871). Alongside his inventive wordplay, Carroll demonstrates a technical mastery of many different verse forms. 'Jabberwocky' (a Wordsworthian parody), with its striking first line ''Twas brillig and the slithy toves', is generally considered to be one of the best nonsense poems in the English language, and 'The Walrus and the Carpenter' is another classic. If (like many of us) you still have a childish sense of humour, you may even smile at the Mad Hatter's song:

Twinkle, twinkle, little bat!
How I wonder what you're at!

Up above the world you fly,
Like a tea-tray in the sky.

It's an antecedent of that old schoolboy favourite 'While shepherds washed their socks by night...' and countless other childhood spoofs.

With Edward Lear, Carroll initiated a tradition of nonsense verse for children that has continued strongly to the present day. With their brilliant use of language Carroll and Lear popularised a much older form of literary expression. Nonsense verse has its origins in the folk tradition of fairy tales, dramas, rhymes, songs and games; it also draws on the intellectual absurdities of court poets, scholars and academics.

Unlike fantasy (where supernatural phenomena are usually explained by some kind of discernible logic), nonsense has no system of logic. In *Alice* the regular rhythms and rhymes of Carroll's verse provide a perfect counterpoint to the illogicality of the sense.

'Everything's got a moral, if only you can find it,' the Duchess tells Alice. Perhaps the human desire to find meanings in everything – even where none exists – helps to explain the continuing popularity of nonsense literature.

Characters

Alice is a bright, observant, conscientious child, intensely curious and questioning. These traits are based on the character of the young Alice Liddell (Tenniel's illustrations do not, however, portray Alice Liddell, who had dark hair and a short fringe). When Alice does or says foolish things it is not her stupidity, but her unfamiliarity with the strange ways of the people and creatures she meets, that gets her into trouble. She breaks the stereotype of the demure, passive Victorian girl. Alice is interested in discovering meanings in life, and she shows that intellectual curiosity is not limited by gender.

The White Rabbit, the March Hare, the Mad Hatter, the Dodo, the hookah-smoking Caterpillar, the grinning Cheshire Cat, the Mock Turtle, Tweedledum and Tweedledee are foremost in a memorable cast of characters, some of them based on real people. The Dodo is a caricature of Carroll himself: he is said to have stuttered, and in pronouncing the name Dodgson he may well have begun 'Do... do...' 'The Pool of Tears' (Chapter 2 of *Alice's Adventures in Wonderland*) also has a Duck, a Lory and an Eaglet: these represent, respectively, the Reverend Duckworth, Lorina Liddell and Edith Liddell, who all accompanied Carroll and Alice on the boat trip to Godstow. The Red Queen ('Look up, speak nicely and don't twiddle your fingers,' she instructs Alice) is based on the Liddells' governess, Miss Prickett. She should be 'formal and strict and pedantic but not unkind', said Carroll, giving directions for a stage version of *Alice*. The Mock Turtle's school studies include 'reeling and writhing' and 'drawling, stretching and fainting in coils' taught by 'an old conger eel'. The latter represents Ruskin, who taught the Liddell girls drawing, sketching and painting in oils.

Themes and influences

Carroll encourages his young readers to question conventional ways of thinking, implicitly criticising the Victorians' solemn, sometimes hypocritical, attitudes towards children. A central theme of *Alice* is the heroine's struggle to adapt to the outlandish ways and rules of the strange new world she has discovered – a metaphor for the peculiar rules and behaviours of the adult world as seen through a child's eyes.

Carroll was a devoted reader of *Punch*, the humorous magazine that often published caricatures of leading politicians, and he kept cuttings that appealed to him in a special book. The Caucus-race can be seen as a parody of competition between the political parties.

Hypocrisy and sloppy use of the English language are also in the firing line of Carroll's satire, as shown by these examples: 'She generally gave herself very good advice (though she very seldom followed it).'

'When *I* use a word,' Humpty Dumpty said in a rather scornful tone, 'it means just what I choose it to mean – neither more nor less. And the moral of that is—Be what you would seem to be—or, if you'd like it put more simply—never imagine yourself not to be otherwise than what it might appear to others that what you were or might have been was not otherwise than what you had been would have appeared to them to be otherwise.'

Sir Humphrey himself (from television's *Yes Minister*) could hardly have put it better.

The plot of *Through the Looking-Glass* is a fantasy game of chess in which Alice has to get from one end of the board to the other in order to become a Queen. The idea of the chess-board came to Carroll during an excursion to Birdlip on the edge of the Cotswold escarpment, when he saw the square fields of Gloucestershire spread out beneath him.

The mock banquet at the end of *Through the Looking-Glass* was inspired by the banquet the Dean of Christ Church hosted in June 1863 in honour of a visit to Oxford by the Prince and Princess of Wales. After the Red Queen has introduced her to the leg of mutton ('Alice – Mutton; Mutton – Alice'), Alice takes up the knife and fork and asks, 'May I give you a slice?' The Red Queen's response is a nice example of Carroll's wit and wordplay: 'Certainly not… it isn't etiquette to cut anyone you've been introduced to.'

Alice is a work of nonsensical fiction. Like all fiction it draws both on the author's creative imagination and on his observations and experiences of life.

> **Learning points**
>
> - Nonsense poems, puns and witticisms can often stand the test of time.
> - Surreal humour strikes a chord when it reflects the absurdities of modern life.
> - While humour based on contemporary people or events can date, it survives when the attitudes it makes fun of are still prevalent. For example, Humpty Dumpty's 'When *I* use a word, it means just what I choose it to mean – neither more nor less' has been used very recently by a cartoonist to lampoon a well-known politician.

RAYMOND CHANDLER
(1888–1959)

'It was a blonde. A blonde to make a bishop kick a hole in a stained glass window.' How's that for an arresting image? Raymond Chandler is the pre-eminent exponent of hard-boiled crime writing, with its gritty realism and terse, whip-crack dialogue. His novels are full of sharp, original similes and metaphors, witty one-liners and selective descriptive detail, which brings a sun-baked Los Angeles, from the grandest of wealthy estates to its underbelly of sordid, down-at-heel bars, vividly to life.

How he began

In 1933 Raymond Chandler lost his job as a top oil company executive in Los Angeles. At the age of 45 he set about turning himself into a writer. He studied the popular pulp magazines of the day and took a correspondence course in fiction writing. He spent five months working on his first short story, 'Blackmailers Don't Shoot', published in the magazine *Black Mask* in December 1933. Influenced by Dashiell Hammett, his predecessor as a writer of hard-boiled crime, he learned his craft by writing short stories for this and other pulp magazines such as *Dime Detective* and *Detective Story*.

Born in Chicago in 1888, Chandler was educated at Dulwich College, London. After leaving school he took the civil service exams, passing third out of 600 candidates, but after six months he left the civil service to join the staff of *The Westminster Gazette*. He worked briefly for the *Daily Express* and the Bristol *Western Gazette*, but he was an unsuccessful journalist. He returned to the United States in 1912 and settled in Los Angeles, where he spent most of the rest of his life.

Looking back on his education and his route into writing, he said:

> It would seem that a classical education might be a rather poor basis for writing novels in a hard-boiled vernacular. I happen to think otherwise. [It] saves you from being fooled by pretentiousness.

How he wrote

With his first novel, *The Big Sleep* (1939), Chandler did what multitudes of writers had done before him: he re-used some of his earlier material. He blended and reworked previously published short stories. It's a method he continued to use in his subsequent novels. He combined and enlarged plots, expanded scenes, adapted or fused characters and added new ones. Sometimes he lifted a whole passage from one of the short stories, just changing a word or two here and there to improve the syntax or change the mood. More frequently he used a scene from a short story as raw material, working on it and transforming it into something quite different from, and often better than, the original. To turn eight separately conceived short stories into three excellent, cohesive novels (which is what Chandler did) was the achievement of a highly skilled craftsman.

Chandler believed that 'the writer should write from the solar plexus', not from an intellectual agenda, and he was dismissive of intellectual claptrap and of much so-called serious literature. He was more interested in 'the creation of emotion through dialogue and description', and in the development of character, than in 'plot'. In 1958, in conversation with Ian Fleming for BBC radio, he said that in writing his crime stories his main interest was not who the killer was, but what the situation really was and what the people were like.

He had an extraordinary flair for strong, original similes and metaphors. Here are a few I particularly like: 'She shot him five times in the stomach. The bullets made no more sound than fingers going into a glove'; 'The sunshine was as empty as a head waiter's smile'; 'A wallet not quite as big as a bale of hay'; 'I looked across at the golden girl. She was getting ready to leave. The white-haired waiter was hovering over her with the check. She gave him some money and a lovely smile and he looked as if he had shaken hands with God.'

There's a lot of wry, often understated, humour: 'One of the velvety tough guys leaned against the middle of my spine with something that was probably not a fishing rod'; 'Hair like steel wool grew far back on his head and gave him a great deal of domed brown forehead that might at a careless glance have seemed a dwelling place for brains'; 'From 30 feet away she looked like a lot of class. From 10 feet away she looked like something made up to be looked at from 30 feet away.'

He was a stylist, a stickler for craftsmanship and precision. In 1948 he wrote to the editor of *Atlantic Monthly*:

> Would you convey my compliments to the purist who reads your proofs, and tell him or her that I write in a sort of broken-down patois which is something like the way a Swiss waiter talks, and that when I split an infinitive, God damn it, I split it so it will stay split.

Chandler's novels

Chandler wrote just seven full-length novels. *The Big Sleep* (1939), *Farewell, My Lovely* (1940) and *The Long Good-bye* (1953) are probably the best known and most highly regarded. *Farewell, My Lovely* (my personal favourite) revolves around two apparently unconnected crimes. Only on page 244 of the book's 253 pages does it become clear that they are, in fact, heavily related. Then everything falls into place and the solution, once revealed, seems inevitable – the most important precept for any crime novel. Some critics prefer *The Long Good-bye*. Its theme is that of one man who, corrupted by money and power, slides into ruin. Gambling, lawyers, the rich and big business all come under the cosh as Chandler examines the pernicious effects they can have on the average man.

Character-driven conflict

'When in doubt, have two guys come through the door with guns,' was Chandler's advice to aspiring writers, but that tossed off comment was almost certainly tongue-in-cheek. There are guns and fights in Chandler's novels, but most of the conflicts are not the sort that can be solved by a bullet or a punch. The central conflict is between Philip Marlowe – cynical, sardonic, contemptuous of pretension and greed – and the powerful, well-heeled people he comes up against. Crimes have to be solved and murderers caught, but establishing some kind of decency is more important to Marlowe. Chandler's hero is both a hard-drinking and a hard-thinking man. He lives by his own moral code, and his observations on and interactions with other characters are at the heart of the stories. It is these that give Chandler's books their depth and their enduring appeal. If you want to write crime fiction, character-driven conflict can be more important than an action-packed plot.

Philip Marlowe

Philip Marlowe, who first appeared in *The Big Sleep*, is the first-person narrator of all seven novels. He's the quintessential tough guy of detective fiction, the epitome of a wisecracking, bottle-loving private eye. Here's how he describes himself in *The Long Good-bye*:

> I'm a licensed private investigator and have been for quite a while. I'm a lone wolf, unmarried, getting middle-aged, and not rich. I've been in jail more than once and I don't do divorce business. I like liquor and women and chess and a few other things. The cops don't like me too well, but I know a couple I get along with. I'm a native son, born in Santa Rosa, both parents dead, no brothers or sisters, and when I get knocked off in a dark alley sometime, if it happens, as it could to anyone in my business, nobody will feel that the bottom has dropped out of his or her life.

Marlowe is tough and cynical. He loathes pretension, greed and betrayal. He's not a superhero: he acknowledges his fallibility. He likes to get up people's noses, rarely missing an opportunity to insult those he dislikes – and sometimes those he likes. But he's principled: he lives by his own moral code and he's more concerned with helping people than he is with making money. As he goes about his business in the murky, corrupt world of Los Angeles, he somehow manages to exude decency and honour. He's also compassionate, as we see at the beginning of *The Long Good-bye*, when he helps and then befriends someone he chances upon, much the worse for drink, outside The Dancers Club on Sunset Boulevard:

> I guess it's always a mistake to interfere with a drunk. Even if he knows and likes you he is always liable to haul off and poke you in the teeth. I got him under the arms and got him up on his feet.

Marlowe's office is a room and a half on the sixth floor of a nondescript building, and his only furniture is a squeaky swivel chair, a glass-topped desk, five green metal filing cabinets and a few chairs. He has no partner or secretary. Fiercely independent, he has a sardonic take on life and his rejection of middle-class values is reflected in his lifestyle and his self-mocking humour: 'I didn't feel very well, but I didn't feel sick as I ought to, not as sick as I would feel if I had a salaried job'; 'I caught the rest of it in one of those snob columns in the society section of the paper. I don't read them often, only when I run out of things I dislike.'

Philip Marlowe is motivated less by the desire to solve the mystery of a murder than by his desire to right social wrongs. The crime needs to be solved and the murderer caught; but for Marlowe it's more important to do everything he can to protect the weak, ease pain, correct social injustices and establish some kind of decency. These are the things that make him risk his life and his reputation; and together with his wry, self-deprecating humour they help to explain why he is such an attractive hero.

Learning points

- Read examples of the sort of work you'd like to write yourself.
- Consider reworking and re-using earlier material, published or unpublished.
- A sardonic tone goes well with an unsentimental, hard-boiled writing style.
- Use sparse, mercilessly observed descriptive detail to bring a location to life.
- Use strong, original similes and metaphors.

TRACY CHEVALIER
(1962–)

'It's about a Dutch artist who paints his servant, and his wife doesn't like it.' That's Tracy Chevalier's succinct description of her bestselling novel *Girl with a Pearl Earring* (1999). She's written eight novels, but I'll concentrate on that bestseller, which has sold over five million copies worldwide, and *The Last Runaway* (2013). Born in Washington DC in 1962, she studied English at Oberlin College, Ohio, before moving to England in 1984. She worked as a reference book editor until 1993 and then studied for an MA in creative writing at the University of East Anglia, where she began work on her first novel: *The Virgin Blue* was published in 1997.

Inspiration and research

Chevalier is an intensely visual writer, and has drawn inspiration from images and objects as diverse as Vermeer's paintings, *The Lady and the Unicorn* tapestries in the Cluny Museum in Paris, an exhibition of the poetry and illustrations of William Blake at the Tate and Mary Anning's collection of fossils in a small museum in Dorchester. All her novels are about strong women who don't quite fit in with the world they exist in and with what's expected of them.

She believes it's very important to convince the reader that you really know what you're writing about and authentic detail is very important to her. She relishes the research she does before writing each book, seeing it as an opportunity to explore and find out about things she previously knew little or nothing about. For *The Last Runaway*, set in nineteenth-century Ohio, she drew on information gleaned from Frances Trollope's 1832 travel book *Domestic Manners of the Americans* and Charles Dickens's *American Notes*, which records his impressions of a trip he made to the United States in 1842.

Sometimes Chevalier is in the middle of writing when she realises that she does not know enough about the subject. For example, when she was working on a scene about a man who was grafting apple trees in *At the Edge of the Orchard* (2016), she realised that she still did not really understand grafting. As she did not want this gap in her knowledge to stop the flow of her writing, she sketched in the scene, putting in asterisks to show that something was missing. Then she was able to go back to it later after she had carried out additional research.

Doing the research

If you want to write a historical novel, researching the period, the people and the subject area will be your first step. Many historical novelists enjoy the research as much as the writing. It's sensible to take the time to gain as much knowledge as you need to give you the confidence to make a start on the book – but not so much time that the task becomes a burden you don't enjoy. Once you're into the book, you can always go back to do more research (as Chevalier does) if you find yourself writing on a subject you don't know enough about. You might even find that your research leads you off in an unexpected direction where you discover something absolutely fascinating – perhaps something that gives you an idea for the next novel.

Girl with a Pearl Earring

Since Chevalier was 19 she's had a poster of Vermeer's painting *Girl with a Pearl Earring* on her bedroom wall. In 1995 she saw the real thing at the National Gallery in Washington DC and a couple of years later she had the idea for the book. The expression on the girl's face is ambiguous, but the intimate look suggests that there's something going on between her and the painter. Is she happy or sad? It's impossible to say. She found herself wondering what Vermeer had done to make the girl look as she does and what the relationship between them was. She did some research and discovered that no one knows anything about any of the models in Vermeer's paintings.

'The power of the painting,' she has said, 'is that we'll never know about her.' She also discovered that very little is known about Vermeer himself. Legal documents provide factual information about when and where he was born, his marriage and how many children he had. He lived with his mother-in-law and family in a particular house in a particular part of Delft, and probably worked in an upstairs room that had three windows. But there are no letters or other documents to give any idea of what he was like as a person.

So despite lots of research and countless books, the identity of the girl in Vermeer's painting remains a mystery – and the same can be said for the personality of Vermeer. This lack of information about both painter and model gave Chevalier a blank canvas when creating her two principal protagonists. She decided against fleshing out the character of Vermeer, deliberately choosing to keep him mysterious. This works really well, compelling readers to interpret his behaviour themselves and to form their own impressions of his character.

Chevalier has recently put on her website some extracts from the notebooks she kept during the novel's gestation:

> Questions about the painting: (1) Why is she wearing the blue turban and yellow cloth? – exotic, not clothing of the time and place; (2) Where did pearl earring come from? She doesn't look like aristocrat. Couldn't afford such a jewel. Given to her? Just for picture (Vermeer 'borrowed' from wife)?

With this starting point, the obvious way for the novel to go would have been an illicit relationship between the painter and his model, who in Chevalier's book is Griet, a 16-year-old girl working as a servant in the Vermeer household. Instead, Chevalier builds tension by the way she depicts their restraint. There's a slow current that carries you gently along, growing in intensity as her controlled writing shows how temptation is resisted for the sake of art.

Griet, the novel's first-person narrator, is a remarkable creation – uneducated but intelligent and perceptive. Vermeer first sees her chopping vegetables for soup and laying them out on the kitchen table.

'Are they laid out in the order in which they will go into the soup?…
I see you have separated the whites,' he said, indicating the turnips and onions. 'And then the orange and the purple, they do not sit together. Why is that?'… 'The colours fight when they are side by side, sir.'

'Griet,' Chevalier has said, 'had an aesthetic eye that simply needed encouragement in order to flourish.' Vermeer's wife Catharina is very jealous of Griet because she is the first and only person to be allowed to act as Vermeer's assistant in his studio. Chevalier was pregnant when writing the book and has said that this made it easy for her to imagine the character of Catharina, who is pregnant throughout the story.

Chevalier undertook extensive research into the social life of seventeenth-century Delft during the Dutch Golden Age – a time when Dutch trade, art and science were among the most acclaimed in the world. She depicts the domestic details of daily life convincingly. There's a lot of technical detail about the way paint was prepared and how Vermeer went about the process of painting. Far from detracting from the storyline, these graphic details add to the novel's verisimilitude.

She believes that Vermeer's famous painting is itself part of the explanation for the novel's extraordinary success. The picture, reproduced on the book's cover, is probably one of the best-known paintings in the world. She decided at an early stage that her aim would be to imitate Vermeer's painting style in words. How ambitious is that?

Writing the book while pregnant and wanting to complete it before her child was born, she decided that it would be short, with a simple, linear structure, a single, first-person viewpoint and a tight focus (as in a Vermeer painting) on her subject. 'Less is more' was her mantra. On writing style, what she put in her notebook was:

> Each word carefully chosen. Not a long book… Images precise and beautiful – lots of light and shade. The aim is when reading it you feel the way you do when looking at Vermeer's paintings.

As it happens, I've seen Vermeer's paintings in the Rijksmuseum, Amsterdam and, to my mind at least, Chevalier achieves her aim. It's a story set at a particular time and in a particular place, but somehow it transcends both time and place.

The Last Runaway

The Last Runaway, which took her four years to write, is the story of a young English Quaker who becomes an American. Honor Bright, jilted by her English fiancé, accompanies her sister to America; but when the sister dies soon after their arrival, Honor, a quiet girl not as outgoing as her sister, finds herself having to choose between returning to England and finding herself a husband.

At the heart of the book is the moral dilemma faced by Quakers, who are opposed in principle to slavery but in practice have to choose between helping runaway slaves and obeying the law (the Fugitive Slave Act made it illegal to help a runaway slave and imposed heavy penalties on those who broke the law). Honor does find a husband; she moves in with his family, but by helping runaway slaves she puts the law-abiding family at risk.

Quilt-making, important to early Quakers, plays a prominent part in the story and Chevalier gives us an enormous amount of technical detail. Honor finds the American style of quilt-making brash and simplistic, while the American women don't appreciate Honor's more subtle English techniques. We can see this as a metaphor for Honor's struggle between her English roots and her American future.

One of Chevalier's strengths is her ability to create very strong female characters. To my mind the strongest and most engaging in *The Last Runaway* is not Honor, but Belle, a tough, whisky-drinking woman. Compassionate and funny, she runs a milliner's shop and is part of the Underground Railway, the secret network of people who give food and shelter to escaped slaves who are making their way north. *The Last Runaway* was followed by *At the Edge of the Orchard* about a pioneer family on the American frontier, as seen through its relationship to trees.

How she writes

Before she starts writing she has an idea of the arc of the whole book – the journey the main character will go on and how she will change – so that when she writes it's a matter of working out how she gets to that end point. Quite often she knows the big scenes in advance, but the smaller ones usually come to her as she is writing: 'It's a combination of knowing where I'm going and the spontaneity of allowing the smaller moments pop out that lead to the big moments.'

Chevalier has the storyteller's knack of making her readers keep turning the page to find out how her heroine will end up. In *Girl with a Pearl Earring* she explicitly presents Griet with eight different choices: 'I reached the centre of the square and stopped in the circle of tiles with the eight-pointed star in the middle. Each point indicated a direction I could take.' She then goes on to spell out each of the eight possible courses of action. Similarly, in *The Last Runaway* Honor is faced with choices about her future, and we can't be sure which way she will turn. In both cases we have to keep on reading to see how things pan out – until we reach an ending that in retrospect seems inevitable. That's the mark of an accomplished writer.

Chevalier begins her writing day by dealing with emails and then re-reading the previous day's work. That gives her the spur to continue. Ideally, she has left something incomplete the previous day – something that she did not quite get down on paper that she can use to get started. Once she begins, she writes in a continuous stream (no editing), using pen and paper, and aims at 1,000 words a day. At the end of each session she types out what's she's written on to her computer, making some changes as she does this. She typically begins around 8 a.m., hoping to finish by early afternoon, but in practice it can be any time between 10 a.m. and 6 p.m. Once the whole book is completed, she goes back to the beginning and starts editing. She attaches great importance to this, believing that almost every sentence can be improved by editing.

Learning points

- Draw inspiration from images and objects you admire.
- Research thoroughly and incorporate authentic period detail into the narrative. The less hard information there is about a historical figure, the more scope you have to create their character.
- Examine every single sentence and consider whether it can be strengthened by editing.

LEE CHILD

(1954–)

'Hey, if this writing thing doesn't pan out, you could always be a reacher in a supermarket,' said Jim Grant's wife. He's well over 6 ft tall, and when they're out shopping in the supermarket it's not unusual for some little old lady to come up to him and say: 'You're a nice tall chap, could you reach me that can?' That's how Lee Child, to give him the name by which millions of readers know him, came upon the name of his hero, Jack Reacher.

He's written 21 thrillers and over a dozen short stories about former military policeman Jack Reacher, a tough guy with universal appeal. Every one of them has been a phenomenal bestseller. It's claimed that a Jack Reacher novel is bought every four seconds somewhere in the world.

How he began

Child has always been a voracious reader. The first books he read were children's adventure and mystery stories, such as Enid Blyton's books about the Famous Five and the Secret Seven. After that it was the Biggles war stories of Captain W. E. Johns. Then he moved on to Alistair Maclean, Raymond Chandler and John D. MacDonald.

He enjoyed acting in school plays and as a teenager had holiday jobs working backstage in small theatres and arts centres. In 1977, after completing a law degree at Sheffield University, he joined Granada Television, where he stayed until 1995, working on iconic series such as *Brideshead Revisited*, *The Jewel in the Crown*, *Prime Suspect* and *Cracker*. Then, at the age of 40, he was made redundant – the result of corporate restructuring. Child has described his Jack Reacher novels as revenge stories driven by his anger at the downsizing at Granada. Losing his job gave him the stimulus to write thrillers with a hero whose main motivation is revenge: someone does a very bad thing and Reacher takes revenge.

For about four or five years before Child began writing, it had been dawning on him that he might be able to write a book and he began to understand how other writers did it. In terms of storytelling, his greatest influence, he has said, was MacDonald's series of crime stories about Travis McGee, a 'salvage consultant' who recovers others' property for a fee. The first Jack Reacher novel, *Killing Floor* (1997), was written in longhand at his dining-room table. He did not own a computer and wanted to wait to buy one with his first advance, which he did.

Jack Reacher

Jack Reacher is an ex-military cop, a former major in the US Army. He's a drifter without roots – a wanderer, alienated from the Establishment he was once part of, who has a strong sense of justice. He's a modern manifestation of the heroic-altruism tradition in English crime fiction exemplified by Leslie Charteris's Simon 'The Saint' Templar. Like many traditional heroes, he sees it as his job to right wrongs and to defend the weak against the forces of evil and oppression. He's like a gunslinging hero of the Wild West: the mysterious stranger who comes into town, cleans things up, gives the baddies their just deserts and then moves on.

Reacher is good at violence. He has the mental and physical attributes both to dish it out and take it, and he doesn't hesitate to use them. He's a very big man, 6 feet 5 inches tall, with a 50-inch chest. A small-arms expert, he's an outstanding practitioner of both man-portable weaponry and hand-to-hand combat. Headbutting seems to be a particular skill. He has no qualms at all about killing those who deserve it, but it's never done gratuitously. Child does not skimp on his descriptions of Reacher's violence:

> Smashed the boss man's balls like I was trying to punt a football right out of the stadium… I jammed my thumb into his eye. Hooked the tips of my fingers in his ear and squeezed.

There are plenty of passages more graphic than that.

Asked how he came to create Reacher's character, Child said:

> I didn't want another drunk, alcoholic, miserable, traumatised hero. I didn't want him to have shot a kid, or his partner, or whatever. I just wanted a decent, normal, uncomplicated guy… I wanted a happy-go-lucky guy. He has quirks and problems, but the thing is, he doesn't know he's got them. Hence, no tedious self-pity. He's smart and strong, an introvert, but any anguish he suffers is caused by others.

How he writes

Child is English, but he deliberately chose to write American-style thrillers. He had visited the US frequently and lapped up American TV. 'It was really a question of mimicking,' he says. 'If you're familiar with the rhythms and the word choices of the country and you can put them down on paper, it actually *becomes* their nationality.' In 1998, after the publication of his first book, he moved with his American wife and his daughter to New York. His wife Jane reads his drafts and takes out any 'Britishisms'.

He gets up late and typically writes from noon until around 6 p.m., chain-smoking and drinking cup after cup of coffee, aiming to produce 2,000 words a day. He has two computers – one just for writing, the other for checking emails and baseball scores. Since 1997 he has written a book a year. He always starts on 1 September, the date on which, having been sacked from his job in television, he went out and bought the paper and pencil (and a pencil sharpener) with which he would write his first Jack Reacher novel. Each book takes him about six months to write; every year he submits the completed manuscript to his publisher in March.

Child begins writing without too much forethought; he has neither a title nor a plot – just a glimmer of what's to come. He does not construct outlines, but begins simply by picturing the climax scene towards which the story will build. 'Then I just start somewhere and let the story work itself out,' he says. He likes his writing to be organic, spontaneous and authentic. Unlike many writers, he does not revise endlessly: 'Not quite "don't get it right, get it written", but close,' he has said.

Child's prose style has been described as 'hard boiled' and 'commercial'. He believes his experience of television drama has helped him to write authentic dialogue. Some Reacher novels are written in the first person and some in the third. Here's how *Killing Floor* begins:

> I was arrested in Eno's diner. At twelve o'clock. I was eating eggs and drinking coffee. A late breakfast, not lunch. I was wet and tired after a long walk in heavy rain. All the way from the highway to the edge of town.

Note the very short, staccato sentences, often without verbs. 'Genre fiction at its most basic,' said one critic, who added 'They're exciting. You can't put them down.' Marilyn Stasio of *The New York Times* said: 'His words are spare, but well chosen; the action is violent, but well calculated; and the ingenuity of the plot is especially well-suited to a cool character like Reacher, who always thinks before he strikes.'

Child believes there are three key elements in a story: character, suspense and education. In the plot-versus-character debate, he's firmly on the side of character. 'Character is, always and forever, the essential primary driver,' he says. That may come as a surprise from a writer whose action-packed stories seem intricately plotted, but if you think about it, it makes a lot of sense. We buy into characters, not plots. Think of Miss Marple, Poirot, Maigret, Rebus, Dalgliesh, Morse, Wexford and all the other heroes of popular crime novels. How many of the plots can you remember? It's always the central character that draws us in and sticks in the mind, not the plot. Child does not believe that his central character needs to grow and develop: 'I prefer other characters around Jack to change and learn and grow… I'll leave Jack as he is.' He believes that readers know what to expect from his novels, and that the consistency of Jack Reacher as a character gives them confidence to stay with him and to continue buying the books.

His second key element is suspense. He's convinced that raising questions and answering them is the way to create suspense. He believes there's something fundamental in human nature that makes us want to endlessly raise and, most importantly, find answers to questions. Let me give you a couple of examples.

We learn in the first sentence of *Killing Floor* that Jack Reacher has been arrested. So the obvious first question is: Why? In the second chapter, we learn that Reacher is being charged with murder. Again, the question is: Why? And so it goes on, one question after another. To take another example, *Never Go Back* (2013) begins with Reacher being attacked by two strangers outside a motel (needless to say, he has no difficulty dealing with them). So the obvious first question is: Why is he attacked? When he visits the headquarters of his old unit in Washington DC, wanting to meet the new commanding officer, Major Susan Turner (because he liked her voice on the phone), he finds that the officer sitting behind his old desk is not Susan Turner. So where is she? Why is she not there? What has happened to her? And so it goes on: a succession of questions raised and answered as the story develops.

There are small questions that may span a paragraph or two, bigger questions that span a chapter or a couple of chapters, and really big questions that are answered only towards the end of the book. 'For me the end of a book is just as exciting as it is for a reader,' he says. He believes a good book should leave its readers knowing more about life than when they began. Hence his third key element – education.

Child does not have much time for most of the advice routinely given to new writers. For example, he does not subscribe to the 'show, don't tell' principle. 'We're not *story showers*,' he says. 'We're *story tellers*… There is nothing wrong with just telling the story. So liberate yourself from that rule.' He believes that reading is the only essential training for a writer.

Spontaneous writing

Novelists can be divided into two broad categories – those who plan ahead (sometimes in enormous detail, with character biographies, timelines, plot points and so on) and those who, like Child, write by the seat of their pants. Those who write with little or no planning often say they would find it really boring if they had to work to a detailed plan. By having no more than a general notion of what the story is about and/or where it will end up, they are free to go down any avenue that suggests itself as they are writing. Of course, it's not necessarily all or nothing: some writers have more than the climax of the story in their head, but much less than a detailed plan. Trial and error will enable you to discover what works for you. If you are able to write effectively without much forethought, your writing time will be exciting.

Learning points

- Very short, staccato sentences can work well in fast-paced crime stories.
- Study and reproduce the speech rhythms and vocabulary of the people in the place where you want to set your story.
- Begin without too much forethought: just a glimmer of what is to come – and a picture of the climax scene – may be enough to get you started.

AGATHA CHRISTIE
(1890–1976)

As a writer, I like to believe that the book is always better than any film or television adaptation. But I'd better confess: I have seen both *Miss Marple* and *Poirot* on television, but I had not read a single Agatha Christie book until I came to write this chapter.

I hurried off to the library and came home with an armful of Agatha Christie novels. There was plenty of choice. In a career stretching over more than 50 years she wrote 80 crime novels and short-story collections, including 33 Poirot and 12 Miss Marple novels. She also wrote 19 plays – among them *The Mousetrap* (1952), based on her novelette *Three Blind Mice* (1950), the longest-running play in history – as well as six romances written as Mary Westmacott. Christie's books have sold over a billion copies in English and another billion in translation.

Beginnings

Agatha Christie was born Agatha Mary Clarissa Miller in 1890 into a comfortably well-off family in Torquay. Growing up surrounded by books, she enjoyed the detective stories of Arthur Conan Doyle and Gaston Leroux (the French writer of detective fiction best known for *The Phantom of the Opera*), both of whom were to influence her writing. In 1914 she married Archibald Christie (they were divorced in 1928; in 1930 she married the archaeologist Max Mallowan) and during World War One worked as a nurse in a hospital dispensary.

The Mysterious Affair at Styles, in which she created Hercule Poirot, the Belgian detective, was written in 1916. The idea for the book came from her dispensing work: a knowledge of poisons is crucial to solving the crime. The manuscript was rejected by two publishers before a third, The Bodley Head, eventually accepted it (they had sat on it for almost two years). They insisted on changes, including a new final chapter, and made her sign a tough contract (she earned little money from her first six novels). The book was published in 1920.

Plotting

The typical Christie whodunnit has a murder committed during the book's early chapters. There is then an examination of the crime scene, followed by the identification and interrogation of suspects. One or more of these often end up dead, usually because they have inadvertently discovered the identity of the murderer and therefore have to be silenced. Towards the end of the book the suspects are gathered together, hidden secrets are exposed and, finally, the murderer's identity is revealed.

Red herrings are used to mislead and confuse the reader. To solve the murder, the reader has to distinguish between the real clues and the red herrings, and Christie makes this fiendishly difficult. The vital clues are often given near the beginning of the book, but they are so underplayed that it is easy to overlook them among all the red herrings. Sometimes she describes a clue which is of little or no significance as 'interesting', and then skates over a clue which is vital to solving the crime. Fake identities are often used to conceal the background of characters who are not whom they seem to be.

The number of possible suspects is usually confined within a closed community, such as a country mansion, hotel, train or boarding school. The reader knows that the murderer must be one of those present and can therefore play the role of detective (Christie never cheats by having another suspect turn up at the last minute). Quite often it is the least likely suspect who emerges as the murderer, sometimes when an apparently watertight alibi is belatedly disproved.

Characterisation

Christie used people she saw on trams, trains or in restaurants as her starting point for creating characters. These are often stereotypical and there is rarely any real character development. As the writer Michael Dibdin put it: 'The characters were all generalised types. There were never any complex psychological characters. They were devoid of any emotional depth.'

Her characterisation may not be deep, but it is often remarkably vivid: Lady Westholme in *Appointment with Death* (1938), who 'entered the room with the assurance of a transatlantic liner coming into dock'; Miss Hinchcliffe in *A Murder is Announced* (1950), winking at the inspector as he prepares to question her sweet-natured lady friend; Miss Bulstrode in *Cat Among the Pigeons* (1959), who 'had another faculty which demonstrated her superiority over most other women. She could listen', and who later sat 'cool and unmoved, with her lifework falling in ruins about her'.

Poirot

Christie made Poirot a Belgian because Torquay had an influx of refugees from German-occupied Belgium during World War One and she wanted a character with whom the reader would sympathise. With his waxed moustache, egg-shaped head, small feet and short stature (only 5 feet 4 inches), he is a curious, rather comic creation. Fastidious and self-important, he has a high opinion of himself. He is obsessed with symmetry, constantly rearranging objects to make them straight-aligned. When he shoots someone dead in *Curtain* (1975) (the final Poirot) the bullet hole has to be in the precise centre of the forehead. He prides himself on his intelligence and powers of analysis – his 'little grey cells'.

Christie gave Poirot a Dr Watson-like sidekick, Captain Hastings, who appears (mostly as the narrator) in just eight of the novels (Christie soon grew tired of him). He frequently asks Poirot questions the reader would like to ask. His statements of the blindingly obvious and his tendency to jump to fanciful conclusions make the reader feel one step ahead of him.

By the late 1930s Christie was finding Poirot 'insufferable' (in the 1960s she described him as 'an egocentric creep'). But she continued writing about him because she saw herself as an entertainer whose job was to produce what the public liked. And the public loved Poirot.

Miss Marple

Miss Marple was originally created for a series of six short magazine stories; the first novel in which she appeared was *The Murder at the Vicarage* (1930). Christie described her as 'fussy and spinsterish' – 'the sort of old lady who would have been rather like some of my grandmother's Ealing cronies – old ladies whom I have met in so many villages'. 'There was,' said Christie, 'no unkindness in Miss Marple, she just did not trust people. Though she expected the worst, she often accepted people kindly in spite of what they were.'

She is acutely observant, often blending into the background as she sits with her knitting, hearing and seeing everything and everyone. She loves gossip and is a shrewd judge of human nature, often using similarities with people she knows, and her recollection of how they have reacted in similar circumstances, to draw conclusions that help to identify the murderer.

Both Miss Marple and Poirot have exceptional intelligence and intuition, and Christie was frequently unsure which of them to use. She quite often replaced Miss Marple with Poirot; in some cases (*Cat Among the Pigeons*, for example) he appears only in the second half of the story. Unlike some of the television adaptations, she does not generally portray the police as fools. In *At Bertram's Hotel* (1965), for example, Chief Inspector Davy is an astute investigator who belies his country bumpkin appearance.

How she wrote

Christie could write anywhere and often typed her stories at the dining-room table. She wrote about the society she was born into and knew well.

Her characters are almost always well-to-do people with a comfortable lifestyle. Many of the stories are set in country houses based on ones she knew and servants often play a part in the plots.

She usually began by deciding on the method of murder. Her next step was to create the murderer and work out the motive, though this sometimes came when she was further into the planning. Then she filled in details of the other suspects and their motives. Finally, she invented the clues and the red herrings.

She used to jot down any ideas on a scrap of paper as they struck her, and the plots were often thought out well in advance of the writing. She uses simple, everyday language and relies heavily on dialogue, most of which is very functional. She maintains pace by limiting the amount of description – and there is much less towards the end of the book. This has the intended effect of making us read faster in order to find out who did it.

Writing what you know

Most of Agatha Christie's characters are comfortably off members of the upper middle class. That was the society she grew up in and those were the kind of people she knew. Country houses with servants feature in many of the stories and these were often modelled on real houses she herself had visited. It's difficult to write convincingly about an environment of which you have no direct experience. So if you've never spent time in a country house, it would be difficult (not impossible, but certainly difficult) to write about it convincingly. You are on safer ground if you create characters based on the kind of people you know and give your story the kind of setting you're familiar with.

Queen of Crime

Agatha Christie, Queen of Crime, became the living definition of classic English mystery fiction – the respectable veneer that hides the mayhem beneath. The ingenuity with which she confounds the reader's expectations is astonishing: the murderer who pretends to be the victim; the murderer who pretends to be a serial killer; the murderer who is the investigating policeman; the murderer who is the narrator; the cast of suspects who are all innocent; the cast of suspects who are all guilty. With bold, imaginative ideas like these, she redefined the traditional whodunnit.

Learning points

- The key ingredients of a traditional murder mystery are: crime, investigation, identification and interrogation of suspects, exposure of hidden secrets and, finally, revelation of the murderer's identity.
- Clues to the murderer's identity are best given near the beginning of the story – hidden among red herrings.
- Confine possible suspects to some kind of closed community and don't cheat by having the murderer turn up at the last minute.
- Characterisation can be vivid even if there is little emotional or psychological depth.

HARLAN COBEN
(1962–)

His books have been translated into 41 languages and he sells around 2.7 million a year worldwide. Harlan Coben has come a long way since he wrote his first two thrillers, *Play Dead* (1990) and *Miracle Cure* (1991); each of them had a print run of fewer than 4,000 copies. It was the 1995 debut of his character Myron Bolitar, a former basketball player turned sports agent, that marked the beginning of his ascent towards popular appeal, though that book (*Deal Breaker*) earned him an advance of just $5,000 and a print run of only 15,000. His breakthrough to bestseller status came with his stand-alone thriller *Tell No One* (2001), which sold more than his first seven books combined.

'Every book I wrote I got better,' he has said, '… in terms of prose, in terms of dialogue and most of the books are a little bit shorter because I know better how to edit. Writing is one of the few activities where quantity will inevitably make quality. The more you write, the better you're going to get at it. That's for sure.'

Suspense

Coben has no time for literary critics who regard crime fiction as some kind of sub-species, unworthy of serious attention:

> Its form compels you to tell a story. That's why I think it's so popular and why I truly believe we are currently living in a golden age of crime fiction… I defy anybody to name any of the truly great authors who have not, in some way, touched on crime. Look at Dickens, Shakespeare and Wilde as just three examples. Suspense is what I love and being able to get my readers to stay up all night turning pages is what drives me.

Coben is a master of the hook, the twist and the surprise ending. There's sex and violence, but his trademarks are fast action, with lots of twists and turns, snappy dialogue, wit, humour and, above all, suspense. His books have been described both as mysteries and as thrillers. Asked to explain the difference, he said:

I guess to the public, the mystery has more of an Agatha Christie, locked-door, solving-the-case connotation, while a thriller is more action-packed. In both cases – and really in the case of any writing, I think – it should be more about suspense, about making people want to read the next word, the next sentence, the next paragraph and the next page, and I think probably the thriller is the purest form of that.

A working man

'I never bought the excuse of not having time to write,' Harlan Coben has said. He believes that if you're a writer, you'll find the time; and that if you can't find the time, then writing isn't a priority and you're not a writer. For him, writing is a normal job. He has compared it with plumbing, pointing out that a plumber doesn't wake up and say that he can't work with pipes today.

Coben was born in New Jersey and his novels play out in the suburban, middle-class setting of his own life: 'We're called New Jersey but we're actually the suburbs of New York. My milieu is the neighbourhood, the family, suburban America – reflective of suburbia all over the world.'

Influences

When he was 16 his father gave him William Goldman's thriller *Marathon Man*. That was when he first had the desire to become a storyteller: 'Man, I couldn't put it down and I remember thinking, I would love to make people feel the way he just made me feel.' He acknowledges that his early books featuring Myron Bolitar were descendants of Raymond Chandler and Robert B. Parker. Other favourite reads include the children's books of C. S. Lewis and Madeleine L'Engle, *Where are the Children?* by Mary Higgins Clark and Philip Roth's *Portnoy's Complaint* and *Zuckerman Unbound*.

Myron Bolitar

Myron Bolitar, the hero of 11 of Coben's novels, is a wisecracking, handsome, 6-feet-4-inches tough guy in the tradition of Raymond Chandler's Philip Marlowe. He's decent, witty and charming, and he lives in the basement of his parents' house in New Jersey. He often finds himself investigating murders involving his clients.

Like many fictional crime heroes, he has a sidekick, his best friend, Windsor ('Win') Horne Lockwood III, the owner of Locke-Horne Investments and Securities. With ice-blue eyes and blonde hair, Win is wealthy and well-connected. He's also ultra-violent – and a holder of the highest category of black belt in the Korean martial art tae kwon do. He's almost like a gun that Myron fires. For Myron and Win, the end justifies the means. They don't hesitate to kill when it's necessary. Myron feels responsible for Win's violence; Win enjoys the violence.

One of Coben's strengths is dialogue. He uses it to propel the plot, develop character, establish the setting and, perhaps above all, entertain the reader. There's a good example in *Deal Breaker*, where the addiction of a mobster (Herman) to golf proves to be the key to the release of a kidnapped girl and the cancellation of a contract taken out on Myron's life:

> Herman put the club back in the bag. 'A man does not force or buy or bully his way onto a golf course,' he explained. '... It would be like putting a gun against a priest's head to get the front pew.'
>
> 'Sacrilege,' Win said.
>
> 'Exactly. No real golfer would do it.'
>
> 'He has to be invited,' Win added.
>
> 'I'd love to be invited to one of the world's great courses... But it is not meant to be.'
>
> 'How about being invited to two of them?' Win asked... 'Merion Golf Club... And Pine Valley.' ... 'I'm a member of both.'

Herman inhaled sharply. Myron half-expected him to cross himself.

…

'Next weekend okay for you?'

Herman picked up the phone. 'Let the girl go,' he said. 'And the contract is off. Anyone touches Myron Bolitar, they're dead.'

Writing dialogue

Dialogue can do a lot. It can reveal character, move the plot along, add humour, and put life and vigour into a scene. Some authors find dialogue easier to write than action or description. You need to have an ear for the way the kind of people you're writing about really talk. Regurgitating a real conversation you've overheard probably won't work: there will be lots of ums and errs and irrelevances which would bore the reader. But if you can capture the right kind of vocabulary, intonation, speech patterns and rhythms, you should be able to write dialogue that sounds natural.

How he writes

Coben's typical routine is to take his children to school before settling down to write in his local coffee shop or library until about 1 p.m. In the afternoon he deals with emails, does interviews and attends to other business-type activities, then goes back to the writing.

Since 1995 he has written a book every year. Each book takes about nine months (he starts in January and delivers it to his publisher by 1 October), but that includes a lot of thinking time. He spends the first three months searching for an idea for the crime that will shape the book. He makes very few notes, keeping it mostly in his head. He settles on the crime, and usually has an idea for the first twist, before he starts writing. Character development and the many twists and turns for which he is renowned come later, as part of the writing process.

'My first book was due October 1, and by spectacular coincidence, I finished it on September 30.' The closer he gets to the deadline, the faster he writes. 'If the book is 400 pages long, I'm rarely past page 250 with one month left. At the end I'll write as many as 150 pages in a week… the last 40 pages of *Promise Me* [2006] were written in a day, which is nothing unusual for me. Once the light's at the end of the tunnel, everything else gets put aside until it's done.'

Coben does not do a plot outline. Before he begins writing he usually knows how the book will end, but he knows very little about what will happen in between. 'It's like driving from New Jersey to California,' he has said. 'I may go Route 80, I may go via the Straits of Magellan or stopover in Tokyo… but I'll end up in California.' One of his favourite quotes is from the novelist E. L. Doctorow, who said that 'writing is like driving at night in the fog with your headlights on. You can only see a little bit ahead of you, but you can make the whole journey that way.'

To write is to communicate

Coben advises aspiring writers to read widely: 'Reading should be to an author what music is to a musician,' he says. He does not believe it's wise to pay much attention to the market or to try to follow the latest trend. Above all, he advocates making your writing compulsive reading – cutting anything the reader is likely to skip. And writing, he says, is about communication:

> To say 'I only write for myself. I don't care who reads it,' is like saying 'I only talk to myself. I don't care who listens.' You can call it art and you can call it business, but without the other side it's playing catch and you're throwing the ball and there's no one there to catch it.

> **Learning points**
>
> - Read extensively.
> - The more you write, the better you'll get.
> - Suspense is vital. Keep asking yourself: 'Is this compelling enough? Will the reader want to turn the page?'
> - No word should be wasted: cut anything the reader would be tempted to skip.

ROALD DAHL
(1916–1990)

Here's a surprising fact. Two of Roald Dahl's best-loved children's books, published initially in the United States, were rejected by at least 11 major UK publishers. It was several years before Dahl was able to persuade one to take them on. *James and the Giant Peach* (1961 in the US, 1967 in the UK) and *Charlie and the Chocolate Factory* (1964 and 1967 respectively) went on to become huge bestsellers. By the 1980s – the most productive decade of his life – Roald Dahl was the world's most successful children's writer. When he died in 1990 he had written a total of 26 short stories, two novels, two books of autobiography, eight screenplays, three books of poetry, six non-fiction books – and 17 children's books noted for ingenious (often grisly) imagination, larger-than-life characters and fantastical plots.

How he began writing

Dahl, a fighter pilot during World War Two, was injured in 1942 and appointed assistant air attaché in Washington DC. The writer C. S. Forester (inventor of Captain Hornblower) interviewed him over dinner about his experiences in the RAF. Seeing that Forester was trying to eat and take notes at the same time, Dahl offered to write them up himself and to send them on to Forester the next day.

The resultant account was his first published work. Dahl was an inexperienced pilot who lost his way disastrously and crash-landed his plane unsuccessfully in the Western desert. In 'Shot Down Over Libya', published in *The Saturday Evening Post*, he became a battle-hardened ace who was trying to land a plane that had been badly damaged by enemy fire. It was not reportage but semi-autobiographical fiction. Dahl wrote another 15 flying stories, most of them semi-autobiographical, and sold all of them to American magazines.

Dahl continued writing after the war and began to make rough notes of possible ideas for future use. His earliest ideas book (1945–48) includes 'the cherry that wouldn't stop growing' – clearly, the genesis of *James and the Giant Peach*. In this book of scribbled notes, which contains many undeveloped or discarded ideas, we can see the embryos of some of his best-loved stories: 'poaching pheasants by filling raisins with Seconal' (*Danny, the Champion of the World*, 1975); 'man who captured and kept in bottles: ideas, thoughts, bits of knowledge, jokes' (*The BFG*, 1982); 'the child who could move objects by looking at them' (*Matilda*, 1988). Let's look at how Dahl developed these ideas into fully fledged stories.

James and the Giant Peach

This is how Dahl described the process:

> … the idea might be what would happen if a peach tree had a peach on it and the peach got bigger and bigger, as peaches do, and then instead of stopping when it got the size of an ordinary peach, it went on getting bigger and bigger. That… is an idea, but it is not a story. Yet it is an interesting little thought, and more important still, no one

had ever thought of it before. So now we have to see if it is possible to build a story around it… And slowly, very, very slowly… you get the idea of having a little boy… and two nasty aunts… and some creatures… But what sort of creatures? I can remember very clearly what happened when I came to that point. I remember saying 'I don't want creatures that have been used before in children's books. I don't want bunny rabbits or squirrels or Mr Toad or little mice. I want new creatures.'

Eventually Dahl fixed on a centipede, earthworm, spider, grasshopper and other creepy crawlies. The story's two villains, Aunts Sponge and Spiker, are comic grotesques described with Dahl's distinctive relish for crude and disgusting detail: 'Aunt Sponge… was like a great white, soggy overboiled cabbage. Aunt Spiker… had a screeching voice and long, wet, narrow lips, and whenever she got angry or excited, little flecks of spit would come shooting out of her mouth as she talked.'

Charlie and the Chocolate Factory

Dahl asked his 15-year-old nephew to read the first draft of *Charlie*. 'I think it's terrible, it's rubbish,' was the reaction. In this first version Charlie falls into a tub of melted chocolate and comes out inside one of the factory's products, a hollow chocolate boy. This finds its way into a shop and is about to be eaten by a little girl when she sees a pair of real eyes looking out at her.

Dahl agreed with his nephew's verdict, discarded the draft and started all over again. In the second draft he introduced the character of Willy Wonka, but there were still no Oompa Loompas or Grandpa Joe. One of Dahl's most memorable characters, Willy Wonka is an adult with the sensibilities of a child and Dahl gave him some of his own character traits. He is devoid of sentimentality; he is self-confident, elusive and mercurial; and he has a sense of fun.

Dahl also invented some beastly children; and he enjoyed writing about these so much that he ended up with 15 of them. In his third draft, he decided that four was the right number. Cutting the cast of beastly children down to four involved some painful decisions. For example, he had to take out Mary Piker ('How could anyone like her / Such a rude and disobedient little kid / So we said why don't we fix her / In the peanut-brittle mixer.'). It's a good example of the 'kill your darlings' principle of writing – expunging a brilliant passage that detracts from the overall storyline. In the end *Charlie* went through six different rewrites.

In both *Charlie* and *The BFG* we can see Dahl's love of language and wordplay. Willy Wonka's factory contains 'cacao beans, coffee beans, jelly beans and has beans' and 'dairy cream, whipped cream… vanilla cream and hair cream'. The BFG's 'gobblefunk' (see below) gives us some lovely made-up words ('snozzcumber', 'whizzpopper', 'swizzfiggle') and some nice spoonerisms ('gun and flames', 'tough and rumble', 'frack to bunt').

Kill your darlings

If you've come up with a turn of phrase or a passage that seems absolutely brilliant, it can be tempting to strain every muscle to find some way of fitting it into your story. Don't do it! If it's not necessary for the story, it will detract from the overall impact – and that's what you should focus on. Dahl's willingness to cut some brilliant lines from *Charlie and the Chocolate Factory,* substantially reducing the number of characters, showed a hugely professional approach to his work.

The BFG

Of all his children's books, *The BFG* (Big Friendly Giant) was Dahl's personal favourite. The first draft of this book had a male hero, 25 giants and almost no 'gobblefunk' – the mangled English that would come to define the eccentric, lovable personality of the BFG, who had made his first brief appearance in *Danny, the Champion of the World*. *The BFG* was the first of Dahl's longer books to be illustrated by Quentin Blake, with whom he had worked on the picture-book-styled *The Enormous Crocodile* (1978). Blake's drawings were then incorporated into new editions of the earlier books. Dahl originally had the BFG wearing a black hat, apron and big black boots, but as soon as he saw Blake's drawings he knew that the BFG had to look softer and more lovable, and so he altered the text. Inventing made-up words for the BFG's 'gobblefunk', Dahl made an alphabetical list of possibilities which ran to 283 words. 'Bundongle', 'bogthumper', 'buzzwangles', 'bottlewort' and 'biffsquiggled' are just a few of the words he invented but did not use.

It's interesting to see Dahl's response to editorial suggestions made by his publisher Jonathan Cape (a letter of 20 January 1982). JC: 'Add "as" – "coming up <u>as</u> red as blood!"' RD: 'No! You are buggering up the cadence of the sentence. These books are all read aloud.' Reading aloud what you have written – to see whether it sounds natural and easy on the ear – is good practice for any piece of writing; in the case of text intended to be read to young children, it's doubly important.

Matilda

In the first draft of *Matilda* (originally called *The Miracle Child*) both the heroine and the plot are totally different from those of the published story. In this version Matilda 'was born wicked and she stayed wicked'. The story climaxed at a racecourse, with Matilda using her telekinetic powers to manipulate the result of a horse race. This first Matilda had no love of reading, and her parents and headmistress were not yet the grotesque characters of the finished book, so that the tricks Matilda played on them (e.g. with the parrot and the superglued hat) were simply the pranks of a very naughty child rather than reactions to the way she was treated.

Writing routine

Dahl wrote most of his children's books in a small, specially built brick hut in the orchard of his house in Great Missenden, Buckinghamshire. His usual routine was to write from 10.30 a.m. until noon and from 4 p.m. until 6 p.m. To avoid distractions he worked with the curtains drawn. He had a paraffin stove and an electric heater hung from the ceiling, and in winter he would climb into a large sleeping bag. He wrote in an old armchair, his feet up on a leather trunk, with a home-made writing board, covered with green billiard cloth, placed across the arms of the chair. He wrote in pencil on lined yellow legal pads ordered from New York. 'The writing always goes slowly,' he said. He worked on *The BFG*, for example, for most of 1981.

Literary influences

Charles Dickens, Ernest Hemingway and Graham Greene were Dahl's literary heroes. As a boy he read Beatrix Potter, A. A. Milne, Frances Hodgson Burnett's *The Secret Garden*, the fairy tales of Hans Christian Andersen and Hilaire Belloc's *Cautionary Tales for Children* – the first thing to leave 'a permanent impression'. At school he developed a taste for exotic action stories (C. S. Forester, G. A. Henty, Henry Rider Haggard), espionage thrillers, Victorian ghost stories and Gothic fantasy (M. R. James, Edgar Allan Poe, Ambrose Bierce).

Norwegian fables and tales (some of them told to him as a boy by his Norwegian mother) struck a particular chord with Dahl, and these were a strong influence. They often featured fantastical, grotesque characters and black humour – elements he was to reinvent and reuse in his own writing.

Dahl's tips on writing for children

All good books have to have a mixture of extremely nasty people – which are always fun – and some nice people. In every book or story there has to be somebody you can loathe. The fouler and more filthy a person is, the more fun it is to watch him getting scrunched.

Dahl knew that children enjoyed stories that contained a threat, and that they loved to see parents or teachers vilified. He kept description to a minimum and constantly asked himself, 'Is this too slow? Is it too dull? Will they stop reading?'

'Children's writers must have a touch of the ridiculous about them, and an ability to giggle...' In a speech at Repton School (which he attended – and hated – before the war) in 1975, he said, 'If some of you do hope to become writers one day, try above all to cultivate very enquiring types of mind and one that is interested in lots and lots of tiny interesting things.'

Dahl ascribed his own success partly to his sense of the comic and the curious, but most of all to his ability to remember and re-imagine his own childhood. He had an instinctive ability to understand and recreate the child's point of view: 'I go down to my little hut... and within minutes I can go back to being six or seven or eight again.'

Dahl viewed writing as more craftsmanship than inspiration. He believed that what a writer needed was 'an infinite capacity for taking pains'. He worked hard on his stories, constantly revising, improving and rewriting.

Fact and fiction, fantasy and reality

In his wartime stories and his second autobiography, *Going Solo* (1986), Dahl was not averse to mixing fact and fiction. His children's books are often described as 'fantasy', but they too were inspired by his own life – events he experienced, people he knew and the Buckinghamshire village in which he spent much of his life. *Charlie and the Chocolate Factory* has plenty of surreal elements, but it was inspired by boyhood memories of his school being chosen to taste new chocolate products for Cadbury's. In *Fantastic Mr Fox* (1970), *Danny, the Champion of the World* and *Matilda*, Dahl makes use of the countryside around his home at Great Missenden (for example, a local beech tree is Mr Fox's home). In the late 1940s Dahl made friends with Claud Taylor, a 'storyteller and a bit of a rogue', who shared Dahl's interest in poaching. Taylor worked for the local nouveau-riche landowner George Brazil, who drove around in a Rolls-Royce and became the victim of a brilliant poaching stratagem based on feeding pheasants raisins laced with sleeping pills – a memorable episode in *Danny, the Champion of the World*.

An uncanny ability to see the world through the eyes of a child, an inventive and ingenious imagination, and lots of nose-to-the-grindstone hard work – these, to my mind, are the ingredients that combined to make Dahl one of the most popular children's authors there has ever been.

Learning points

- Children's books should have a mixture of nasty and nice people: the nastier the characters, the more children enjoy seeing them get their comeuppance.
- Children like to be threatened and spooked, and they enjoy magic, treasure, chocolates and toys.
- Reading aloud what you have written enables you to see whether it sounds natural and easy on the ear.
- Work hard, take endless trouble over the detail of your manuscript, and be prepared to rewrite and rewrite and rewrite.

JAMES ELLROY

(1948–)

His gun-happy cops shoot first and ask questions later. Life is cheap and the cops of Los Angeles Police Department are as crooked and corrupt as the criminals they chase. He's known for his dense plotting and his pared-down, staccato writing style full of street slang and profane language.

Influences and beginnings

As a ten-year-old, Ellroy read boys' mystery books; when he had got through the ones his father had bought, he began to steal them. During his teens and 20s he drank heavily, used drugs, was engaged in crime (especially shoplifting and burglary) and was often homeless.

According to Ellroy, his greatest cultural influences were the Lutheran Church and *Confidential*, a racy US magazine which pioneered the publication of celebrity scandal in the 1950s. When he began to write, the hard-boiled police and detective novels of Dashiell Hammett and James M. Cain were powerful influences, along with the works of Joseph Wambaugh, a former policeman who mixed novel-writing with true crime.

As a delinquent, homeless 17-year-old, Ellroy dreamt of becoming a great literary writer, but soon realised that the only books he really enjoyed were crime stories. After spending time in prison he found work as a golf caddy. He gradually realised that he would not be able to write a novel unless he gave up drink and drugs – which he eventually did. In an interview for *The Paris Review* he explained how, in January 1979 when he was almost 31, he began to write:

> I was on the eighth hole at Bel-Air Country Club and I said, 'Please, God, let me start this novel tonight.' And I did. Standing

up at the Westwood Hotel, where I had a room. Using the dresser as a desk, I wrote: 'Business was good. It was the same thing every summer. The smog and heat rolled in, blanketing the basin; people succumbed to torpor and malaise; old resolves died; old commitments went unheeded. And I profited...' I sat down and did it... I felt like I had created myself entirely out of sheer will, egotism, and an overwhelming desire to be somebody. All of a sudden I knew what I was going to do for the rest of my life. I haven't stopped since.

While a caddy he also worked serving notices initiating legal action and this provided him with the idea for his first novel *Brown's Requiem* (1981). This revolves around an ex-policeman (based loosely on Ellroy) and a psychotic, anti-Semitic arsonist, Fat Dog Baker. Ellroy said the book was 'wish fulfilment... crime... autobiography... but mostly a work of imagination'.

Brown's Requiem was followed by *Clandestine* (1982), his first police saga set in 1950s Los Angeles, containing a fictionalised account of his mother's murder (see below) and the introduction of one of his most memorable creations, the corrupt Irish policeman Dudley Smith. Then came *Silent Terror* (published as *Killer on the Road* in 1986) and the Lloyd Hopkins Trilogy (1984–85). He continued caddying while writing his first five books; the job allowed him to be home by early afternoon and to spend the rest of the day writing.

L.A. Quartet

These early novels earned him a cult following, but it was his L.A. Quartet, described by one critic as 'an epic pop culture history of Los Angeles from 1947 to 1959', that established his reputation. *The Black Dahlia* (1987), *The Big Nowhere* (1988), *L.A. Confidential* (1990) and *White Jazz* (1992) were international, critically acclaimed bestsellers.

Fictional characters (most of them pretty unpleasant) rub shoulders with real-life figures; and there are prodigious amounts of sex, drugs, violence, mutilation, mayhem and inventive foul language. Here's how Ellroy introduces gangster Mickey Cohen:

> The Mick was a soft touch for crippled kids, stray dogs, the Salvation Army and the United Jewish Appeal. The Mick also ran bookmaking, loansharking, gambling, prostitution and dope rackets and killed an average of a dozen people a year. Nobody's perfect, right, Hepcat? You leave your toenail trimmings on the bathroom floor, Mickey sends people on the night train to Slice City.

The Black Dahlia fused the real-life murder of Elizabeth Short with a fictional story of two police officers investigating the crime. Ellroy's own mother was raped and strangled when he was ten years old. A few months later he was given a book containing an account of the unsolved murder of Elizabeth Short, a would-be starlet (dubbed 'The Black Dahlia' on account of her lustrous black hair) whose mutilated corpse had been found in LA. Ellroy became obsessed with the case and in his imagination he merged The Black Dahlia murder with that of his mother. Written as an homage to his mother, the book recreates the world in which she lived and died. 'I didn't openly mourn my mother,' he said, 'but I could mourn Betty Short.'

The Black Dahlia required a substantial amount of research. Unable to get access to the police files, he obtained copies of the *Los Angeles Times* and the *Los Angeles Herald-Express* on microfilm. He made notes from the newspaper articles and on the basis of these extrapolated a fictional story with an autobiographical element. The story is narrated by LAPD officer Dwight 'Bucky' Bleichert, a former boxer whose physical appearance is similar to Ellroy's, who becomes obsessed with a woman's death.

L.A. Confidential is regarded by many as Ellroy's best book. A shoot-out in an all-night diner is central to the story, but it begins at Christmas 1951 with six prisoners being beaten senseless in their cells by drunken LAPD officers. For three of the cops involved, it's a pivotal incident that leads to the exposure of past secrets on which they have built their careers. Ed Exley tries to do his job without bending the rules, but when it comes to advancing his own career he does not have too many scruples. Jack Vincennes has a glamorous sideline as consultant to a popular TV crime series and revels in his celebrity. Bud White is young, brash, with a predilection for violence, and eager to make his mark in the LAPD.

When it comes to questioning suspects, the police don't use kid gloves:

> Dudley smiled. 'You came along peacefully, which is to your credit. You did not give us a song and dance about your civil rights, which, since you don't have any, speaks well of your intelligence. Now, my job is to deter and contain organized crime in Los Angeles, and I have found that physical force often serves as the most persuasive corrective measure. Lad, I will ask questions, you will answer them. If I am satisfied with your answers, Sergeant Wendell White will remain in his chair.

White's preferred method of interrogation (other than with women) is physical violence. Here's a snippet of a conversation he has with a prostitute:

> 'There's blood on your shirt. Is that an integral part of your job?' 'Yeah.' 'Do you enjoy it?' 'When they deserve it.' 'Meaning men who hurt women.' 'Bright girl.' 'Did they deserve it today?' 'No.' 'But you did it anyway.' 'Yeah, just like the half dozen guys you screwed today.'

The plot of *L.A. Confidential* is complex and fast-moving, but it's the exploration and gradual revelation of the psyches and characters of the three principal, very different protagonists that makes it more than a run-of-the-mill crime novel.

Underworld USA Trilogy

American Tabloid (1995) was the first novel in an ambitious trilogy Ellroy has called a 'secret history' of the mid-to-late twentieth century. With its follow-up novels *The Cold Six Thousand* (2001) and *Blood's a Rover* (2009), it chronicles American history from the JFK assassination to Watergate through the interconnected stories of government agents, informers, mobsters, ideologues, film stars and politicians.

American Tabloid, inspired partly by Don DeLillo's novel *Libra* (1988) about Kennedy's assassin, Lee Harvey Oswald, covers the aftermath of JFK's assassination, the plotting of the Martin Luther King and Robert Kennedy assassinations, and Howard Hughes's takeover of Las Vegas. The overarching moral voices of the trilogy are Robert Kennedy and Martin Luther King, while J. Edgar Hoover is the principal baddie. *The Cold Six Thousand* is the best known and most highly regarded of the trilogy, but Ellroy later thought it too long and its extreme telegraphic style too rigorous for such a complex story.

My Dark Places

After *American Tabloid* Ellroy interrupted the trilogy to write a memoir, *My Dark Places* (1996), based on memories of his early life and his investigation of his mother's unsolved murder. Allowed access to LAPD files on the case, Ellroy and investigator Bill Stoner spent 15 months following up lines of enquiry, but gave up after they came to believe that any suspects were dead. The memoir is partly a journey of reconciliation with his mother and partly a candid autobiography; he does not skate over the delinquency of his youth. He later said:

I can describe depravity without being depraved. I wrote *My Dark Places*, a memoir about my own slimiest actions, but I've refrained from such actions for many years. Breaking into houses was a thrill, peeping was a thrill. But these practices need to be curbed and regulated in order to ensure a safe society. There has been a great deal of chaos in my life, and there remains chaos in my creative life, so I crave order… even as I describe flagrant disorder in wondrous detail.

Perfidia

Perfidia (2014) is the first volume of a projected Second LA Quartet featuring fictional and real-life characters from his earlier books as much younger people. It takes them from the day before the Japanese attack on Pearl Harbour to V-J Day: 'Hirohito's heathen hornets are now heading across the high seas' (Ellroy likes alliteration). There's the apparent suicide of a Japanese American family, the wholesale internment of all Japanese Americans and war profiteering. Against this backdrop, events are viewed through the different perspectives of four characters over a period of 23 days in December 1941: Hideo Ashida, a gay Japanese American police chemist; Kay Lake, a feisty character from *The Black Dahlia* who infiltrates a ring of Communist sympathisers in Hollywood; real-life William H. Parker, a police captain who became head of the LAPD from 1950 until 1966; and the evil, Machiavellian Dudley Smith. The supporting cast of real-life characters includes (to name just a few) Bette Davis, Joan Crawford, Bertolt Brecht and Sergei Rachmaninoff.

How he writes

Ellroy begins a new novel by sitting in the dark and thinking. He then makes some notes; these usually include story ideas, character profiles and some kind of historical perspective. Next he writes a synopsis: key actions, love interests, intrigues and conclusion. He writes this as quickly as he can; the synopsis for *Blood's a Rover,* to give one example, took him six days. This synopsis serves as a prospectus for the crucial next step: a detailed outline of the novel, which will enable him to keep track of the plot and the chronology.

He works as rigorously on the outline as he does on the text of the novel. The outline begins with a descriptive summary of each character. Next is a description of the book's overall design and intention. The third and final element is a detailed description of each chapter of the book. The completed outline includes everything he needs to know; it serves as a superstructure, allowing him to keep the whole story in his mind as he writes the book. The outline of *Blood's a Rover* was almost four hundred pages long and took him eight months to write.

Each day he sets himself a target based not on the number of words he will write but on the number of outlined pages he will convert into text. The ratio of finished text to outlined pages varies from book to book, depending on the density of the outline. When writing *Perfidia,* five pages of outline (an average day's target) was typically turned into eight pages of text.

He writes in longhand on legal pads, making corrections in red ink. He then goes through the completed text, editing 50 pages a day. After this it goes to a typist. He then proofreads the typed text, making more additions and subtractions. Once he has a draft he's happy with, this goes to his agent who checks the logic of the dramatic scenes and makes sure that each character's motivations and actions are convincing. Ellroy continues to make small changes at the copy-editing stage.

He sometimes uses document inserts between chapters – tabloid copy, police reports, FBI transcripts, etc. This technique enables him to get outside the perspectives of his viewpoint characters to convey information they don't have and to provide historical facts and/or occasional editorial comments in a compressed, direct way.

L.A. Confidential marked a significant stylistic change, with the adoption of a terse, telegraphic style with extremely short, clipped sentences. This came about when his editor asked him to cut more than a hundred pages from the text – without removing any of the subplots or changing any of the scenes. His solution was to go through the novel from beginning to end, deleting every unnecessary word from every single sentence. The result was a distinctive staccato style that, together with period-appropriate street slang, proved highly effective for the fast-moving, action-packed story. 'I love slang,' he said. 'I love hipster patois, racial invective, alliteration, argot of all kinds.'

Slang and jargon

Ellroy makes extensive use of the street slang of Los Angeles. Giving your characters appropriate speech, whether that's the vernacular of the Los Angeles underworld or the jargon of a university common room, makes them believable. Whether your story is set in the past or the present, the words and expressions you put into the mouths of your characters, as well as their speech rhythms, need to reflect their origins, education, occupation, social status and so on. If you're writing a YA novel set in the present day, for example, your characters will have to use the kind of language – and the kind of slang – that young people today really use. Many occupations and professions have their own language and their own slang. Actors, aristocrats, bankers, builders, servicemen, civil servants – from time to time they all use words that are double Dutch to the rest of us. Using slang that's vigorous and apt will bring your characters to life.

> **Learning points**
>
> - A terse style with very short sentences can work well with a fast-paced crime story.
> - Creating fictional characters who rub shoulders with real-life figures may give your narrative the appearance of reality.
> - A true crime, researched or read about in a newspaper, may provide raw material you can use in your fiction.
> - By inserting documents into a story you can give the reader information that's unknown to your viewpoint characters. Examples include newspaper extracts, emails, letters, diary extracts and courtroom transcripts.

J. G. FARRELL
(1935–1979)

'The really interesting thing that's happened during my lifetime has been the decline of the British Empire,' said J. G. Farrell. He died in 1979 (killed in a fishing accident at the age of 44) and is best remembered for three books which became known as the Empire Trilogy. The book he was working on at the time of his death, *The Hill Station*, was intended to complete a quartet of historical novels linked by the loss-of-Empire theme.

How he became a writer

In 1956, following an injury on the rugby pitch during his first term at Oxford, Farrell was diagnosed with polio. It nearly killed him and left him permanently weakened. It may also have turned him into a writer. His convalescence lasted nearly two years and he later said it was during his long stay in hospital 'that I started writing and doing some thinking'.

He consciously eschewed marriage and material comfort in order to devote himself to writing novels.

His time in hospital formed the basis for *The Lung* (1965), which described the horror of being incarcerated in an iron lung for lengthy periods. This and two other early novels with contemporary settings, *A Man From Elsewhere* (1963) and *A Girl in the Head* (1967), have long been overshadowed by the highly successful and critically acclaimed Empire Trilogy – *Troubles* (1970), *The Siege of Krishnapur* (1973) and *The Singapore Grip* (1978), three historical novels connected by theme rather than character, period or geography. The settings range from Ireland immediately after World War One, to the India of the 1857 rebellion, to the besieged Singapore of World War Two.

The follies of the British Empire provide the central theme of all three novels. 'I may start out with the most serious and measured intentions,' he wrote to a friend in August 1969 (when he was finishing *Troubles*), but 'everything I touch has a habit of turning to the absurd.' The tone is ironic and humorous. Farrell pokes fun at the occupying elites, largely unaware of, and uninterested in, the local populations they rule. He satirises the blundering, insensitive, and at times farcical way in which the British rulers respond to events they don't understand and cannot control.

Krishnapur

The Siege of Krishnapur, Farrell's best-known novel, won the Man Booker Prize in 1973. It portrays an India controlled by the East India Company, which had its own private armies and administrative units. The company effectively ruled India from 1757 until 1858, when the Government of India Act brought the country under the direct control of the Crown and established the British Raj.

Based on the Indian mutiny of 1857 and inspired by real events – the sieges of Cawnpore and Lucknow – it is set in the fictional town of Krishnapur, an isolated outpost where a besieged British garrison manages to hold out for four months against an army of native sepoys. Well-researched descriptive detail, such as the procedures and techniques for loading and firing cannons, helps to establish a convincing authenticity. As the siege intensifies and the attacking sepoys move ever closer, the inhabitants are gradually but inexorably broken down by starvation, stench, cholera and despair. Fortitude co-exists with absurdity in a novel which pokes fun at imperial pride, Victorian conventions, the British class system and religious fanaticism.

The Collector of Krishnapur, Mr Hopkins, is an idiosyncratic figure, absurd but heroic. He has visited the Great Exhibition of 1851 and believes fervently in progress, represented by the inventions on show at the exhibition. He treasures his countless models of experimental machines and the Residency's many allegorical statues. As the siege intensifies and the Residency collapses, its priceless furniture is used to reinforce the defences and the much-loved artefacts are used as ammunition. By the end of the novel, steep clefts have opened in the Collector's assumptions about progress and the civilised order.

Farrell's uncompleted novel, *The Hill Station*, is set in India a few years after the mutiny; we have already met its main protagonist, Dr McNab, in *Krishnapur*. One of the principal characters is a clergyman who, during the heyday of anti-Ritualism, is made to suffer for his High Church convictions. In one memorable scene protesters turn a church service into a riot. This is based on what actually happened at St George-in-the-East, Stepney in 1859: Farrell simply transposed the action to Simla.

Troubles

In 2010 *Troubles* was retrospectively awarded the 'Lost' Man Booker Prize for novels published in 1970 (the year when a rule change meant that the prize, inaugurated in 1969, was never awarded). Set in 1919, the book tells the darkly comic story of Major Brendan Archer, an upper-class English war veteran who travels to a grand but shabby hotel on the County Wicklow coast to meet a woman he believes to be his fiancée. The Majestic Hotel of *Troubles* was inspired by the burnt-out shell of a hotel Farrell saw on Block Island during a visit to Rhode Island in the United States. The Majestic Hotel's hundreds of rooms are disintegrating on a grand scale; its few remaining guests thrive on rumours and games of whist; herds of cats have taken over the Imperial Bar and the upper stories; bamboo shoots threaten the foundations; and piglets frolic in the squash court. The Major watches from the confines of the decaying hotel – a metaphor for the dying empire and failing British power in Ireland – as the growing independence movement loosens the imperial grip on the country.

The Singapore Grip

Farrell's last completed novel revolved around the economics of Empire – a subject he researched extensively, studying economic textbooks and reading works of Marx and Engels. In 1939 business is booming for Walter Blackett, head of Singapore's oldest and most powerful firm. With the war in Europe, the Allies are desperate for rubber and helpless to resist his price-fixing and market manipulation. But it's not all plain sailing for Blackett: his daughter keeps entangling herself with unsuitable boyfriends and his native employees repeatedly go on strike. Neither he nor anyone else suspects that the world they know is about to come to an end. *The Singapore Grip* satirises corporate power, imperial greed, and military arrogance. It was criticised at the time for its heavy-handed critique of global capitalism. With the financial crash of 2008 and its aftermath, the novel is arguably more pertinent today than when it was written.

> **Historical events**
>
> Important historical events (in Farrell's case, the Indian mutiny, Irish home rule and the fall of Singapore) can provide a stimulating setting for a work of fiction. You'll probably need to undertake extensive research – and ideally visit the location(s) where the event took place. If you've become fascinated by a specific event that happened in the past (from the Battle of Hastings to the execution of Charles I, from the Great Fire of London to the French Revolution), think about using it as the stimulus and setting for a historical novel.

Influences

Born in Liverpool of Irish parents, Farrell was a writer whose fiction was strongly affected by his family background (his father served in India) – as well as by his own political leanings and a wide range of literary influences. These included Tolstoy's *War and Peace,* Malcolm Lowry's *Under the Volcano* and the works of Joseph Conrad, Vladimir Nabokov, Stendhal and Thomas Mann. His Indian Diary shows him reading Charles Dickens's *David Copperfield* and *Hard Times*, Mrs Gaskell's *Cranford* and Jane Austen's *Emma*, as well as Elizabeth Bowen's *The Last September* (about life at a country mansion in Cork during the Irish War of Independence). A lot of his reading was in French (he was fluent and taught for a period in Paris), and included Marcel Proust, Jean-Paul Sartre and Albert Camus. Farrell's interest in colonial affairs was sharpened, and his views about colonial rule were informed, by the time he spent in France during the later stages of the Algerian War in the early 1960s and by a visit he made to Morocco.

How he wrote

Farrell was a disciplined author with a strict writing routine. He worked in the morning, and compared himself to a clockwork mouse which gradually ran down during the day. In the afternoon he would go for walks in London's parks or visit the British Museum Reading Room.

He researched his books meticulously, typically spending more than a year examining British Museum and other archives before he began to write. He searched out old books for material he might be able to make use of, such as a Victorian guide with tips on travel to India and nineteenth-century volumes of the *British Medical Journal* (discovered on a street barrow) which provided him with a detailed, blow-by-blow account of the furious dispute within the medical profession about the causes of cholera – something Farrell made extensive and effective use of in *Krishnapur*.

Early in 1971 he spent several months in India as part of his preparation for *Krishnapur*. He flew to Bombay and then travelled by train to Jaipur, Agra, Delhi, Dehradun, Hardwar, Lucknow and Calcutta, soaking up the sights, sounds and smells of India as background for the novel. From 23 January to 2 April he kept a diary, recording his impressions of the people he saw and the places he visited. One entry lists the contents of a Maharajah's palace, and he makes good use of this in *Krishnapur*.

In another diary entry he writes:

> Among the Indians encountered was a young chap, a nice fellow, I went round the caves with who kept saying 'Correct!' in places where 'I see' or 'Yes' would have been more appropriate. The guide would say something about one of the frescoes and the young man would bark 'Correct!' No doubt rather alarming for the guide.

Farrell uses this in *Krishnapur*, where the Maharajah's son, Hari, constantly responds to statements with an inappropriate 'Correct!'

Learning points

- Serious subjects can be written about with ironic humour.
- Visit the place(s) you're going to use as a setting for your novel and soak up the sights and sounds.
- Well-researched descriptive detail will give your writing the stamp of authenticity.
- If you overhear a striking bit of conversation, think about attaching it to one of your fictional characters.

HELEN FIELDING
(1958–)

Who would ever have thought that a neurotic 30-something, with low self-esteem and an obsession with her weight, would spawn a whole new literary genre? *Bridget Jones's Diary* (1996) was the trail-blazer for the genre we now know as 'chick lit'.

The Diary first appeared as a column in *The Independent* on 28 February 1995, when the ladette culture of young women drinking and behaving badly was in its early days. When it was published the following year as a hardback novel, with a plot based very loosely on Jane Austen's *Pride and Prejudice*, it sold modestly. But once it had appeared in paperback, word of mouth put it on to the bestseller lists – and it stayed there for many months.

The book 'was bought by readers who wouldn't otherwise buy many books', said Ian Jack, former editor of *The Independent on Sunday*. 'It enlarged the reading class.' Its popularity can be explained in part by Helen Fielding's ability to key into contemporary obsessions about image and health – and to do so with a deliciously light-hearted irony.

A flawed character

'I think that almost accidentally I hit on something that is quite fundamental to women, which is this gap between how we feel we're expected to be and how we actually are,' Fielding has said. 'That's why Bridget struck such a chord with women, because she is human and she has these flaws which most of us have.'

'Even though I have spent a lot of time denying that Bridget was me, she was,' said Fielding, speaking in 2009 at the Oxford Union. She believes that many young women today are left bewildered as they struggle to 'have it all' and to live up to an idealistic society: 'Look at how many self-help books are sold, especially in America... They have become a religion.' People are made to feel that they should aspire to have this perfect life: 'They feel they should be getting up at six in the morning and going to the gym, then doing a full day's work and coming back late and have to feed 12 people for dinner.'

Bridget, obsessed with body image and appearance, takes to heart advertisements telling women they need to dress and look and groom themselves in a certain way:

> Being a woman is worse than being a farmer – there is so much harvesting and crop spraying to be done: legs to be waxed, underarms shaved, eyebrows plucked, feet pumiced, skin exfoliated and moisturised, spots cleansed, roots dyed, eyelashes tinted, nails filed, cellulite massaged, stomach muscles exercised... Is it any wonder girls have no confidence?

A devotee of lifestyle magazines and self-help books, Bridget worries constantly about her weight and her 'singleton' status. She is fed up with friends and relations who are always reminding her that her biological clock is ticking and suggesting that it is high time she found a partner:

At dinner Magda had placed me, in an incestuous-sex-sandwich sort of way, between Cosmo and Jeremy's crashing bore of a brother. 'You really ought to hurry up and get sprogged up, you know, old girl,' said Cosmo. 'How's your love life anyway?' Oh God. Why can't married people understand that this is no longer a polite question to ask? We wouldn't rush up to them and roar, 'How's your marriage going? Still having sex?'

When we first meet Bridget she is working in publishing PR. She then gets a job as an interviewer for a television news programme, working for an editor who is determined to trivialise and sensationalise everything. He plans a live-action special about the emergency services: 'Bridget!... Fire... I'm thinking mini-skirt. I'm thinking fireman's helmet. I'm thinking pointing the hose.' Predictably, the broadcast is a hilarious disaster.

Bridget smokes and drinks too much, and spends wine-guzzling evenings with her best friends, grouching about 'smug marrieds', slagging off men and griping about 'emotional fuckwittage' – male commitment phobia. Neologism (the coining of new words) is one characteristic of Fielding's writing; another is bathos, with Bridget's absurdities and pratfalls frequently offsetting situations which could otherwise be sublime.

After hearing how brilliant Tina Brown of *The New Yorker* is at dealing with parties, 'gliding prettily from group to group', Bridget laps up a magazine's advice about party-going:

... one must never go to a party without a clear objective: whether it be to 'network', thereby adding to your spread of contacts to improve your career; to make friends with someone specific; or simply to 'clinch' a top deal. Understand where have been going wrong by going to parties armed only with objective of not getting too pissed.

Everyday problems

One explanation for the success of *Bridget Jones's Diary* lies in the way it chronicles Bridget's unending struggles against the rest of the world. She is constantly fighting to meet her peers' expectations and to survive the kind of day-to-day problems faced by many young women. With the daily grind to survive, she juggles career, friendships, her obsessions about appearance and weight, and her romantic life. In a world where striving for the perfect life seems to be encouraged, readers can relate to a character who, like them, has difficulty coping with the demands of daily life. By writing about everyday problems that everyone faces, you can connect with your readers.

A strong beginning

Bridget Jones's Diary gets off to a cracking start with a list of New Year's resolutions which give the reader an entertaining snapshot of Bridget's character. These include: 'I will not... sulk about having no boyfriend, but develop inner poise and authority and sense of self as woman of substance, complete *without* boyfriend, as best way to obtain boyfriend.'

Before we have read more than the first three resolutions ('stop smoking; drink no more than fourteen alcohol units a week; reduce circumference of thighs by 3 inches... using anti-cellulite diet'), we're pretty sure there is not a hope of Bridget sticking to any of them. In fact she doesn't even manage to get through the first day. Her list of food consumed on 1 January includes '12 Milk Tray (best to get rid of all Christmas confectionery in one go and make fresh start tomorrow)'.

At 11.45 p.m. she writes in her diary 'Ugh. First Day of New Year has been day of horror. Cannot believe I am once again starting the year in a single bed in my parents' house. It is too humiliating at my age.' Within the book's first three pages we have a vivid pen-picture of Bridget, her lifestyle, her flaws and foibles – all of this setting the scene for what is to follow.

Chick lit

Typical chick lit (usually a paperback with a pastel-coloured cover) has a female protagonist (often, but not always, in her 20s or 30s) who is trying to make it in the modern world, struggling against everyday issues and problems, and going through the kind of traumas with which many women can identify. The subject matter may include boyfriends, dating, sex, love, marriage, infidelity, relationships, friendships, working environments, shopping and myriad other present-day addictions.

But most of these subjects can be read about in romantic novels, family sagas and other fiction. So what's different about chick lit? To my mind there are two answers to that – two defining characteristics. First, the writing style is light, breezy and, above all, humorous: humour is a very important element. Secondly, there is a distinctive tone – confiding, confessional and personal. At its best, chick lit makes you feel as if a bosom friend is telling you about the day-to-day problems in her life.

After the phenomenal success of *Bridget Jones's Diary* critics re-categorised a few earlier novels, such as H. B. Gilmour's *Clueless* (1995) and Terry McMillan's *Waiting to Exhale* (1992), as chick lit, and suggested that Jane Austen was the original inventor of the genre.

The route into writing

Fielding read English at Oxford and then she spent ten years at the BBC, helping to make Comic Relief television documentaries about Africa, before going into freelance journalism and then working for *The Independent on Sunday*. Her distinctive, telegraphic writing style owes much to her journalistic apprenticeship and the need to produce regular, high-quality, easy-to-read copy, to length and to a tight deadline.

Fielding had always wanted to be a writer, and her work for the BBC provided her with the material for her first novel, *Cause Celeb* (1994). Set in a fictitious country in East Africa, it satirises the juxtaposition between the image-obsessed Western media, making smart television documentaries about refugees, and the struggling, poverty-stricken developing world.

The bestselling novel which made her name was followed by its sequel, *Bridget Jones: The Edge of Reason* (1999), and then by *Olivia Joules and the Overactive Imagination* (2003), a comic spy novel, set in Miami, Los Angeles, England and the Sudan, which chronicles the adventures of a young female freelance journalist who is very different from Bridget Jones. Olivia Joules is intelligent and multi-lingual, speaking Arabic as well as French, German and Spanish, and she has a trim figure. Fielding admires the novels of Ian Fleming, and Olivia Joules has been described as a female James Bond.

In the third Bridget Jones novel, *Bridget Jones: Mad About the Boy*, published in 2013 to mixed reviews, Bridget is a 51-year-old wealthy widow – a character to whom many readers have struggled to relate in the way they did to the younger Bridget. Fielding also contributed to the screenwriting as a member of the team which scripted three hugely successful films starring Renée Zellweger as Bridget Jones.

Chick lit has been criticised as 'frothy and trivial'. It may be breezy and light-hearted, but it often deals with the kind of day-to-day dilemmas young women face. And it can be very funny.

Learning points

- Readers like to read about characters with the kind of flaws and problems they have themselves.
- Neologism (the coining of new words) can work well in humorous writing.
- A book must have a strong beginning in order to grab the reader's attention from the first page.
- Chick lit novels have a confiding, confessional, conversational tone – and humour.

IAN FLEMING
(1908–1964)

'I am going to write the spy story to end all spy stories,' said Ian Fleming.

One morning in January 1952 he sat down at his desk and set about creating a fictional secret agent. One of the books Fleming, a keen birdwatcher, kept close by at his house in Jamaica was a standard field guide, *Birds of the West Indies*, written by an American ornithologist, James Bond. In Fleming's hands he became British Secret Service agent 007.

'I wanted the simplest, dullest, plainest-sounding name I could find,' said Fleming. 'Brief, unromantic, Anglo-Saxon and yet very masculine.' He was to become the most famous fictional secret agent of all time. The Bond books have sold over 40 million copies, and more than five out of every ten people in the world are estimated to have seen a Bond film.

Fleming wrote four James Bond novels before he made his big breakthrough. This came with *From Russia, with Love* (1957). In 1961 newly elected President Kennedy named this among his ten most favourite books and it became a worldwide bestseller. Between 1952 and his death in 1964 Fleming wrote 12 James Bond novels (plus two collections of short stories). The books were given a huge fillip by the spate of films, which began with *Dr No* in 1962 with Sean Connery playing James Bond.

Fleming was 43 when he created James Bond. In 1931 he had taken and failed the civil service entry examinations: his lowest mark (20 out of 100) was for his English essay. He worked briefly as a journalist in Moscow before going into banking and stockbroking. A commander in naval intelligence during the war, in 1945 he was appointed foreign manager of Kemsley Newspapers (owners of the *Daily Express*), a position he held until 1959. He negotiated two months' paid annual leave so that he could spend January and February of every year writing at Goldeneye, his house on the North Shore of Jamaica.

James Bond

There has been endless speculation about real-life inspirations for the character of Bond. In fact Fleming gave him some of his own characteristics. Like Bond, Fleming was a 70-cigarettes-a-day man, a heavy drinker and had a weakness for pretty women. Bond, the same height as Fleming, wears the same black moccasins, dark-blue Sea Island cotton shirts and lightweight blue suits. He has Fleming's black hair, blue eyes, longish nose and 'slightly cruel mouth'. In two of the books Bond's physical appearance is likened to that of the American songwriter, singer and actor, Hoagy Carmichael.

One leading contender as model for Bond is Patrick Dalzel-Job, whom Fleming knew during the latter part of the war. Dalzel-Job was a crack marksman who not only parachuted behind enemy lines in World War Two but also taught himself to ski backwards and to pilot a miniature submarine. He wore an airman's jacket with a compass hidden inside one of the buttons and had a pipe with a hidden chamber containing maps. He had a Bond-like streak of rebellion and a reputation for bravery just short of lunacy. Another contender is Michael Mason of Naval Special Operations, who was based in Romania for part of the war and killed two Nazi agents sent to assassinate him. Other possible models include: Sidney Reilly, a British spy who disappeared in Russia in the late 1920s; the Serbian–British double agent Duško Popov (code name Tricycle), who shared Fleming's taste for casinos, fast cars, strong drink, women and expensive clothes; and agent William Stephenson (code name Intrepid), a Canadian who ran British Intelligence in North America. Yet another contender is Bill 'Biffy' Dunderdale, an MI6 agent and close friend of Fleming's whose persona and sophisticated tastes also matched those of Bond. Fleming declined to comment on all this speculation; but he once said that 'James Bond was a compound of all the secret agents and commando types I met during the war.'

For all his sophisticated tastes, physical attributes and gung-ho bravery, Bond is a two-dimensional character without any real depth – something which Fleming himself acknowledged. In a letter to his friend William Plomer, written shortly after completing *From Russia, with Love*, he said '... although I still enjoy writing about Bond, I constantly find myself piling on adjectives... to fill the vacuum created by my waning enthusiasm for this cardboard booby.' If you like your spy stories to have subtle characterisation, psychological insight and intellectual depth, Fleming is not your man. Bond is, above all, an action man: he succeeds through a mixture of physical prowess and suave one-upmanship.

Villains and others

Bond's women are physically very attractive, but most of them are rather wooden characters. Some of his accomplices, such as Kerim (*From Russia, with Love*) and Quarrel (*Dr No,* 1958), are more colourful and convincing. But it's the villains – outrageously over the top, deliciously despicable – who stand out and stick in the mind. They often have physical characteristics which mark them out as evil or psychologically damaged (usually both). Among the most memorable are lesbian Rosa Klebb, with her knife-tipped shoes, poisonous knitting needles and love of torture; Red Grant, a psychopath who loves killing and is very good at it; Blofeld, whose 'compressed, dark lips, capable only of false, ugly smiles, suggested contempt, tyranny and cruelty'; and Dr No, with mechanical pincers for his hands, who says, 'You are right, Mister Bond. That is just what I am, a maniac.'

Plots

The James Bond books were inspired largely by Fleming's wartime experiences and stories he read in the newspapers. The plots are typically simple, with few of the Byzantine twists and turns favoured by some thriller writers. He mingled fact and fiction in a deliberate and highly effective way. He once said:

> My plots are fantastic, while being based on the truth. They go wildly beyond the probable, but not, I think, beyond the possible. Every now and then there will be a story in the newspapers that lifts a corner of the veil from Secret Service work. A tunnel from East to West Berlin... Crabb's frogman exploit to examine the hull of a Soviet cruiser... the Russian spy Khokhlov with his cigarette case that fired dumdum bullets... this is all true Secret Service history.

The plot of the first James Bond book, *Casino Royale* (1953), was inspired by a visit Fleming and his boss, Admiral Godfrey, made to the casino in Estoril while they were in Lisbon. Fleming, a keen but cautious gambler, played a long but unsuccessful game against some 'sombre Portuguese in their dark suits'. He whispered to Godfrey, 'Just suppose those fellows were German agents – what a coup it would be if we cleaned them out entirely!' In reality, it was Fleming who was cleaned out by the Portuguese. In *Casino Royale* Soviet secret agent Le Chiffre is cleaned out, humiliated and destroyed by Bond. The assassination attempt on Bond in the same book is based on the attempted Soviet assassination of a former German spymaster by Bulgarian agents who (as in *Casino Royale*) missed their target and blew themselves up.

Composite characters

James Bond was an amalgam of several people (mainly secret agents and military men) Fleming came across during the war. When you're creating a character, you can draw on the physical, behavioural and personality traits of your acquaintances. By drawing inspiration from a number of different sources – people you know or have met – you can create a unique fictional character. Don't base a character on a single individual: if it's a recognisable and unflattering portrait, you could risk a libel action. Composite characters, drawing on several real-life sources, are the stock-in-trade of many successful novelists.

Settings, set pieces and descriptive detail

Fleming had an acute sense of pace, but the Bond books also have a rich evocation of place. The settings are exotic and coloured with authentic first-hand description grounded in reality. The Royale-les-Eaux of *Casino Royale* draws on Fleming's pre-war visits to Le Touquet and Deauville. *Dr No* gives us the authentic flavour of Fleming's Jamaica, with his love of snorkelling, wildlife and the cocktail hour. The Istanbul scenes of *From Russia, with Love* drew on his visit to that city in 1955. The golf match in *Goldfinger* (1959) takes place at Royal St Marks, which bears a strong resemblance to Royal St George's, at Sandwich in Kent, where Fleming, who had a house nearby, was a member.

There are memorable set pieces, such as the torture scene in *Casino Royale*; M's insistence (in *Dr No*) on replacing Bond's beloved Beretta automatic ('Ladies' gun, sir,' says the Secret Service armourer) with a more powerful weapon; and Bond's encounters with the deadly centipede and the giant squid (*Dr No*).

Fleming makes extensive use of top-notch brand-named products, such as Bond's Morland cigarettes with their triple gold band and his favourite breakfast of strong coffee from De Bry in New Oxford Street, brown eggs from French Marans hens, Cooper's vintage Oxford marmalade, and Norwegian heather honey from Fortnum & Mason. Fleming's specific, often sensuous, descriptive detail and his use of distinctive mannerisms, such as the way Bond likes his martinis 'shaken, not stirred', convey authenticity and realism.

When and where he wrote

When in Jamaica Fleming usually wrote every morning from 9 a.m. until noon. Later in the day (from 5 p.m. until 6.30 p.m.) he read through what he had written, making corrections and improvements. He tapped out the words of his first James Bond novel, *Casino Royale*, on his 20-year-old Imperial portable typewriter. It took him just seven weeks to complete the 62,000-word draft. The manuscript is a maze of corrections, with many paragraphs rewritten and pages retyped and pasted in. After completing the book (but before revising it again prior to publication) Fleming bought something to remind himself of his hoped-for future as a writer – a gold-plated typewriter. Fleming – like Bond – loved luxury.

A winning formula

The James Bond books have been criticised on many counts: violence, materialism, racism, snobbery, sadism, misogyny, sexual coldness. Bond has been described as 'a licensed criminal who, in the name of false patriotism, approves of nasty crimes'. Fleming said that Bond was 'not a bad man', but he agreed that he was ruthless and self-indulgent, and 'not very likeable or admirable'. The Bond books – many of them, rather well-written – are full of violent action, brutal deaths, fast cars, hairbreadth escapes, bizarre electronic gadgetry, beautiful women, sex and sadistic villains. It's a powerful combination.

Learning points

- Idiosyncratic physical characteristics and habits, marking them out as evil or damaged, make villains stand out and stick in the mind.
- A character's physical attributes can compensate for a lack of psychological depth.
- You can mix fact and fiction. You can set your story in a location you know well; and real-life events can inspire fictional incidents.
- Exotic settings can work if they are coloured with authentic first-hand description grounded in reality.
- Brand names and distinctive mannerisms which define the tastes of your protagonist (such as the way Bond likes his martini shaken, not stirred) can help to fix a character in the mind.

FORD MADOX FORD
(1873–1939)

'A neglected Modernist master' is how Ford Madox Ford has been described. He wrote more than 80 books, but made his name with just two of them, *The Good Soldier* (1915) and *Parade's End* (1924–28), which was adapted for television in 2012. He's not an easy read. 'Impressionism' was the word he used to describe his method of writing.

The Good Soldier

'This is the saddest story I ever heard.' That's *The Good Soldier*'s famous opening line. *The Saddest Story* was Ford's preferred title for the book, but his publisher demurred, believing that such a title would have made the book unsaleable – especially coming out, as it did, shortly after the outbreak of World War One.

The narrator explains:

'I have, I am aware, told this story in a very rambling way so that it may be difficult for anyone to find their path through what may be a sort of maze… And, when one discusses an affair – a long, sad affair – one goes back, one goes forward. One remembers points that one has forgotten and one explains them all the more minutely since one recognizes that one has forgotten to mention them in their proper places and that one may have given by omitting them, a false impression. I console myself with thinking that this is a real story and that, after all, real stories are probably told best in the way a person telling a story would tell them. They will then seem most real.'

So the story is not told chronologically. The narrator, John Dowell (an American millionaire), studs the text with personal anecdotes and numerous digressions – geographical, topographical and cultural. It soon becomes clear, moreover, that he is an unreliable, untrustworthy narrator. There are confusions, uncertainties and ambiguities, and, as US critic and academic Sondra J. Stang said, 'overstatements, understatements, denials, lies, evasions, contradictions, accusations, exaggerations, puns, apparent irrelevancies, logical fallacies, omitted links, digressions, sharp anticipations, delayed explanations, swings of mood… He… confuses and tests the reader.'

The Good Soldier chronicles the tragic lives of two 'perfect couples' during the years before World War One. For nine years Dowell is the odd man out in a close foursome. He tells us that he knows the other three with 'extreme intimacy'. Yet he does not realise that two of the quartet (one is his wife) are having an affair. He appears to be utterly inept at understanding his predicament. His friend, the good, noble soldier of the title, Edward Ashburnham, is a hopeless philanderer and Dowell's wife, Florence, the seemingly helpless invalid who must be guarded against any undue emotional strain, turns out to be an unfaithful libertine. The story is driven by perfidy and passion, and culminates in two suicides. Dowell recounts his impressions of how things first appeared, and then changes the story as viewpoints and understanding shift with later revelations.

The unreliable narrator

An unreliable narrator is a narrator (usually first person) whose credibility has been seriously compromised. The narrator's understanding of what is going on is typically less than that of the reader. The unreliability may be apparent immediately, perhaps by some false or delusional claim, or it may become clear only later in the story – in which case the reader will need to think again about what has gone before. It is therefore a literary device that can confuse and test the reader. Since the unreliable narrator gives a distorted view of events, readers are obliged to reconsider the story and provide their own interpretation. If you want to stretch or challenge the reader, consider using an unreliable narrator.

Parade's End

Parade's End comprises four volumes: *Some Do Not...* (1924), *No More Parades* (1925), *A Man Could Stand Up* (1926) and *The Last Post* (1928). Ford began it in 1922 when he was living on the French Riviera. Writing to H. G. Wells, he said: 'I've got over the nerve tangle of the war and feel able at last really to write again – which I never thought I should do.' His experience of concussion and shell shock after the Battle of the Somme had a profound effect on him. He had been suffering from amnesia and for a time feared he would be unable to write the epoch-defining novel he felt he had to write. The book was written over a period of five years and was finished in New York on 2 November 1927.

Parade's End is the culmination of Ford's experiences as an infantry officer during World War One, but it is much more than that. It's a portrait of an age with the social and moral order in turmoil: the war is just the symptom of a wider malaise. After his first spell at the front, the hero, Christopher Tietjens, returns with partial memory loss: Ford gives us a convincing and effective portrayal of how the brain works when it is either damaged or over-excited and at the end of its tether. The novel has two unforgettable characters: Tietjens and his wife Sylvia. They dominate the story regardless of whether or not they are centre stage.

Christopher Tietjens (lumpish and clumsy, with immense hands) is an extraordinary, multi-layered creation. He is, as one critic said, 'humane in his relationships, feudal in his outlook, Christian in his beliefs, a classicist by education, a Tory in politics'. He is 'synonymous with the character of an ordered, bounded, and harmonious past... the England of gentry and farms' with 'a code of honour and self-respect' – a gentleman 'clinging to noble ideals in an age of hypocrisy and materialism'. He is highly intelligent, with an encyclopaedic memory, and is frequently described as 'the most brilliant man in England'. But men sponge off him and women generally find him repellent: 'his looks and his silences alarmed them'.

During part of the war, Tietjens, a conscientious and caring officer, is in charge of an infantry company preparing soldiers for the front:

> He said, with tears in his voice: 'Damn it all, I gave them that extra bit of smartness... Damn it all, there's something I've done...' getting cattle into condition for the slaughterhouse... They were as eager as bullocks running down by Camden Town to Smithfield Market... Seventy per cent of them, would never come back... But it's better to go to heaven with your skin shining and master of your limbs than as a hulking lout... The Almighty's orderly room will welcome you better in all probability.

Ford's inspiration for Tietjens was his one-time friend Arthur Marwood, son of a good Yorkshire county family, a sceptical Tory who was a brilliant mathematician in the office of government statistics. According to Ford, Marwood had an 'acute and scornful' mind, and was, 'beneath the surface, extraordinarily passionate – with the abiding passion for the sort of truth that makes for intellectual accuracy'.

'Surely the most possessed evil character in the modern novel,' was Graham Greene's take on Christopher's wife, Sylvia. A modern woman, bored and promiscuous, she's the exact opposite of her husband. She undermines and humiliates him with malicious rumours and bare-faced lies – socially, financially and psychologically. Her final act of malice is the cutting-down of the Great Tree of Groby at Tietjens's ancestral home – 'as nasty a blow as the Tietjens had had in generations'. The paradox is that Christopher, whom she detests so much, is the only man in the world Sylvia can love.

Reading *Parade's End*, I found myself asking: 'But did I know that? Have we been told that already or not? In what sense did Christopher "kill" his father? Did we know that Mrs Macmaster was even pregnant, let alone that she had lost a child? Have we been told Tietjens is under arrest?' It's a book you have to read with great attention.

Impressionism

Ford was notorious for the liberties he took with facts. In the preface to one of his books (*Ancient Lights*, 1911) he wrote: 'This book… is full of inaccuracies as to facts, but its accuracy as to impressions is absolute… I don't really deal in facts, I have for facts a most profound contempt. I try to give you what I see to be the spirit of an age, of a town, of a movement. This cannot be done with facts.'

Speaking about the British novel, Ford said its problem was that:

... it went straight forward, whereas in your gradual making acquaintance with your fellows you never do go straight forward. You meet an English gentleman at your golf club. He is beefy, full of health, the moral of the boy from an English Public School of the finest type. You discover, gradually, that he is hopelessly neurasthenic, dishonest in matters of small change, but unexpectedly self-sacrificing, a dreadful liar but a most painfully careful student of lepidoptera and, finally, from the public prints, a bigamist who was once, under another name, hammered on the Stock Exchange... To get such a man in fiction you could not begin at his beginning and work his life chronologically to the end. You must first get him in with a strong impression, and then work backwards and forwards over his past.

Putting a character on the page with a strong first impression and then developing him or her by means of flashbacks and, especially, by dipping into the character's consciousness to show things from his or her point of view, is a favourite technique of Ford's. This is precisely what he does with his principal characters in both *The Good Soldier* and *Parade's End*.

In both books the narrative goes round and round, backtracking and criss-crossing. A fact, an opinion or a memory will be dropped in and often not explained for a dozen or a hundred pages. Sometimes a character is left in a state of emotional crisis while the novel goes off for several pages in another direction. Sometimes a vital piece of information is casually mentioned, whereupon the narrative backs off, as if shocked by anything stated with such certainty. The narrative, in other words, acts in the same way as the mind often works.

Influences and contemporaries

Ford's writing was heavily influenced by Henry James and Joseph Conrad (he collaborated with Conrad on three novels). Prior to

The Good Soldier, his best-known achievement was *The Fifth Queen* trilogy of historical novels (1906–08), based on the life of Catherine Howard. He also wrote essays, poetry, memoirs and literary criticism.

Publisher as well as writer, in 1908 Ford founded *The English Review,* in which he published work by Thomas Hardy, Joseph Conrad, H. G. Wells, Henry James, John Galsworthy, W. B. Yeats, Wyndham Lewis and D. H. Lawrence. He moved to Paris in 1922 and two years later founded the influential *Transatlantic Review,* whose contributors included James Joyce, Ezra Pound, Ernest Hemingway, Gertrude Stein and Jean Rhys.

Ford was born Ford Hermann Hueffer, but changed his name in 1919 (because it sounded too German) in honour of his grandfather, the painter Ford Madox Brown, whose biography he had written. His later years were spent partly in France and partly in the United States (he taught at Olivet College in Michigan).

Learning points

- You don't need to tell the story chronologically.
- Introduce a character with a strong first impression and then develop him or her through flashbacks and by dipping into the character's consciousness.
- Impressionistic fiction is driven by actions, thoughts and dialogue rather than narrative. It blurs reality by focusing on a particular character's perception of events.

KENNETH GRAHAME
(1859–1932)

Publishers have never been much good at picking bestsellers. *The Wind in the Willows*, now regarded as one of the classics of children's literature, was turned down by every publisher it was sent to. These included John Lane at The Bodley Head, publisher of two of Grahame's earlier books, and *Everybody's*, the American periodical that originally solicited it. When Methuen finally picked it up in 1908, they were so sceptical that they refused to pay Grahame any advance. In America the publisher Scribner took it on only after a personal appeal from President Theodore Roosevelt.

The Wind in the Willows also received the thumbs down from the critics: reviews were almost universally hostile. Most of them had praised Grahame's earlier books and had no doubt expected it to be in a similar vein. *The Times*'s critic was caustic: 'Grown-up readers will find it monstrous and elusive. Children will hope, in vain, for more fun.' Arthur Ransome judged it to be an out-and-out failure, 'like a speech to Hottentots made in Chinese'. The only reviewer who saw its merits was the novelist Arnold Bennett.

Published in 1908, the year that Grahame retired from his position as secretary at the Bank of England, *The Wind in the Willows* was to endure much longer, and to become much more famous, than anything he ever wrote. When he retired he moved back to Cookham in Berkshire, where he had been brought up. There, he spent much of his time by the Thames, 'simply messing about in boats', as one of the most famous phrases from the book puts it. He began to write down the bedtime stories he had started to tell his son, many years earlier, on his fourth birthday.

Grahame had written four books when *The Wind in the Willows* was published. The most notable of these were *The Golden Age* (1895) and

Dream Days (1898), collections of stories he had written as a young man for London periodicals such as the *St James Gazette*. Though the stories were about children, they were not written *for* children. They are very much of their time. Based on reminiscences of childhood, they use imagery and metaphor rooted in the culture and mythology of Ancient Greece. The world depicted is one in which children are locked in perpetual warfare with adult 'Olympians' who have forgotten how it feels to be young.

The original English and American editions of *The Wind in the Willows* were published without illustrations, but these were soon followed by several illustrated editions. The best-known and most popular illustrations are probably those by E. H. Shepard, which first appeared in 1931. These are believed to have been authorised by Grahame, who was pleased with the initial sketches but did not live to see the completed work.

The Wind in the Willows can be read either as separate stories or as a complete account of the adventures of Rat, Mole, Badger and Toad in their world alongside the river. It begins with a striking example of hospitality, as Rat invites Mole to accompany him on the river for a picnic. He has only met Mole that day, but he takes him into his home – and this ends up lasting at least a year. Throughout the book there are examples of animals offering one another food or shelter (Rat's dinner engagement with the Otters; Rat's call on Toad to introduce his friend Mole; Badger bringing Rat and Mole, followed by a pair of lost hedgehogs, into his house out of the cold of a snowstorm).

Character

The characters of Toad, Ratty, Mole, and Badger are clearly drawn and each has its own distinct personality. Perhaps the most memorable is the boastful and vain Toad, who sings:

... the most conceited song that any animal ever composed: 'The world has held great Heroes / As history-books have showed / But never a name to go down to fame / Compared with that of Toad! / The clever men at Oxford / Know all that there is to be knowed / But they none of them know half as much / As intelligent Mr Toad!'

Toad's impulsive and generally short-lived enthusiasms (boats, gipsy caravans, motor cars) may reflect adult interests, but they are reminiscent of the kind of crazes that many of us will remember from childhood. The other protagonists are also sharply drawn: practical and clever Ratty, who relaxes by writing poetry; emotional, loyal and home-loving Mole, always wanting to please; and stodgy Badger, who is lazy and speaks 'in that rather common way ("I want some grub, I do"),' but is very wise. He knows about life and acts almost as the village elder: 'The Wild Wood is pretty well populated by now; with all the usual lot, good, bad, and indifferent – I name no names. It takes all sorts to make a world,' he tells Mole. He commands great respect as well as fear among the animals. Rat is the first to mention him: 'Dear old Badger! Nobody interferes with him. They'd better not.' By the end of the novel, he is especially feared by the Weasels, who quieten their infants by telling them that 'if they didn't hush them and not fret them, the terrible grey Badger would up and get them'.

Anthropomorphism

Each creature retains its own animal habits, but they converse and philosophise and behave like humans, and we almost forget that they are animals. Giving animals human personalities and characteristics – anthropomorphism – is a literary device which goes back to ancient times. It dates from before *Aesop's Fables* in sixth century BC Greece and the collections of fables from India which employ anthropomorphised animals to illustrate principles of life. Many of the stereotypes of animals we recognise today, such as the wily fox and the proud lion, can be found in these ancient scripts.

Toad may tell Ratty that 'I'm going to make an animal of you, my boy!' but Grahame's idiomatic dialogue makes us see the protagonists not as animals, but as people: 'How are you today, old chap?' (Rat to Toad); 'Now, pitch in old fellow' (Rat to Mole); '"O, you silly ass, Mole!" cried Toad'; 'You're the best of fellows! Just cut along outside' (Badger to Mole); 'Stir your stumps, Toad, and look lively!' (Badger).

Viewpoint

The Wind in the Willows is written in the omniscient third person. Mole is the main protagonist, followed by Toad, whose adventures can be read as a separate book. But Grahame also uses Ratty and Badger as viewpoint characters to drive the storyline. None of the four principals is perfect. They are shown both at their best and at their worst, dealing with problems to which we can all relate, such as losing a home or getting into trouble for acting foolishly.

Mole makes an ideal protagonist. He is eager and innocent, and he has an open-minded attitude to life, constantly seeking new experiences. Through Mole, the reader can see life through the fresh eyes of childhood. Naïve and inexperienced, he learns from his mistakes. His disregard for the advice of the more experienced Ratty often lands him in trouble: his ill-advised attempt to row ends with him overbalancing and capsizing the boat; and when he ignores Ratty's warning against going into the Wild Wood, he gets completely lost. By the end of the book, the reader has followed Mole through a succession of learning experiences, and has seen him grow into a more mature and worldly character/animal.

Mole is not the only creature to benefit from experience of the real world. In the end even the arrogant Toad humbles himself and puts aside his conceited ways. The reader may wonder whether this change of character will last, but the signs are good. In the final chapter he refuses to make a speech or to sing. And, after consultation with his three friends, he recompenses the people (the gaoler's daughter, the engine-driver and the barge-woman) who have helped him, willingly or unwillingly, to extricate himself from his difficulties. 'He was indeed an altered Toad!' concludes Grahame.

Enduring popularity

The book's charm owes a good deal to the pastoral setting and Grahame's (rather idealised but nonetheless convincing) evocation of the Thames Valley; and to the central importance attached to 'home' as a place of comfort and safety, with good food and a cosy fireside the indispensable props.

But it is the four principal characters, above all, who linger in the mind. They are not perfect and they make mistakes. But for all their weaknesses, Mole, Toad, Badger and Rat epitomise some of the best characteristics of human behaviour, and they are good role models. *The Wind in the Willows* is crammed with passages that show the enduring value of friendship and of qualities such as generosity, humility, forgiveness and compassion. Perhaps it is this, together with its four unforgettable protagonists, that explains its enduring popularity.

Character development

The characters of the four animals develop and change as the story progresses. Mole becomes less naïve and more mature; Toad becomes less boastful. The development of human characters involves more complex personality traits, but the principle of character development is the same. There may be exceptions in the case of some fast-paced thrillers (heroes such as James Bond and Jack Reacher are the same at the end of the story as they are at the beginning), but most fiction depends for its success upon, among other things, creating believable characters who develop and change as the story progresses.

> **Learning points**
>
> - A bedtime story told to a child can be written up many years later.
> - Make your animal protagonists distinct, clearly drawn personalities – and give them human characteristics we can recognise.
> - Put your animals into situations that have parallels with the kind of difficulties human beings have to face.
> - Home can be important in a children's story as a place of safety and comfort.

GRAHAM GREENE
(1904–1991)

Cast an eye over the list of bestselling fiction in your Sunday newspaper. You'll be hard-pressed to find anything that's not a thriller, a romantic novel or a whodunnit. Yet it's literary fiction that gets most of the critical acclaim and scoops most of the prestigious prizes. Graham Greene's special achievement was to square that circle. He was not only one of the most critically admired writers of the twentieth century; he was also one of the most popular.

Be popular and serious

I'm suspicious of the way fiction tends to be divided into popular genre novels and literary works. Isn't a good book a good book? In recent years many crime writers have proved that a gripping whodunnit can be a mechanism for exploring all kinds of serious issues. If you're a novelist, you're in the entertainment business and you need to keep readers turning the page. But they'll probably get more out of the experience if they're also made to think a little bit about life.

Writing style

Evelyn Waugh said that Greene's writing style was 'not a specifically literary style at all. The words are functional, devoid of sensuous attraction.' The opening sentence of *Brighton Rock* (1938) is a good illustration: 'Hale knew, before he had been in Brighton three hours, that they meant to murder him.' The prose is lean, realistic and readable. Its purpose is to interest and excite the reader. 'Excitement is a situation, a single event,' said Greene. 'It mustn't be wrapped up in thoughts, similes, metaphors… Action can only be expressed by a subject, a verb and an object, perhaps a rhythm – little else. Even an adjective slows the pace or tranquilizes the nerve.'

Another hallmark of Greene's writing is the strong visual sense (it's no coincidence that most of his novels have been made into films). As Waugh said of the opening scene of *The Heart of the Matter* (1948), 'It is the camera's eye which moves from the hotel balcony to the street below, picks out the policeman, follows him to his office, moves about the room from the handcuffs on the wall to the broken rosary in the drawer, recording significant detail.'

Influences

Graham Greene began to write after reading Marjorie Bowen's *The Viper of Milan* (1906), a story about the hatred between two princes in fourteenth-century Italy. The book is a mingling of charm and almost unbelievable cruelty. The black-hearted Visconti, Duke of Milan, has a genius for evil; his antagonist, della Scala, Duke of Verona, is an honest man but he betrays his friends and dies a traitor.

Greene read the book, which he said 'made evil interesting', when he was 14. He could identify with the two protagonists. In the evil Visconti he recognised personality traits of a fellow pupil who bullied him at Berkhamsted School, while he himself identified with the character of della Scala, the traitor. The lingering (and often malign) influence of childhood experiences was to be a recurrent feature of Greene's writing.

Themes and characters

The Viper of Milan foreshadowed two of the dominant themes of Greene's fiction. One is the juxtaposition of antagonistic values – what Greene called 'cleavage' and others have called 'the dangerous edge of things'. 'The world is not black and white. More like black and grey,' he said. So his villains are often kind-hearted, his heroes weak and flawed; the guilty are frequently innocent, and the innocent guilty. In the war-ravaged Vienna of *The Third Man* (1950) Harry Lime has no difficulty reconciling his dilution of stolen penicillin (fatal to its victims) with his Catholicism: '"Oh, I still believe, old man. In God and mercy and all that. I'm not hurting anybody's soul by what I do. The dead are happier dead. They don't miss much here, poor devils," he added with that odd touch of genuine pity.'

The other theme foreshadowed by *The Viper of Milan* is that of loyalty – something that preoccupied and obsessed Greene for much of his life. At Berkhamsted School, where his father was headmaster, Greene 'belonged to neither side. I couldn't side with the boys without betraying my father, and they regarded me like a collaborator in occupied territory.' For Greene, disloyalty was both a virtue and a necessity. He believed that the writer's duty was to subvert and make trouble for the Establishment. As the protagonist of *Our Man in Havana* (1958) puts it, 'I don't care a damn about men who are loyal to the people who pay them, to organizations... I don't think even my country means all that much. There are many countries in our blood, aren't there, but only one person.'

We can divide Greene's novel-writing into three phases. In his early stories he gets the reader to question conventional notions of good and evil. His second period has an explicitly religious dimension, as he explores the dilemmas of Catholic characters torn between their religious beliefs and the demands and temptations of human existence. Both Scobie (*The Heart of the Matter*) and the Whisky Priest (*The Power and the Glory*, 1940) are guilt-ridden characters who struggle to reconcile their religion with their human weaknesses and their compassion for others. Pinkie, the teenage gangster of *Brighton Rock*, is Greene's most unrelievedly evil creation, but a romantic film has him in tears. In his later fiction Greene concentrates on secular rather than religious themes. Protagonists such as Fowler (*The Quiet American*, 1955), Brown (*The Comedians*, 1966) and Plarr (*The Honorary Consul*, 1973) are rootless, faithless, world-weary characters. They live in strife-torn environments and often come into conflict with someone, such as Pyle in *The Quiet American*, who (unlike them) tends to see the world as black and white.

Many of the fictional characters Greene created were based on people he met, but he was conscious of the influence his own character had on his writing:

The main character in a novel must necessarily have some kinship to the author, they come out of his body as a child comes from the womb, then the umbilical cord is cut, and they grow into independence. The more an author knows of his own character the more he can distance himself from his invented characters and the more room they have to grow.

'Greeneland'

Throughout his life Greene travelled a great deal, often to 'wild and remote places'. Liberia, Mexico, Sierra Leone, Cuba, Vietnam, Haiti and Argentina are the settings for some of his best-known books. The geographical settings change, but the fictional world of 'Greeneland' remains much the same. It's a world of seediness and darkness, misery and humiliation, failure and disappointed hope, loyalty and betrayal – a world epitomised by *Brighton Rock*'s thugs and razor gangs and the down-at-heel pubs and rundown boarding houses of a town where 'the pale green sea washed into the scarred and shabby side of England'.

How and why he wrote

In his early youth Greene read lots of adventure stories and he later said that these had a great influence on his writing. He admired T. S. Eliot and Herbert Read, but the writers who influenced him most were probably Henry James, Joseph Conrad, Evelyn Waugh (friend and fellow Catholic) and, especially, Robert Louis Stevenson.

From an early age Greene thought of himself, and lived, as a writer:

> The great advantage of being a writer is that you can spy on people. You're there, listening to every word, but part of you is observing. Everything is useful to a writer, you see – every scrap, even the longest and most boring of luncheon parties.

During his 86 years Greene wrote 26 novels, as well as many short stories, plays, screenplays, autobiographical works, essays, reviews and children's books. 'I have no talent,' he said. 'It's just a question of being willing to put in the time.' While many readers will disagree with the first sentence, all published writers will agree with the second. Without hours of sustained effort – the hard slog of turning out words, day after day – nothing is achieved.

For most of his life Greene wrote to a daily target of 500 words and stopped as soon as that was reached. In the 1970s he reduced this to a minimum of 350 words a day, but still produced a book every two years or so. He kept up the discipline of daily writing into his early 80s.

For Greene, writing was a form of therapy. 'Sometimes I wonder,' he said, 'how all those who do not write, compose or paint can manage to escape the madness, melancholia, the panic and fear which is inherent in a human situation.'

For many years he divided his full-length fiction into serious novels and 'entertainments' (a distinction he eventually abandoned). In fact, much of what he wrote is both entertaining and thought-provokingly serious. By adding moral and psychological depth to the thriller, and elements of adventure to the intellectual novel, Graham Greene succeeds as few others have done in combining popular and literary fiction.

Learning points

- A lean, functional writing style makes for easy reading.
- Painful childhood experiences can provide compelling insights and raw material for your writing.
- Loyalty and betrayal are powerful themes.
- The juxtaposition of antagonistic values (e.g. kind-hearted murderers, deeply flawed heroes) can produce compelling characters.
- Everything is useful to a writer.

JOHN GRISHAM
(1955–)

'Unputdownable'. It's a word publishers often use to promote their latest thriller. The book does not always live up to the hype, but John Grisham's legal thrillers justify that description. He has written 30 bestselling novels for adults, plus six legal thrillers for children, short stories and non-fiction. Worldwide sales of his books exceed 275 million.

Why and how he began

John Grisham began writing because he had a story that he wanted to tell. He was a young lawyer when he heard a 10-year-old girl telling a jury what happened when she was beaten and raped: 'Her testimony was gut-wrenching, graphic, heartbreaking and riveting. Every juror was crying.' He found himself musing about what would have happened if the girl's father had taken the law into his own hands and murdered her attackers. With that thought, the story that was to become *A Time to Kill* (1989) was born.

Writing was not a childhood dream and as a student Grisham had no desire to write. But as a child he had always been surrounded by books:

> My mom didn't believe in television. She just didn't. We moved around a lot when I was a kid, a lot of little small towns in the Deep South, and first thing we'd do was always join the local Baptist church, and the second thing would be to get our library cards. We would judge the quality of the town by the number of books you could check out… We always had stacks of books around the house… And I grew up loving to read… Right from the start, I loved the works of Mark Twain.

Born in Jonesboro, Arkansas, in 1955, Grisham graduated from Mississippi State University, attended the University's School of Law and practised criminal law for about a decade. When he began in 1981 he volunteered for as much 'indigent work' as he could get: 'little people fighting big corporations'. This experience fed directly into his writing. The abuse of power, especially by large multinational companies or federal government, is a recurrent theme in many of his novels.

The story he wanted to tell became an obsession, but he had never written fiction before and he was unsure how to begin. He spent many weeks refining his plot outline and fleshing out his characters, and then took several days over the first chapter. Encouraged by his wife's reaction to this, he settled down to three years of very early mornings, getting up at 5 a.m., and late nights.

Getting ideas

The idea for Grisham's first book came from a harrowing experience when he was working as a lawyer. Could something unpleasant you've seen or heard or experienced at work – something you feel strongly about – provide the stimulus or starting point for a novel? Think back over your own career and identify half a dozen incidents or experiences that made a strong impression on you. Making a few notes about these may enable you to identify the one with most potential. Then think about how it might be worked up into a story.

A Time to Kill

Set in the Deep South in the early 1980s, the story is played out against a background of racial tension in Clanton, Alabama, a small town still struggling to free itself from lingering prejudices, where the influence of the Ku-Klux-Klan is not far beneath the surface. The fast-moving story culminates in a tense courtroom drama. The main protagonist is Jake Brigance, the young lawyer engaged to defend the girl's father, a black man who has killed two white men. Grisham has said: 'There's a lot of autobiography in this book. I no longer practise law, but for ten years I did so in a manner very similar to Jake Brigance... Much of what he says and does is what I think and would say under the circumstances.'

Brigance (also the central character of *A Time to Kill*'s sequel, *Sycamore Row* – 2013) is white, handsome, liberal, comfortable with all races and social classes, and moderate in his habits and tastes. His almost flawless character is seen by some critics as a major weakness. Some of the supporting cast, such as the old soak Lucien Wilbanks (Brigance's one-time boss) and the obese divorce lawyer Harry Rex Vonner, are more memorable.

Getting published

Once the book was finished, Grisham spent a year submitting it to New York publishers. He made multiple approaches to agents and publishers, and followed the standard advice to submit the first three chapters. The book was rejected 28 times. When his wife pointed out that the first three chapters were not the best, he tried submitting the first, the third and the seventh chapter (in which the pivotal killing takes place). This did the trick.

Wynwood Press, a small, unknown publisher, agreed to a modest print run of 5,000 copies. Once the book had been accepted, Grisham worked under his editor's guidance through several revisions (he also tried half a dozen different titles). Published in June 1989, it did not sell well. Grisham himself bought 1,000 copies, selling these over the following year to friends, bookshops and libraries.

The Firm

As soon as *A Time to Kill* was finished he began work immediately on a second novel, the story of an ambitious young attorney lured to an apparently perfect law firm that was not what it seemed. Its route to publication was very different from that of his first book. In the autumn of 1989, just after *A Time to Kill* was published, he sent the manuscript to his agent. 'The book sort of languished in New York throughout the fall of '89,' Grisham has said. '... And unknown to us – and this is the luckiest break I've had in publishing, and I think everybody at some point has to have a lucky break – unknown to my agent, unknown to anybody, a copy of *The Firm* was stolen from a publisher in New York – a publisher who hadn't read it yet – and it surfaced in Hollywood, sort of a bootleg copy of the manuscript. And a guy got it out there, and made twenty-five copies of it, and gave it to every studio.'

In the first week of January 1990 Grisham heard that four major companies were locked in a bidding war for the book's film rights. Paramount won, and a couple of weeks later the hardback and paperback rights were sold. When *The Firm* came out in March 1991 it was a major publishing event. It became that year's bestselling novel, staying on *The New York Times*'s bestseller list for 47 weeks. It was the cue for Grisham to give up being a lawyer and start being a full-time writer.

A Painted House

A Painted House (2001) was Grisham's first departure from legal thrillers, as he broadened his canvas to focus on more general issues of the rural South (he also wrote some sports and comic fiction, but continued with his legal thrillers). *A Painted House* is a semi-autobiographical story set in the cotton fields of Arkansas where Grisham himself spent his early childhood. Here's how it begins:

> The hill people and the Mexicans arrived on the same day. It was a Wednesday, early in September 1952. The Cardinals were five games behind the Dodgers with two weeks to go, and the season looked hopeless. The cotton, however, was waist high to my father, almost over my head, and he and my grandfather could be heard before supper whispering words that were seldom heard. It could be a 'good crop.'

The narrator is Luke Chandler, a seven-year-old farm boy who (like Grisham) loves baseball and lives with his parents and grandparents in a little house that's never been painted. He sees things that no seven-year-old should see and finds himself keeping secrets that will put an end to his childhood innocence. 'I really like *A Painted House*,' Grisham said recently. 'It's just a different kind of book; it's a childhood memoir, it's a lot of family lore, and there's a lot of autobiography in it.' *The Times* described *A Painted House* as 'a lyrical, gritty and personal novel... his best work'. It is very different from his fast-paced legal thrillers, with (according to *Publishers Weekly*) 'characters no reader will forget... and a drop-dead evocation of time and place that mark this novel as a classic'.

How he writes

In an interview for *The Telegraph* in 2009, Grisham said:

> I know what I do is not literature. For me, the essential component of fiction is plot. My objective is to get the reader to feel impelled to turn the pages as quickly as possible. If I want to achieve that, I can't allow myself the luxury of distracting him. I have to keep him hanging on and the only way to do it is by using the weapons of suspense. There is no other way... I can't change overnight into a serious literary author. You can't compare apples to oranges. William Faulkner was a great literary genius. I am not.

With his love of suspense and intrigue, it's no surprise to learn that his favourite author is John le Carré (John Steinbeck and Raymond Chandler are other writers he admires).

'When you write suspense,' says Grisham, 'you have to sacrifice certain things you would like to explore: people, relationships, setting, places, culture, food.' He believes his best novels are those in which a fast-paced story is linked to the exploration of a serious issue, such as capital punishment in *The Chamber* (1994), tobacco litigation in *The Runaway Jury* (1996), homelessness in *The Street Lawyer* (1998) and insurance fraud in *The King of Torts* (2003).

His usual routine is to begin work at 6 a.m. and to write for five or six hours, finishing around noon. He takes only six months to write a book, but this is preceded by an extensive outline. 'The outlining process can go on for a long time, even a year or two.' Once he is sure that he has a story strong enough to sustain a novel of between 375 and 500 pages (40 chapters of around ten pages each), he starts work on a full, chapter-by-chapter outline. He attaches great importance to this because 'it makes you see the whole story'.

He believes that writing a thriller is similar to writing a murder mystery, because of the need to insert clues. Before he begins writing Grisham makes sure that he has a robust main plot that works, as well as a core subplot. He does not pre-plan every incident and every character, but he puts a great deal of effort into the outline, knowing that if this is as good as he can make it, the book will be easy to write.

He always sticks closely to his outline. 'You've got to start with your principal character, it's got to be somebody that your reader cares about. And that's the hardest one. You've got to get them in trouble, and you've got to get them out. And your readers have got to care about that person when they're in trouble, or you've lost them. That's basic suspense, and I did not invent it.'

Once the first draft is complete, he spends a month revising it. The first draft of *A Time to Kill* was almost twice the length of the published novel. He enjoys neither outlining nor revising, but always advises aspiring writers that without these disciplines they are unlikely to succeed. His other piece of advice is: 'Don't quit your day job. Pursue a real profession first and write as a hobby. Very few aspiring writers survive on words alone.'

> **Learning points**
>
> - Writing while holding down a full-time job will probably mean getting up very early, and/or staying up very late, to write, but you'll be able to pay your bills as you learn the craft of writing.
> - Submit the best three, rather than the first three, chapters of your book.
> - Make your principal character someone the reader cares about.
> - Don't give up the day job until you are sure you can make it as a full-time writer.

THOMAS HARDY
(1840–1928)

'Write what you know' is the advice routinely given to new writers. Thomas Hardy grew up in an agricultural community in rural Dorset. That was the world he knew – and that was what he wrote about. He wasted no scrap of his own experience – a valuable lesson for any writer.

Hardy has the unusual, if not quite unique, distinction of being both a great novelist and a great poet. 'The business of the poet and novelist,' he said, 'is to show the sorriness underlying the grandest things, and the grandeur underlying the sorriest things.' As a novelist – and that's the focus of this chapter – Hardy's strength and appeal derive from the power with which he depicts both landscape and character.

Beginnings

The son of a small-time builder and a domestic servant, Hardy spent his childhood in a two-up, two-down cottage in Higher Bockhampton, near Dorchester. At the age of 16 he became an architect's apprentice; he taught himself Greek, and read Latin and Greek poetry before work each morning. He was deeply affected by the insecurity of the lives of the rural poor, and his first-hand experience of their constant, year-round struggle to survive underpinned much of his writing.

Hardy's first attempt at a novel was in 1867. *The Poor Man and the Lady* attacked the hypocrisy of the middle and upper classes and the indifference they showed towards workers who aspired to better themselves through education (it can be seen as a dry run for *Jude the Obscure* – 1895). Hardy himself described it as 'strikingly socialistic'. It took him five months to produce a first draft of the novel and another five to produce a revised version ready for submission. He then spent 14 months trying – unsuccessfully – to find a publisher. Determined to succeed as a novelist, he took all the advice he could get both from publishers and published writers. One of the people who read the manuscript was the novelist George Meredith. He advised Hardy to discard it, on the grounds that it would be fiercely attacked and would damage his future chances as a novelist, and to write a less polemical novel – one 'with a purely artistic purpose' and more of a plot.

First successes

Hardy took Meredith's advice. Resolving to write a different sort of novel, he searched *Dorset County Chronicle* for stories from the 1820s that he might make use of (throughout his career his eye for poignant detail often came from clippings from newspaper reports of local events: the spreading bloodstain at the end of *Tess of the D'Urbervilles* (1891), and little Jude's suicide note are just two examples). His plan was to use the country life he knew and to dream up a thrilling plot, and he put this into practice in his first two published novels, *Desperate Remedies* (1871) and *Under the Greenwood Tree* (1872). His third novel, *A Pair of Blue Eyes* (1873), was the first published under his own name; its serialisation in a popular magazine is believed to be the origin of the term 'cliffhanger' (one of the characters is left literally hanging off a cliff). Hardy recognised the importance both of serialisation and of the US market, and was always ready to accept cuts and changes imposed by his editors. His next novel, *Far from the Madding Crowd* (1874), established his reputation and enabled him to give up his work as an architect to concentrate wholly on his writing.

Landscape

The Dorset landscape, described with a naturalist's eye, and village life in the first half of the nineteenth century (before it was changed for ever by the industrial revolution) was the foundation for Hardy's novels. He gave the towns and villages of his 'Wessex' fictitious names, but his descriptions are based on reality and they are easily identifiable. His writing shows a deep passion for the countryside and nature plays a significant role in his stories, but his descriptions are never sentimental. Time and again he demonstrates the harshness of nature and the calamitous effect it can have on human lives. In *The Mayor of Casterbridge* (1886) Henchard's financial ruin is caused partly by his own impulsive character, but is ultimately brought about by a disastrous change in the weather.

Sometimes the landscape is humanised, as in this description of Egdon Heath in *The Return of the Native* (1878):

It was at present a place perfectly accordant with man's nature – neither ghastly, hateful, nor ugly; neither commonplace, unmeaning nor tame; but, like man, slighted and enduring; and withal singularly colossal and mysterious in its swarthy monotony.

In *The Woodlanders* (1887) he sets the scene by melding the landscape with the human drama that is to follow:

It was one of those sequestered spots outside the gates of the world... where, from time to time, dramas of a grandeur and unity truly Sophoclean are enacted in the real, by virtue of the concentrated passions and closely knit interdependence of the lives therein.

Character

Hardy had an acute sense of drama; and the heroes and heroines of his major novels are some of the most compelling and dramatic characters in all literature. Henchard, Tess and Jude, in particular, are magnificently conceived, brilliantly portrayed, unforgettable figures who dominate their stories.

The Mayor of Casterbridge is Hardy's most powerful study of character and destiny. Although some incidents in the novel strain credibility, Henchard leaps off the page. He is an extraordinary creation, full of contradictions: strong, ignorant, energetic, uneducated, driven, lovable, self-destructive, depressive, volatile, bad-tempered. He craves affection, but has an explosive temperament that drives it away.

Tess, on the other hand, is an innocent whose downfall is brought about not by her own character but by the society in which she lives. By giving the novel the deliberately provocative subtitle *A Pure Woman*, Hardy made his own position clear and waved a red rag in the face of conventional views. Tess was condemned by society as a fallen woman, a kept mistress and finally a murderess; but for Hardy she was pure of heart, with all the virtues of charity. With a plot that revolves around rape, illegitimate birth and adultery against a background of rural spoliation, *Tess* attacked Christian hypocrisy, Victorian double standards and the exploitation of cheap labour, and it provoked a furious reaction. Always ready to adapt his writing to the demands of the market, Hardy produced a heavily cut and changed text for serialisation in *The Graphic*, for which he removed anything likely to offend its Christian readers. *Tess* was written, revised, cut, restored and revised again before the final, complete version was published in November 1891.

Bitter at his own failure to attend university, in *Jude the Obscure* Hardy hits out at the class system's denial of education and opportunity to the intelligent poor, and the resultant wastage of human resources and talent. The novels which most critics regard as Hardy's masterpieces (*The Return of the Native*, *The Mayor of Casterbridge*, *The Woodlanders*, *Tess of the D'Urbervilles* and *Jude the Obscure*) are generally sad stories with bleak (but somehow inevitable) endings. *Jude*, the most unremittingly gloomy, was savaged by the critics as 'a shameful nightmare' and 'Jude the Obscene'. But there was also praise for 'the most powerful and moving picture of human life which Mr Hardy has given us', and for the *Saturday Review* Jude's final words represented 'the voice of the educated proletarian, speaking more distinctly than it has ever spoken before in English literature'.

After *Jude* Hardy gave up fiction and devoted himself to his first love, poetry. Explaining this change of tack, he pointed out that he had always tried to keep close to natural life and poetry in his novels.

Strong characters

Characters full of contradictions, like Henchard, can make a strong impression on the reader. They are often more interesting – and more memorable – than characters with consistent, uniform personality traits. It does not matter much whether these character traits are positive or negative: vividly drawn 'bad' characters often stick more in the mind.

Reflecting human nature

Hardy's subject matter was often controversial and groundbreaking. His style was of its time: his prose, influenced by Greek tragedy, is peppered with classical allusions and biblical references which contemporary readers may find tedious or incomprehensible. There are coincidences and improbabilities of plot which jar, and descriptive passages which may be too lengthy for present-day tastes. The agricultural communities Hardy wrote about are long gone, and the nineteenth-century landscape has changed. His novels remain popular because, with their powerful depictions of character and landscape, they reflect human nature.

'I never let a day go by without using a pen,' said Hardy when he was in his 80s. 'Just holding it sets me off; in fact I can't think without it. It's important not to wait for the right mood. If you do it will come less and less.'

Learning points

- Write what you know and waste no scrap of your own experience: use it to inform and underpin your writing.
- If at first you don't succeed, try, try again (Hardy's first novel was unpublishable).
- Research old newspapers and other media for material you can use in your fiction.
- Take all the advice you can get from published writers and publishers, and be open to accepting any cuts or changes suggested by an editor.
- Get into the habit of writing something every day.

ROBERT HARRIS
(1957–)

His sales are measured in millions and his books have been translated into 37 languages. From the Nazis to Stalin's legacy in today's Russia, from Ancient Rome to global financial markets – Robert Harris has written a string of diverse, fast-paced thrillers. His books are both serious and entertaining; that's a trick few novelists can pull off.

Determined from an early age to be a writer, Harris edited his school magazine and went on to read English at Cambridge. He became a BBC news reporter and then a political journalist. Before turning to fiction he wrote several non-fiction books including, most notably, *Selling Hitler* (1986), an investigation into the scandal of the 'Hitler Diaries'. Published by a West German magazine in 1983, they were later proved to be forgeries.

Fatherland

Harris used his considerable knowledge of World War Two in his first, and arguably his most satisfying, thriller. If things had gone slightly differently in 1941–1942, the outcome of the war could easily have been different. What would Germany have been like if the Nazis had won World War Two? That's the fascinating 'what if' question to which *Fatherland* (1992) provides one possible answer.

Fatherland was an instant international bestseller. The compulsive, fast-paced plot and believable characters make the book a gripping read. Harris's portrayal of what a victorious Germany might have been like is plausible – and deeply chilling. 'Robert Harris has created the whole structure of a totally corrupt society in a way that makes the flesh creep,' said John Mortimer. In Harris's Germany of 1964 the Jews have been wiped out and there are 100 million German settlers in Ukraine. Britain and the rest of Western Europe are demoralised, weak and irrelevant. The world's two superpowers are the United States and the Greater German Reich.

Harris's models for the Greater German Reich of *Fatherland* were George Orwell's *Nineteen Eighty-Four* (1949) and Martin Cruz Smith's *Gorky Park* (1981). The total subservience to the SS-dominated hierarchy he describes in *Fatherland* has clear parallels both with the world of Big Brother depicted in Orwell's masterpiece and with the Soviet totalitarianism of *Gorky Park*. The world Harris created was so chillingly realistic and controversial that the book caused a furore in Germany and was turned down by 30 publishers before being accepted there and becoming a bestseller.

It's worth considering why a novel that depicts such a horrific scenario has given so much pleasure and been enjoyed by so many people, including many who tend to read 'literary' fiction rather than crime novels or thrillers. Harris believes the explanation lies in sheer relief that the terrifying nightmare he describes did not materialise.

Counterfactual history

Fatherland belongs to a genre known as counterfactual, or alternative, history – books that explore 'what if' questions. One of the best-known early examples is *If It Had Happened Otherwise* (1931), which includes an examination by Winston Churchill of what could have happened if Robert E. Lee's Confederate Army had won at the Battle of Gettysburg, the turning point of the American Civil War.

Two more recent examples of counterfactual novels are Kingsley Amis's *The Alteration* (1976), which explored what might have happened if the Reformation had never taken place, and Len Deighton's *SS-GB* (1978), based on a successful German invasion of Britain in 1941. So Harris's starting point of German victory in World War Two was no new invention. What was different was setting the novel not in Britain, but in Germany.

Other historical fiction

Harris's follow-up novel *Enigma* (1995) is also rooted in World War Two. Set in the hidden wartime world of signals intelligence and cryptography, it's a story of codes, secrets, love and betrayal. For me the book's strength lies in Harris's ability to recreate the feeling of what it must have been like to work at Bletchley Park, where the 'need to know' principle was rigorously applied and most people knew little or nothing about what others were doing. As the code-breakers wrap up and rub their hands together, trying to keep warm in an English winter, you can almost feel the cold and taste the revolting wartime food. There's a feeling of actually being there, waiting for the reports to come in from doomed convoys out in the North Atlantic.

At the heart of *Archangel* (1998) is Harris's ability to conjure up the authentic feel of post-Communist Russia. The book is a clever blend of historical fact, accurate contemporary reportage and creative, imaginative fiction. 'I have never read a better description of the death of Stalin, anywhere,' said the eminent historian Norman Stone.

In 2003 Harris's fiction took an unexpected turn with *Pompeii*, the first of his novels set in Ancient Rome. This was followed by his Cicero trilogy, described by one critic as 'like watching a political, multi-chariot pile-up'. *Imperium* (2006), *Lustrum* (2009) and *Dictator* (2015) are set in the final days of the Roman Republic.

To go from Stalin's legacy in modern-day Russia to Ancient Rome is a radical change of tack, but perhaps the leap is not as enormous as it might seem. The power struggles of competing rival groups were as much a feature of government in Roman times as they were in Nazi Germany or Communist Russia. 'Human beings haven't changed much in 2,000 years,' says Harris. He also points to parallels between Ancient Rome and Nazi Germany – astonishing feats of engineering, military marching and stamping feet, the symbol of the eagle and the existence of high culture alongside inhumane brutality. There were shady dealings in Ancient Rome, in Nazi Germany and in Communist Russia; and there are shady dealings today.

An Officer and a Spy (2013) is based on the infamous Dreyfus affair. It tells the true story of Georges Picquart, who fights to expose the truth about the evidence that wrongly convicted Dreyfus for espionage.

> **Power struggles**
>
> Power struggles between competing groups and/or individuals have been a recurring feature of government – and of life – from the earliest times to the present day. And from Shakespeare to J. K. Rowling, they have formed the basis of countless works of fiction. The setting need not be exotic. In almost every office and every family in the country, you're likely to find a power struggle of some kind, whether it's over a triviality or something of real, lasting significance. For a few people, achieving and exercising power becomes an all-consuming passion. People like that can make compelling fictional characters.

Contemporary political fiction

In another departure from his previous works, *The Ghost* (2007) features a former Prime Minister remarkably similar to Tony Blair. Harris was at one time close to Blair and the novel reflects Harris's opposition to Blair's decision to support US military action in Iraq.

The Fear Index (2011) achieves the remarkable feat of making some sense of the puzzling world of global financial markets. 'Nowhere in fiction – either in films or in novels – has anyone really written about how the financial world is ticking,' says Harris. His research led him to conclude that the key to the world of hedge funds – and the key to his novel – was not the banker or the financial whiz-kid, but the clever geeky scientist:

> Of course there have been novels set in hedge funds, but… [no] novel that shows it as it really is – which is so dependent on science; physicists and mathematicians and computer programmers. It was an absolute eye-opener for me; to go into these hedge funds and find that the people [working] there were all PhDs.

The Fear Index is set in Geneva. It's a tale of scientific hubris, with computers at its heart. Harris has described it as 'Gothic realism' – a sort of twenty-first-century *Frankenstein*. 'The Gothic novel is generally about the hinterland between human beings and the other, the supernatural. But our hinterland, in quite a realistic way, is now between being human and being a machine.' *Conclave* (2016) goes behind the scenes at the Vatican in the near future, following the death of a Francis-like leader of the Roman Catholic Church, to tell the story of a power struggle to elect a new pope.

How he writes

All of Robert Harris's books – fiction and non-fiction – are based on facts. He begins by recreating specific, concrete details. In *Fatherland* many of the characters whose names he uses actually existed, and their biographical details are correct up to 1942 (after that he plays around with them and gives them fictitious life histories according to the needs of his plot). *Enigma* incorporates the content of original decoded signals of U-boats attacking the North Atlantic convoys. *The Fear Index* includes authentic details about the operation of hedge funds and the workings of global financial markets – the result of Harris's extensive research. When he began work on the book he knew nothing about the financial world.

> As a novelist I quite like – I suppose because I was a journalist – to go into worlds and discover new things about them, and to try and take the reader into a world in a procedural way. So you're on the shoulders of people who are doing their jobs, be it an aqueduct engineer [the Cicero Trilogy] or a code-breaker [*Enigma*], or in this case [*The Fear Index*] an algorithmic hedge fund manager.

Harris has the rare ability to make complex material accessible, comprehensible and compelling. The reader invariably ends his books better informed as well as hugely entertained. Whether recreating Ancient Rome or speculating on possible versions of history, he has the ability to fuse a fascination for politics with a strong storytelling instinct. The result is compelling fiction.

Harris uses straightforward prose to write intelligent thrillers full of narrative tension, believable characters and well-researched, spot-on atmospheric detail. Carefully crafted suspense produces page-turning entertainment. He has a clear, direct style and a respect for traditional storytelling techniques: 'I'm a journalist at heart,' he says. 'So it's telling the story that matters.'

Learning points

- You can blend historical fact and contemporary reportage with your own imagination to create compelling fiction.
- Incorporating concrete facts, true biographical information and spot-on descriptive detail gives your writing a feeling of real authenticity.
- If you write in an accessible and compelling way, you can not only entertain your readers but also leave them better informed – even about complex subjects.

ERNEST HEMINGWAY
(1899–1961)

A Farewell to Arms (1929), Hemingway's first bestseller, was based on the time he spent as an ambulance driver on the Italian front. Written in the first person, it's a semi-autobiographical love story set against the background of World War One. His first novel, *The Sun Also Rises*

(1926), had caused a stir with its modernist, pared-down style, and *A Farewell to Arms* cemented his reputation.

The novel ends with the stillborn birth of the hero's son and the death of his lover Catherine – and this final sentence: 'After a while I went out and left the hospital and walked back to the hotel in the rain.' It's a simple enough sentence, but in an interview for *The Paris Review* in 1958 he said, 'I rewrote the ending to *A Farewell to Arms*, the last page of it, 39 times before I was satisfied.' He was a perfectionist. When the interviewer asked what had stumped him, he said 'Getting the words right.'

Hemingway produced no fewer than 47 different endings. In 2012 these were reproduced, together with early drafts of other passages, in a new edition of the novel published by Scribner. We can see that a writer regarded as one of the giants of American fiction was uncertain about the kind of ending he wanted, and he had great difficulty finding the right words.

That low-key, matter-of-fact final sentence is typical of Hemingway's lean, spare prose. Coming at the end of an epic story of war and love, to have Henry walking away from the hospital in the rain – and to describe this in simple, everyday language, leaving almost everything unsaid – seems right.

The alternative endings that Hemingway considered range from several paragraphs to a short sentence or two. They show how the novel could have concluded on a very different note. Some of them are more optimistic: 'He [Henry's son, who lives in this version] does not belong in this story. He starts a new one. It is not fair to start a new story at the end of an old one but that is the way it happens. There is no end except death and birth is the only beginning'; 'Finally I slept; I must have slept because I woke. When I woke the sun was coming in the open window and I smelled the spring morning after the rain and saw the sun on the trees in the courtyard and for that moment it was all the way it had been.'

One ending is uncharacteristically spiritual: 'The thing is that there is nothing you can do about it. It is all right if you believe in God and love God.' And some are bleaker: 'In the end it is better not even to remember things but I know that'; 'That is all there is to the story. Catherine died and you will die and I will die and that is all I can promise you.'

This 2012 edition, which also lists the alternative titles he considered (some straightforward, others cryptic), shows the enormous trouble Hemingway took over his prose. There are handwritten notes and long passages crossed out, giving us an insight into his thinking and a real sense of his writing process. We can see that he did not get it right first time.

Leaving it out

Knowing how much information to give the reader – what to put in and what to leave out – is a difficult skill to learn: trial and error is probably the only way. That final sentence of *A Farewell to Arms* makes no attempt to describe Henry's feelings or to say anything profound about the loss of his lover and child. It leaves it all unsaid, but the contrast between that matter-of-fact sentence and what has gone before only serves to heighten the latter's impact. Using the analogy of an iceberg, Hemingway habitually kept the meaning hidden. He avoided explanations, believing that if the writing was strong enough, the reader would see below the surface and understand what he was getting at.

For Whom the Bell Tolls

In 1937–1938 Hemingway reported on the Spanish Civil War for the North American Newspaper Alliance. He was present at the battle of the Ebro, the last republican stand, and was among the journalists who were some of the last to leave the battle. *For Whom the Bell Tolls* (1940), generally regarded as his finest book, graphically describes the brutality and inhumanity of the civil war. Probably the most unforgettably horrific scene is his description of an execution line of baying villagers, armed with clubs, flails and pitchforks, which fascist supporters are forced to go through before being thrown over the edge of a cliff. Hemingway based the scene on events that took place in Ronda in 1936, when a mob threw some 500 suspected fascists into a gorge.

The book's title is taken from John Donne (1624): 'any man's death diminishes me, because I am involved in mankind; And therefore never send to know for whom the bell tolls; It tolls for thee.' Death is a main preoccupation of the novel. The hero, Robert Jordan, knows that his assignment to blow up a bridge held by the fascists will inevitably mean his own death, and the guerrilla leaders he is working with also see their own deaths as inevitable. Camaraderie and sacrifice in the face of death permeate the novel, and suicide also looms large. Robert Jordan and many of the other characters would prefer to die rather than to be captured. To avoid it they are prepared to be killed or to kill themselves.

The book ends with Robert Jordan, wounded and unable to go any further, awaiting a final attack that will end his life. If he is not killed, he faces the choice of capture, followed by torture for the extraction of information and eventual death at the hands of the enemy, or suicide. He understands suicide but doesn't approve of it, and thinks 'you have to be awfully occupied with yourself to do a thing like that'. In 1961 Hemingway took his own life.

A Moveable Feast

Towards the end of his life Hemingway recorded his memories of Paris, where he lived in the 1920s with other expatriate writers such as James Joyce, F. Scott Fitzgerald, Wyndham Lewis, Ford Madox Ford, Ezra Pound and Gertrude Stein. 'If you are lucky enough to have lived in Paris as a young man, then wherever you go for the rest of your life, it stays with you, for Paris is a moveable feast,' he wrote. *A Moveable Feast*, published posthumously in 1964, is a memoir consisting of sketches of Hemingway's experiences in 1920s Paris. It includes specific details and locations of the cafes, bars, hotels and apartments that Hemingway knew (some of which survive today). It is based on notebooks he had filled during the years he lived in Paris and had stored in a trunk left in the basement of the Ritz Hotel. His memories are personal, affectionate and full of wit, and the sketches give us a fascinating glimpse of Hemingway's life at a time when he was finding his feet as a writer. They recall a time when, poor, happy, unknown and writing in cafes, he discovered his vocation.

How he wrote

'My aim is to put down on paper what I see and what I feel in the best and simplest way,' said Hemingway.

> When I am working on a book or a story I write every morning as soon after first light as possible. There is no one to disturb you and it is cool or cold and you come to your work and warm as you write. You read what you have written and, as you always stop when you know what is going to happen next, you go on from there. You write until you come to a place where you still have your juice and you stop... You have started at six in the morning, say, and may go on until noon or be through before that.

As a novice writer and journalist in Paris, Hemingway was influenced by Ezra Pound. He learned to write in the modernist style, using understatement, distrusting adjectives, eschewing sentimentalism, and presenting images and scenes without explanation of their meaning. He began by writing short stories and learned how to prune language, how to get the most from the least, and how to build intensity. Meaning is established through dialogue, through action and through silences. The prose is tight and lean. He discards many common punctuation marks (colons, semicolons, dashes, parentheses) in favour of short declarative sentences that build on each other, and in place of commas he habitually uses 'and'.

His distinctive style has sometimes been called the theory of omission, but Hemingway preferred the analogy of an iceberg:

> If a writer of prose knows enough of what he is writing about he may omit things that he knows and the reader, if the writer is writing truly enough, will have a feeling of those things as strongly as though the writer had stated them. The dignity of movement of an iceberg is due to only one eighth of it being above water.

When he was awarded the Nobel Prize in Literature in 1954, it was for 'his mastery of the art of narrative… and for the influence that he has exerted on contemporary style'.

What does it mean to be a writer? Here's Hemingway's definition:

> All good books are alike in that they are truer than if they had really happened and after you are finished reading one you will feel that all that happened to you and afterwards it all belongs to you: the good and the bad, the ecstasy, the remorse and sorrow, the people and the places and how the weather was. If you can get so that you can give that to people, then you are a writer.

> **Learning points**
>
> - Put down on paper what you see and feel in the simplest way you can.
> - A lean, pared-down writing style, with simple language and few adjectives and punctuation marks, can be effective.
> - Always stop a writing session when you know what is going to happen next, so that you can pick it up easily in your next session.
> - Present scenes without explanations: establish meaning through dialogue, action and silences.
> - Do not expect to get it right first time: learn from the trouble Hemingway took over *A Farewell to Arms*, with its 47 alternative endings and a final page rewritten 39 times.

JAMES HERBERT
(1943–2013)

'Herbert was by no means literary, but his work had a raw urgency,' said Stephen King (the world's number one horror writer). 'His best novels, *The Rats* and *The Fog*, had the effect of Mike Tyson in his championship days: no finesse, all crude power. Those books were bestsellers because many readers (including me) were too horrified to put them down.'

James Herbert wrote 23 novels. Published in 34 languages, they sold 54 million copies. Five of them were adapted for cinema, television and radio, and in 2010 he was made Grand Master of Horror by the World Horror Convention. Herbert had the ability to grab his readers on the first page and keep them glued to the page with a rising crescendo of genuinely chilling suspense. '[He] comes at us with both hands, not willing to simply engage our attention, he seizes us by the lapels and begins to scream in our faces,' said King.

How he became a horror writer

Asked in a radio interview what got him into horror, Herbert said: 'I lived in a very spooky house in a very spooky street and I used to watch spooky films.' Half of the street, at the back of Petticoat Lane in London, had been bombed and the house he lived in had been condemned. If his parents went out in the evening he was left alone in the house.

> My greatest fear was being plunged into darkness when the electricity failed. Then I had to go down to the cheerless cellar clutching a shilling for the meter with nothing but a candle. That's if I had a shilling. If I didn't I hurried to bed, because my Gothic imagination ran riot with thoughts of Dracula and other monsters. That environment fuelled the macabre side of my imagination. I might not have become a writer had I not been born there.

In another interview he said that his love of storytelling came from his mother, who 'had an ability to see things with a child's eye and told us wonderful stories'.

> I hate violence and I didn't plan to write horror; it just poured out of me. The great thing is that you can write humour, romance or political thrillers under that genre. You can write about a mundane situation and take a mental leap to something outrageous.

The Rats

After school and art college, Herbert joined the art department of an advertising agency (he was to design many of his own book covers). He was 28 when he began writing his first and most famous novel, *The Rats*, in his spare time. It took him ten months and when it was completed he sent it off to half a dozen publishers. Five rejected it but the sixth recognised its appeal. Within three weeks of publication it sold 100,000 copies. The novel broke new ground with its depiction of ordinary people caught up in horrific events and its graphic descriptions – unusual at the time – of gore and bloodshed.

The Rats (1974) had two sources of inspiration. The first was a piece of ground, where there had formerly been stables, behind his house in the East End of London. His parents ran a fruit stall in Bethnal Green market, and this was where the market traders dumped rotting fruit and vegetables. It was alive with rats. The second inspiration was watching a scene from the vampire horror film *Dracula* in which one of the characters says he has seen a thousand rats with red eyes looking up at him.

The Rats is relatively short, just under 200 pages, but it packs plenty of sex, violence and gruesome action into those. It begins and ends in a derelict old house by the canal, which is the physical centre of the story and the key to the horrific series of attacks. It begins when the rats attack, and eat alive, a down-and-out drunkard who takes refuge in the house. Herbert chooses familiar settings – an underground train, a school, a cinema, a zoo – and victims (including a baby and a schoolboy) with whom readers cannot help but sympathise, as he ratchets up the suspense with attacks that become more and more horrific. Some of the writing makes the flesh creep: 'He couldn't rise now for the sheer weight of writhing, furry vermin feeding from his body, drinking his blood.'

Three-quarters of the way through the book Herbert uses an old trick of the trade, making the reader believe, at least for a short time, that the problem has been solved: 'The danger had passed. So everyone thought.' But of course everyone was wrong. The danger had not passed; the vermin had not been vanquished. The rats survive to wreak more havoc and death over London until the book's gripping finale. The one-page epilogue sees the survival of just one rat. That is enough to pave the way for the book's two sequels, *Lair* (1979) and *Domain* (1984).

The Rats received a lot of stick from critics revolted by Herbert's stomach-turning descriptions and his graphic anatomical portrayals of mutilation caused by the giant, black, flesh-eating rats. Some critics were also alienated by the book's implicit (and occasionally explicit) criticism of governments' lack of care towards those at the bottom of the social scale and failure to react promptly to tragedy. He once said in an interview: 'The subtext of *The Rats* was successive governments' neglect of the East End of my childhood; the house I lived in was an old slum that had to be pulled down.'

Ordinary protagonists

The impact of Herbert's stories derives not only from his graphic descriptions of horrific events and the page-turning suspense, but also – and especially – from the way they affect ordinary people. When the lives of a baby and a schoolboy are threatened by huge rats, any parent is bound to feel a pang of terror and sympathy. Protagonists to whom the reader can relate, and with whom he or she cannot help but sympathise, are an appealing feature of any novel, regardless of genre.

The Fog

Herbert's reputation was cemented by his second book, *The Fog* (1975). The peaceful life of a Wiltshire village is shattered by a yawning, bottomless crack, out of which creeps a fog that drives people insane. In one famous scene the entire population of Bournemouth walks into the sea. In another, a teacher comes to a sticky end in the school gymnasium, strung up on the bars, trousers down and looking at the wrong end of a pair of shears. An old lady is shredded and eaten by her pet cats. Students assault and mutilate their teachers before turning on one another. And so it goes on.

Ash

His last novel, *Ash* (2012), is a thumping book, almost 700 pages long, very different from *The Rats* and *The Fog*. It involved a lot of research and investigation, and he relaxed his usual avoidance of planning (see below) in order to fit the book's different elements together. His starting point was something the Queen was alleged to have said (though it seems rather unlikely): 'There are dark forces at work in this country about which we know little.'

A ghost hunter and parapsychologist, David Ash, is sent to a remote Scottish castle ('a desolate, ancient place with a dark heart') to investigate a series of bizarre happenings. A man is found crucified in a locked room, and the drama intensifies with repeated sightings of a mysterious hooded figure. Described by one reviewer as 'part horror story, part mystery, part conspiracy thriller, part political diatribe', *Ash* had a mixed reception.

How he wrote

Herbert wrote in longhand with a felt-tip pen on to jumbo pads of A4. He set himself a rigid, disciplined writing routine.

> The more you work, the more intense you are about it, the better you become. I'm terrible in the mornings, but I'm always at my desk by 10 a.m. You have to be disciplined as a writer. I never plan my novels because if I know what is going to happen it bores me rigid. I let the story tell itself. At 1 p.m. Eileen [Herbert's wife] buzzes me on the intercom for lunch. I'm back at my desk by 2.30 p.m. and work on for three hours, then I reward myself with a large vodka before settling down for *The Simpsons*. People laugh at this because I'm supposed to be dark and mysterious.

Chilling and thrilling

Herbert was prone to vivid dreams and his novels are the stuff of nightmares spiced up with sex – both chilling and thrilling. It's a combination that made him the number one novelist for adolescent males in the 1970s and 1980s. What is more remarkable is that the readers of his early novels stayed with him over four decades. Herbert retained the ability to shock, horrify and entrance readers to the end. His depiction of violence was unremitting but he insisted the violence was real: 'I was very much against the Tom and Jerry and John Wayne types of violence where no one is ever really hurt.'

He is remembered as a pre-eminent writer of horror novels, but many of his books contain elements of fantasy, science fiction, crime and, of course, the supernatural. He was adept at writing gruesome, spine-chilling scenes and causing his readers acute discomfort they can hardly bear – but cannot bear to put down. The fact is that many of us (although, sales figure suggest, many more men than women) enjoy being frightened.

In contrast to Stephen King's treatment in the United States, Herbert rarely received serious attention from critics in Britain. His characterisation and dialogue may not be of the highest order, but as a writer of page-turning suspense and gruesome but gripping set pieces, sometimes combined with sharp social comment, he is in a class of his own.

I'll let Jeremy Trevathan, Macmillan publisher and Herbert's editor for ten years, have the last word:

> Jim Herbert was one of the keystone authors in a genre that had its heyday in the 1970s and 1980s. It's a true testament to his writing and his enduring creativity that his books continued to be huge bestsellers right up until his death. He has the rare distinction that his books were considered classics of the genre within his lifetime.

> **Learning points**
>
> - An unpleasant childhood experience (such as Herbert's being left alone when his parents went out at night) could provide the stimulus for a novel.
> - Ordinary people caught up in extraordinary events can be a powerful combination.
> - Setting horrific events in settings with which the reader is familiar may heighten their impact.
> - Making the reader believe that the problem has been solved and then showing that it has not (and is perhaps even worse than was thought) increases the intensity of the suspense.
> - Even a horror story can be used to make a political point.

JAMES HERRIOT
(1916–1995)

There's a special noise a rejected manuscript makes when it comes through the letter-box and hits the doormat. It's more recognizable than that of a ewe in labour or a cow with a prolapsed uterus. I would call it a sickening thud and it was a noise I learned to hate.

In the 1970s James Herriot (aka Alf Wight) became a publishing sensation. But success did not come quickly or easily. He had been writing seriously and trying to get published for almost ten years before his first book was accepted. Years later, whenever he was asked for advice about getting into print, he would always respond with the same words: 'Don't give up.'

That's just one of the things I learned when I met Alf's son, Jim Wight. 'He had plenty of rejections,' said Jim, 'but he just kept going. He had determination and self-belief.' I met Jim at 'The World of James Herriot' in Thirsk, North Yorkshire. Now a museum, it was the house from which Donald Sinclair and Alf Wight (aka Siegfried Farnon and James Herriot) ran their veterinary practice for more than 50 years.

I asked Jim about the process by which his father had turned the everyday incidents of his working life into bestselling stories. 'He must have kept a diary,' I suggested. 'No, he only kept a notebook,' said Jim. He just wrote down headings – nothing more. He had an excellent memory, and these headings were enough to remind him of the smallest details. Most of his writing was done sitting in front of the television.

> He did not have a study, but simply tapped away on his typewriter among the rest of us in the sitting-room. If something interested him on the television, he would stop and enjoy it before effortlessly switching himself back into writing mode. He could just shut off his mind and concentrate on the words in front of him.

A perfect birthday present

In 1955, on the eve of Alf Wight's thirty-ninth birthday, his wife Joan wrote to his parents in Glasgow: 'Guess what I have bought for him – a typewriter! I'm sure he will be writing to you much more often now; he may even get down to writing that book he has been talking about for thirteen years!'

Alf bought himself a few how-to writing books and started to tap away at the typewriter. His first efforts, in the late 1950s and early 1960s, were stories about some of the farmers he knew and vets he'd worked with; and he connected these together, rather tenuously, into a novel written in the third person. It was full of florid adjectives and long sentences, and he spent many months reworking it and trying to improve it. In the end he realised that it was unpublishable. 'It was,' he said, 'like a schoolboy's essay, and a poor one at that.'

Submissions, rejections

His next tack was to have a go at short stories. He was well-read (favourite authors included Charles Dickens, Walter Scott, Samuel Pepys, H. Rider Haggard, Ian Fleming and, especially, P. G. Wodehouse) and he enjoyed the short fiction of Arthur Conan Doyle, H. G. Wells and O. Henry. He wrote seven or eight short stories, mainly about sport and other outdoor activities, and submitted them to selected magazines and to the BBC. And every one of them came back to him with that 'sickening thud' on the doormat.

Finally, he decided that instead of writing about topics like sport that simply interested him, he had to write about something on which he was a real expert. 'Write what you know' is advice often given to new writers, and that's exactly what he decided to do. There was only one possible subject – veterinary practice. In the autumn of 1965 he dusted down his abandoned novel and set about rewriting it. He ditched the flowery language, the florid style and the complicated sentences of his first effort, and wrote in a simpler, more conversational style. This process took some 18 months. When it was complete, early in 1967, he had produced something that was much more readable.

He submitted the rewritten novel to Collins. Juliana Wadham, their reader, liked it, but asked 'Why have you written this as a novel? These stories are, quite obviously, based upon real incidents so why turn them into fiction? Why don't you rewrite it in the first person as an autobiographical work? The stories will be all the more appealing to your readers if they realise they are ones that are based upon fact.'

So in September 1967 he began rewriting it for the third time, now turning it into a semi-autobiographical work with a new title suggested by one of his client friends – *If Only They Could Talk*. It's interesting to compare the text of the unpublished novel with that of the published book. In Chapter 8, Siegfried takes James to a farm to perform a post-mortem. He forgets his knife and has to borrow a carving knife from the farmer's wife. In the unpublished novel this incident is described as follows: 'When he arrived at the house he found that he had forgotten to take his p.m. knife and decided that he would have to borrow a carving knife.' The prose is plain and easy to read. He had got rid of the flowery language and the complicated sentences. But it's flat and unexciting.

In the published version, the episode is told very differently:

> We arrived at the farmhouse with a screaming of brakes. Siegfried had left his seat and was rummaging about in the boot before the car had stopped shuddering. 'Hell,' he shouted, 'no post mortem knife! Never mind, I'll borrow something from the house.' He slammed down the lid and bustled over to the door.

Here we have a lively narrative, with dialogue that illustrates Siegfried's eccentric character.

He resubmitted *If Only They Could Talk* to Collins in July 1968. He must have been bitterly disappointed when – once again – it was rejected.

Published at last

Wight's wife Joan suggested that he should try Michael Joseph, publishers of Richard Gordon's humorous 'Doctor' books. Instead, he submitted it to an agent, Jean LeRoy at David Higham Associates, whose book *Sell Them a Story* he had just read. She took it on and it was accepted by the first publisher she sent it to – Michael Joseph!

With advertising contrary to the code of practice of the Royal College of Veterinary Surgeons, Alf Wight needed to find a pseudonym. He also hoped to hide his authorship from his veterinary clients, believing that, 'These people may not like to be portrayed as they have been.' On 11 February 1969 he was watching his favourite television programme, *Match of the Day*. Manchester United were playing Birmingham City in an FA Cup tie, and he saw City's goalkeeper, the Scottish international

Jim Herriot, make a string of outstanding saves. He had found his pseudonym.

The first two James Herriot books, *If Only They Could Talk* (1970) and *It Shouldn't Happen to a Vet* (1972), sold very modestly. But when these were combined and published as one book in 1972 for the US market, with the title *All Creatures Great and Small*, this became a huge bestseller. Phenomenal success in the US had a knock-on effect in the UK and the books shot up the bestseller lists. Two films and a memorable television series, which ran from 1978 to 1990, helped to make him one of the country's most popular authors. By 1979 he was the recipient of six Golden Pan awards – each of his first six books sold more than one million copies in paperback – an achievement equalled only, at that time, by Ian Fleming. Not until 1980 did the bestselling author stop practising full time. He always saw himself as, first and foremost, not a writer but a vet. 'I want to continue to be known as a vet round here,' he said. 'If a farmer calls me to a sick animal, he couldn't care less if I were George Bernard Shaw.'

Fact and fiction

Alf Wight qualified for veterinary practice in 1939, but 1937 is given as Herriot's year of qualification. The first four books have a pre-war setting, with the remainder set mainly in the 1940s and 1950s. Most of them were written in the 1970s, and in reality many of the incidents recorded took place then – some passed on to the author by his son (who joined the practice in the late 1960s) or one of the other veterinary assistants. The stories are based on real incidents and real people – subtly embellished, as in this example:

> Some dogs crossed to the other side of the road when they entered Trengate and slunk past the surgery with their tails down, but Blanco nearly tugged Mr Bendelow off his feet as he fought to drag him through our door.

The books are set in the Yorkshire Dales, some 30 miles from Thirsk, where most of the incidents really took place. We can explain this geographical shift partly by Wight's love of the Dales (from time to time he worked in Wensleydale – and spent part of his honeymoon there), and partly by a desire to put some distance between his writing and the real people and places of his immediate working environment. Wight's Thirsk becomes Herriot's Darrowby, and the Golden Fleece is changed to the Drovers' Arms. Brawton, where Herriot and his wife spend their Thursday afternoons, is Harrogate; and Hartington, where the hospitable Granville Bennet has his practice, is Darlington.

His characters are based on real people but, with just one exception (John Crooks, his assistant from 1951–1954), he gave them fictitious names, hoping to hide their identities. James Herriot's beagle, Sam, is an amalgam of Danny and Dinah, two of Alf Wight's dogs.

Changing time, place, incidents

Herriot changed the times and locations of his stories. Changes in time and/or place can sometimes improve the narrative and increase the appeal of a story, as well as put some distance between stories and the people who inspired them. Real-life incidents can be subtly changed or embellished to make them more colourful and memorable. Any skilled raconteur or teller of jokes knows how, by exaggerating some of the detail and perhaps adding a little invention, a story can be made more amusing and appealing. In the same way, a writer can change or exaggerate real-life events in order to improve the narrative and strengthen the humour.

Why is Herriot's writing so popular?

How can we explain the phenomenal popularity of the James Herriot books? Here are half a dozen answers:

Unforgettable characters, brought vividly to life by Herriot's shrewd observation and skilful description: 'While Olive drew the milk by almost imperceptible movements of her fingers and with a motionless wrist, her father hauled away at the teats as though he was trying to ring in the new year.' Siegfried and Tristan are just two among a whole galaxy of memorable characters who stick in the mind.

Empathy with animals. Respect for animals permeates almost every page. It's no coincidence that the books have achieved their greatest sales in countries (the UK and US) where a fondness for animals and pet-keeping, and concern for animal welfare, are strong national traits. But there is little sentimentality: we see the lows as well as the highs of veterinary practice.

A strong sense of place. We're captivated by the author's infectious love of the Yorkshire Dales. The descriptive writing is simple and unpoetic, but effective: 'Ted's smallholding was a grey smudge high on the hillside near the top of the dale.'

Self-deprecating humour. We laugh at the foibles and idiosyncrasies of Siegfried, Tristan and Herriot's veterinary clients, but it's the author's willingness and ability to tell a good story against himself that makes him such a congenial companion.

Easy to read. The books are well-written, in a simple style which combines deft description with authentic dialogue.

Feel-good. Above all, perhaps, the stories are full of warmth and humanity: as one reviewer put it, 'a celebration of life itself'.

Learning points

- Don't give up in the face of repeated rejections (Herriot, like many other authors, had been trying to get published for many years before he succeeded).

- Write about something you know and love – and on which you're an expert.
- Clearly drawn, larger-than-life characters stick in the reader's mind.
- Simple, unpoetic description can create a strong sense of place.
- Self-deprecating humour can make the reader warm to an author.

ALDOUS HUXLEY
(1894–1963)

Brave New World (1932), like Orwell's later novel *Nineteen Eighty-Four,* offers us a frightening vision of the future. In place of Orwell's nightmare of a boot stamping on the human face for ever, Huxley gives us a less violent, but no less terrifying, dystopia. It's a consumption-based society of people bred in test tubes who are unable to experience human emotions or to appreciate beauty. There is nothing but perpetual, drug-induced contentment.

During his prolific career Huxley produced 47 books, encompassing poetry, drama, essays, short stories, travel books, screenplays and novels. He was arguably a better essayist than novelist, because he was more interested in ideas than in the development of plot or character. But he is remembered mainly for his novels – especially the one that has become a bestselling popular classic, *Brave New World.*

How he began

Huxley was educated at Eton and Balliol College, Oxford, graduating in 1916, the year in which he published his first collection of poetry. After a short, unhappy period as a schoolmaster (teaching French at

Eton and Repton), he resolved to make his living as a freelance writer. Half-blind in one eye when he began to write, he learned to touch-type. A well-connected member of the intellectual upper crust, he spent time during World War One working as a farm labourer at the home of Lady Ottoline Morrell, where he met Katherine Mansfield, Robert Graves and Siegfried Sassoon, as well as Bloomsbury figures such as Clive Bell and Bertrand Russell.

He wrote for the literary magazine *The Athenaeum,* reviewed plays for *The Westminster Gazette* and wrote articles for *Vogue, Vanity Fair, House and Garden* and the Condé Nast publications. 'I heartily recommend this sort of journalism as an apprenticeship,' he said in an interview years later. 'It forces you to write on everything under the sun, it develops your facility, it teaches you to master your material quickly, and it makes you look at things.' In the 1920s he lived with his wife and young son in London, France and Italy, where he visited his friend D. H. Lawrence.

His first two novels, *Crome Yellow* (1921) and *Antic Hay* (1923), established him as a major author. *Crome Yellow*, the story of a house party at an English country house, satirises the fads, fashions and social decadence of the time. *Antic Hay* is a comic novel depicting the aimless, self-absorbed life of London's cultural elite in the years following World War One. Both novels demonstrate Huxley's ability to introduce intellectual ideas into fiction. With their mixture of satire and earnestness, these and his later works were seen by some critics as symptoms of a hollow age, and by others as liberating and provocative novels of ideas.

Brave New World

According to Huxley, *Brave New World* began as a parody of H. G. Wells's *Men Like Gods*, a scientific fantasy in which the hero is transported into another world some 3,000 years in the future. But he found himself wandering farther and farther from his original purpose and ended up with something quite different.

Much of the character of *Brave New World* stemmed from Huxley's first visit to the United States in 1926. He was dismayed by the extravagance of America's consumer society and by the way people used their free time not to improve their minds, but to pursue what he regarded as trivial, worthless activities. On the sea journey to America he had found and read Henry Ford's book *My Life and Work*, and he came to believe that Ford's principles of mass production to satisfy a consumer-driven society applied to everything he saw. The visit made him pessimistic about the future of European culture, which he feared would become trivialised.

Set 600 years in the future, the novel envisions a world that, in its quest for social stability and peace, has created a society devoid of emotion, love and beauty. The world is in the hands of ten World Controllers who administer a global society, bred in test tubes, tranquillised by the mind-numbing drug soma and divided into rigid castes, each with its own level of intelligence, going from Alpha double plus at the top, through Beta, Gamma and Delta down to Epsilon minus (semi-moron) at the bottom. It's a world dominated by a government-enforced obsession with consumerism; a world of no-strings-attached pleasure, where contraception is compulsory and promiscuity is a virtue.

The starting point for Huxley's *Brave New World* was Henry Ford, with his Model T motor car marking the beginning of mass production. Ford is revered as founder of the world order depicted in the novel, and the dialogue is sprinkled with almost-familiar expressions such as 'Oh, Ford!', 'for Ford's sake', 'Ford help me' and so on. Most of the characters' names are clever derivatives drawn from history, philosophy and psychology. So we have, among many others, Bernard Marx (from George Bernard Shaw and Karl Marx),

Henry Foster (Henry Ford), Lenina Crowne (Vladimir Lenin), Mustapha Mond (Mustafa Atatürk, founder of Turkey after World War One, and Sir Alfred Mond, industrialist and founder of ICI) and Morgana Rothschild (bankers JP Morgan and the Rothschilds).

The title is an ironic line from Shakespeare's *The Tempest*: when Miranda sees other people for the first time she is overcome with excitement and utters the famous line. But what she is seeing is not men acting in a civilised manner, but men representing the worst aspects of humanity. Huxley employs the same irony in *Brave New World* when 'the savage' John refers to what he sees as a 'brave new world'. John, raised on the Savage Reservation in New Mexico, has read nothing but Shakespeare and his dialogue is full of Shakespearian quotations. He lives by a moral code based on his life in the Reservation and his reading of Shakespeare.

John 'the savage' cannot accept the reality of this 'brave new world'. Here's how 'His Fordship Mustapha Mond, Resident World Controller of Western Europe' describes it:

> The world's stable now. People are happy; they get what they want, and they never want what they can't get. They're well off; they're safe; they're never ill; they're not afraid of death; they're blissfully ignorant of passion and old age; they're plagued with no mothers or fathers; they've got no wives, or children, or lovers to feel strongly about; they're so conditioned that they practically can't help behaving as they ought to behave. And if anything should go wrong, there's soma.

In *Nineteen Eighty-Four* people are controlled by inflicting pain; in *Brave New World* they're controlled by inflicting pleasure.

> **Unfamiliar cultures**
>
> Huxley's visit to the United States was the catalyst for *Brave New World*. Visiting a country you don't know and experiencing unfamiliar customs and cultures can leave a strong impression. Make a note of aspects of the new environment that seem particularly strange or interesting. Contrasting those with the world you know could spark your imagination and stimulate your creativity.

How he wrote

Huxley wrote *Brave New World* over just four months in 1931. He worked in the mornings, and then again for a short time before dinner, usually for four or five hours a day. He did a great deal of rewriting, usually correcting and rewriting each page several times as he went along. Before he started on a novel he had a dim general idea of what would happen, but no detailed plan, and he developed the story as he went along. He liked to finish one chapter to his satisfaction before beginning on the next, and he was never entirely certain what would happen in the next until he started on it.

Huxley himself thought that his most successful novel was not *Brave New World*, but *Time Must Have a Stop* (1944), the story of a young poet who holidays with his hedonistic uncle in Florence, because, as he put it, 'it seemed to me that I integrated what may be called the essay element with the fictional element better than in other novels'. In an interview for *The Paris Review* in 1960 (three years before his death) he said:

> I have great difficulty in inventing plots. Some people are born with an amazing gift for storytelling; it's a gift which I've never had at all... The great difficulty for me has always been creating situations... even then I'm not very good at creating people; I don't have a very wide repertory of characters. These things are difficult for me.

After 1937, when Huxley moved to California, he wrote fewer novels and turned his attention more to philosophy, history and mysticism. He had a lifelong interest in the impact (both positive and negative) of science and technology on twentieth-century life. He became interested in the effects of consciousness-changing drugs and in *The Doors of Perception* (1954) wrote about his experiences with the hallucinogenic drug mescaline. A humanist and a pacifist, he was much concerned with spiritual subjects such as parapsychology and philosophical mysticism.

By the end of his life, Huxley was widely acknowledged as one of the pre-eminent intellectuals of his time. But he continued to believe in the importance of fiction which, together with history and biography, he saw not only as a means of providing an authentic picture of life both past and present, but also as the most effective vehicle for expressing ideas. He was nominated seven times for the Nobel Prize in Literature.

Learning points

- Journalism can be excellent training for anyone who wishes to become a novelist.
- A novel can be an effective vehicle for expressing and exploring ideas.
- It is possible to start a novel having only a general idea of what will happen, and to develop the story as you write.

HOWARD JACOBSON
(1942–)

'An English writer who happens to know about Jews and would like to write like Jane Austen, with a little bit of Yiddish.' That's how Howard

Jacobson has described himself. He would rather be known as 'the Jewish Jane Austen' than 'the English Philip Roth'.

The Finkler Question

In 2010 Jacobson won the Man Booker Prize with his eleventh novel, *The Finkler Question*. Andrew Motion, chair of the Booker judges, described it as 'very funny… very clever, very sad and very subtle… absolutely a book for grown-ups, for people who understand that comedy and tragedy are linked'.

The trigger for the book was Jacobson's meeting with a man who had just lost his wife of 60 years.

> I thought there was something particularly Jewish about the way this widower was grieving and I thought it would be interesting to have somebody not Jewish looking at that. And amid all the worrying about anti-Semitism I thought how, nevertheless there is so much goodwill towards us; how much I love being in England. How English I feel.

The book follows a year or so (with occasional flashbacks) in the lives of three friends – Sam Finkler and Libor Sevick, two Jewish widowers, and Julian Treslove, who is not Jewish but yearns to be. It explores the nature of friendship and what it means to be an English Jew in the twenty-first century.

At 68, Jacobson was the oldest writer to win the Man Booker Prize since William Golding in 1980. He has said that the prize matters to him because it's an award for good writing. As he put it in an interview in *The Telegraph*, 'It's a prize for bloody writing. We desperately need it because fewer and fewer people know what writing is. They are not taught it any more. They are not taught to read.' He deplores the false categorisation of writing into 'literature' and 'entertainment' as if the two were mutually exclusive.

How he began writing

Jacobson was 40 when he wrote his first novel. As a younger man he had tried – and failed – to write like some of his literary heroes (D. H. Lawrence, Henry James, Leo Tolstoy). Then he found himself teaching English at Wolverhampton Polytechnic – 'which was a job to me so humiliating, in a city so ghastly, at a rubbishy time of my life, that I started to write about it'. *Coming from Behind* (1983) is a satirical campus novel which has been compared with the work of David Lodge and Malcolm Bradbury.

The plot revolves around a West Midlands Polytechnic forced to share facilities with the local football club. The novel's hero, Sefton Goldberg, is – perhaps more than any of Jacobson's heroes – defined by his Jewishness. There are countless sentences that begin: 'Being Jewish, he didn't know that...' or 'Being Jewish, he couldn't understand how...' He uses his Jewishness to make himself a victim – because he enjoys the amusement and the power which, paradoxically, this gives him. One example of this is his friendship with fellow cynic Peter Potter. As 'the first Jew Peter had ever struck up a friendship with', Goldberg 'wanted to make the experience easy for him. As long as he remained hunched and dejected he was fairly sure Peter could cope.'

Other novels

His second novel, *Peeping Tom* (1984), was described by *Time Out*'s reviewer as 'the funniest book about sex ever written'. It's a comedy of sexual jealousy and a satire on literary biography. Subsequent books include *The Very Model of a Man* (1992), a reworking of the Cain and Abel myth; *No More Mister Nice Guy* (1998), the story of a television critic's mid-life crisis; and *The Mightly Walzer* (1999), set in the Jewish community in Manchester during the 1950s, which won the Bollinger Everyman Wodehouse prize for comic writing. Two later books, *Who's Sorry Now?* (2002) and *Kalooki Nights* (2006), were both long-listed for the Man Booker Prize, and in 2014 his futuristic love story *J*, featuring two main characters where the past is not spoken about, was shortlisted for the same prize.

The Mighty Walzer is a good example of the way Jacobson uses failure as a major theme in many of his books. He described it as 'a coming of age novel of a young man dreaming of conquering the world as a ping-pong player and winning untold wealth and the adoration of beautiful women'. In fact the hero's journey ends in obscurity. 'Obscurity is a very good subject for a writer,' says Jacobson. 'Failure is a very good subject for a writer. You don't want to write about success... no one really wants to read a novel about somebody for whom it's all gone right. The stories we love are the stories about people for whom it's all gone wrong and may go right, but mainly goes wrong.' Much of Jacobson's humour comes from his characters' failures in life and their own awareness of these.

Serious comedy

For Jacobson the novel is 'essentially a comic medium', but he sees comedy as something very serious: 'I don't mean a light medium... I don't mean something very trivial. I mean something very serious, the medium in which we show disdain for religion, for our leaders, for belief systems... Comedy and seriousness are friends, they're not enemies.'

Jacobson has said that his sense of humour is:

English partly but I think it's more Jewish than it's English, and the characteristic there is that Jews are funny because they know that life isn't, and that's not true of the English. The English think life can be very amusing and boisterous and vitalistic, and they're extremely good at expressing that. Jews are not boisterous and vitalistic in that way, Jews are melancholy and reflective, and the jokes that we make are anguished, bitter jokes about the fact that life is not funny. Life is not funny, that's why we make a joke about it. And that I see as distinctly Jewish.

> **Comedy and seriousness**
>
> For Jacobson, comedy and tragedy are two sides of the same coin. Writing a novel, you can put humour to good use for a serious purpose. You can use comedy not only to entertain your readers but also to challenge and make fun of all kinds of things: ideas, beliefs, thoughts, practices, people, etc. Nothing is outside the ambit of the novelist. Wit and humour can be used to explore every aspect of human nature.

Influences

He has described himself as 'an old-fashioned English lit man, straight down the line – it's George Eliot, it's Dickens, it's Dr Johnson, it's Jane Austen'. Other writers he especially admires include Fyodor Dostoyevsky and Ivan Turgenev. He studied literature at Cambridge under the influential literary critic F. R. Leavis, who famously cited Jane Austen, George Eliot, Henry James and Joseph Conrad as the principal torch bearers of the traditional English novel – and amazingly excluded such writers as Charles Dickens, Laurence Sterne and Thomas Hardy (though he later changed his position on Dickens). Jacobson has a special liking for books about women who are desperate to be treated justly, to be acknowledged and to find fulfilment in love: his favourites among these are *Persuasion* (Jane Austen), *Jane Eyre* (Charlotte Brontë), *Middlemarch* (George Eliot), *Little Dorrit* (Charles Dickens) and *Anna Karenina* (Leo Tolstoy).

Comic novelist?

Jacobson has been described as a comic novelist, but to my mind that's a rather misleading epithet. There are few of the farcical, laugh-out-loud scenes you'd expect to find, for example, in a Tom Sharpe novel.

Jacobson himself has said:

To my ear the term 'comic novelist' is as redundant and off-putting as the term 'literary novelist'. When Jane Austen rattled off the novel's virtues in *Northanger Abbey* – arguing that it demonstrated 'the most thorough knowledge of human nature, the happiest delineation of its varieties, the liveliest effusions of wit and humour... conveyed to the world in the best chosen language' she wasn't making a distinction between the literary novel and some other sort, or between the comic novel and the not so comic. The liveliest effusions of wit and humour are simply what the reader of a novel has the right to expect.'

He believes it's the writer's job not only to entertain, but also to challenge and stretch the reader.

Jacobson also writes non-fiction and journalism, and has written and presented several television programmes (including the Channel 4 series *The Bible: A History*). But for my money it's the novels, above all, for which he will be remembered. They show us that comedy and tragedy are two sides of the same coin.

Learning points

- A painful period of your life can be put to good use if you write about it or use it to stimulate your writing.
- Obscurity and failure can be good subjects for a writer because many readers will relate to them.
- Comedy can be used to provide a scathing insight into a serious subject and perhaps even to reveal deep truths about it.
- Don't be afraid to stretch and challenge the reader.

STEPHEN KING
(1947–)

'Not since Dickens has a writer had so many readers by the throat,' said *The Guardian*'s review of one Stephen King bestseller. In a career stretching over four decades the world's leading horror writer has completed more than 50 books (in the genres of horror, science fiction and fantasy). The easy-going narration and clean, unpretentious style of his writing contrast with the horrific content of many of his stories. Cliffhanging chapter endings keep us turning the pages, and realistic detail helps us to suspend disbelief and accept the supernatural elements.

Unlike most bestselling authors, King has written extensively about the process of writing. 'If you want to be a writer,' he says, 'you must do two things above all others: read a lot and write a lot. There's no way around these two things that I'm aware of, no shortcut.'

How to become a good writer

King divides writers into four categories: bad, competent, good and great. He believes it's impossible to turn a bad writer into a competent one, or a good writer into a great one; but that 'it is possible, with lots of hard work, dedication and timely help, to make a good writer out of a merely competent one'. He does not pull his punches: 'Read and write four to six hours a day. If you cannot find the time for that, you can't expect to become a good writer.' That may seem hopelessly unrealistic if you are holding down a full-time job or have children or parents to care for. But remember that most bestselling authors began writing when they were doing other work to pay their bills. Stephen King was teaching when he wrote his breakthrough novel, *Carrie* (1974).

King identifies three essential writing tools:

(1) Vocabulary – 'Use the first word that comes to your mind, if it is appropriate and colourful.' King believes that plain and direct writing is

best, and that it's important to avoid clichéd similes and metaphors and to use fresh images.

(2) Grammar – 'You need at least a rudimentary grasp,' says King, who likes the simplicity of just putting a noun and a verb together to make a sentence. His pet hates are adverbs (Don't say 'He closed the door firmly' say 'He slammed the door') and the passive voice (which he describes as 'weak, circuitous and frequently tortuous'). He also dislikes using verbs like 'shout', 'plead' or 'gasp' to pump up the dialogue attribution. If you need to attribute dialogue, 'say' is, he believes, the best word to use.

(3) Style – King likes short paragraphs because they 'make the reader welcome', and he often uses the single-sentence paragraph because this 'more closely resembles talk than writing, and that's good'.

Much of this echoes George Orwell's views on writing. King believes that a writer needs a room without distractions, the determination to shut the door and a concrete goal (he suggests a daily target of 1,000 words).

King's route into writing

King's first story (about a teenage grave robber) was published when he was a teenager, but this was followed by lots of rejections. His first truly original story idea – about counterfeit trading stamps – came to him while he was watching his mother stick her collected green stamps into a book and noticed that her tongue was green from licking the stamps. He sent the story to *Alfred Hitchcock's Mystery Magazine*, but it came back with a routine rejection slip and just one manuscript piece of advice: 'Don't staple manuscripts. Loose pages plus paperclip equal correct way to submit copy.' But before long he had progressed to receiving rejection slips with manuscript notes which gave him some encouragement to continue submitting.

King studied composition, fiction and English literature at school and college, but says that he learned more about writing in ten minutes from the editor of his local newspaper, for which he wrote sports reports while he was still at school. His first piece of copy was handed back heavily amended, with several superfluous or overblown phrases deleted.

Before *Carrie* was accepted in the spring of 1973, King, now with a wife and two children, almost despaired of making it as a full-time writer. Although he was selling short stories to magazines, the market for these was becoming smaller as horror and science fiction were becoming less popular. His teaching was also leaving him increasingly exhausted. His first two published novels were written on his wife's portable Olivetti typewriter in the laundry room of a doublewide trailer where he and his wife were living at the time.

A job like any other

King's approach to writing is uncomplicated: 'Don't wait for the muse… This isn't the Ouija board or the spirit world we're talking about here, but just another job like laying pipe or driving long-haul trucks.'

He advises new writers to begin by writing the kind of stuff they like to read, whatever the genre. 'Write what you like, then imbue it with life and make it unique by blending in your own personal knowledge of life, friendship, relationships, sex and work. Especially work.' He believes that readers are drawn into a book when they can recognise the people, their behaviours, their surroundings and their talk – in short, when they hear echoes of their own lives and beliefs.

Narration, description and character building

King's approach is to put a group of characters in some sort of predicament and see how they can extricate themselves.

> The situation comes first. The characters come next. Then I begin to narrate. In some instances, the outcome is what I visualised. In most, however, it's something I never expected. And if I'm not able

> to guess... how the damned thing is going to turn out... I can be pretty sure of keeping the reader in a state of page-turning anxiety.

King has no time for 'the tiresome tyranny of the outline and the notebook filled with character notes'. Most of the situations he has created can be expressed as a *what if?* question. For example, what if a policeman in a remote Nevada town went berserk and started killing everyone in sight? (the premise for *Desperation*, 1996). Although King has written some plot-driven books, he distrusts plotting on the grounds that (a) people's lives are largely plotless and (b) plotting is incompatible with the spontaneity of real creation.

King sees narration, description and dialogue as the three elements of a story, and believes that good description is a skill that can be learned. He dislikes exhaustive descriptions of characters' physical features or clothing. Carrie White, for example, is described as a high school outcast with a bad complexion and a fashion-victim wardrobe. King leaves his readers to fill in the detail in their own heads. In *The Shining* (1977) Stuart Ullman, manager of the Overlook Hotel, moves with 'the prissy speed that seems to be the exclusive domain of all small plump men. The part in his hair was exact, and his dark suit was sober but comforting.' In *The Drawing of the Three* (1987), the second in The Dark Tower sequence, Eddie Dean is first seen with 'the cuff of a blue shirt, slightly pulled back to reveal crisp curls of black hair. Long fingers.' Later he is described as 'a guy of about twenty, tall, wearing clean slightly faded blue jeans and a paisley shirt' who 'looked like a college kid'. 'Description begins in the writer's imagination but should finish in the reader's,' says King. 'For me, good description usually consists of a few well-chosen details that will stand for everything else.'

Character building, says King, involves paying close attention to how real people act and talk. The writer's job is to make characters behave in ways which both help the story and seem reasonable to the readers, given what they know both about the characters and about real life.

Effective description

Reading tastes and attention spans have changed a great deal over the years. How many readers today have the patience to cope with the exhaustive descriptive passages to be found, for example, in Thomas Hardy's novels? Many genre novelists keep their descriptions to a minimum because they want to maintain pace and avoid anything that could delay the action or bore the reader. Whether you are describing a person or a place, the use of a few well-chosen details is likely to be the most effective technique. If those details have been carefully selected, they will stand in for everything else and enable the reader to use his or her imagination to paint the rest of the picture.

Writing regime

King writes his first draft as quickly as he can, and has a daily target of 2,000 words (completed anytime between 11.30 a.m. and late afternoon). Only in the most dire circumstances does he allow himself to get up from his desk without meeting that target. It takes him three months to produce a draft of around 180,000 words. When that first draft is complete he has a couple of days off and then begins immediately on a new project. He does not look at the draft again for at least another six weeks. Then he reads it through, looking for mundane mistakes (inconsistencies, spellings, typos) and any holes in plot or character development. He then asks himself: What is this story about? Is it coherent? What are its recurring elements? What can I do to make them clearer? So in the second draft he corrects mistakes, plugs holes and adds scenes and incidents that reinforce the story's coherence. Importantly, the second draft is also the time to remove words that do not enhance the story. 'Second draft equals first draft minus 10 per cent,' was the advice King was given by one magazine editor, and he believes that's a pretty good guideline.

For more detail about Stephen King's approach to writing, read his fascinating memoir *On Writing* (2000).

Learning points

- Read a lot and write a lot – four to six hours a day, if you expect to become a good writer.
- Use the first word that comes to mind if it is appropriate and colourful.
- Set yourself a concrete goal – perhaps a daily target of 1,000 words.
- Begin by writing the kind of stuff you like to read yourself – then blend in your own personal knowledge and experience.
- Read Stephen King's book *On Writing*.

HARPER LEE
(1926–2016)

Bookshops on both sides of the Atlantic opened their doors at midnight on 14 July 2015. It was described as the biggest publishing event of the decade – the release of Harper Lee's *Go Set a Watchman*. Written before *To Kill a Mockingbird* and hidden away in a safe deposit box for more than 50 years, it had the critics scratching their heads – and comparing it with *Mockingbird*. The theme – racial inequality in America's Deep South – is the same, but it's treated very differently.

> ### Old material
>
> The text of *Watchman* was hidden away for half a century. Anyone who's been writing for any length of time is likely to have stuff in the bottom drawer or in an old computer file that for one reason or another has never seen the light of day. It could be a novel you started but never finished. Something you abandoned half-finished, perhaps to concentrate on a different project. Stuff you completed, but never felt sufficiently confident about to submit. Or some rejected manuscript you never got around to dusting down and submitting somewhere else. Why not dig it out and take a fresh look at it? The time lapse might enable you to spot things you did not see at the time. You might find that you can improve it – and use it.

How the books were written

Nelle Harper Lee was born in Monroeville, Alabama, in 1926. She had a vivid imagination and from an early age composed stories on an old typewriter her father had given her. She went to law school, believing this would be a good discipline for someone hoping to become a writer, but did not complete the course. In 1947 she moved to New York (she lived there for the next 60 years – until her stroke in 2007), where she took a job as an airline agent and started to write fiction in her spare time. She met up with her childhood friend, the writer Truman Capote, who introduced her to his friends Joy and Michael Brown. In 1956 she found herself an agent and in November of the following year she received the best Christmas present any aspiring writer could wish for: the gift of a year's salary. It came with a note from the Browns, which read: 'You have one year off from your job to write whatever you please. Merry Christmas.'

In 1957–1958, when Lee was writing *Go Set a Watchman*, America's Civil Rights Movement was in full swing. In 1955 Rosa Parks of Montgomery, Alabama, was jailed after refusing to give up her seat to a white bus rider. This led to the year-long Montgomery bus boycott of 1955–1956, a protest against segregated public facilities in Alabama, led by Martin Luther King. When, in 1956, the Supreme Court ruled that segregation on public transport was unconstitutional, the Alabama legislature voted 91–1 to close Alabama's public schools rather than integrate them.

This was the background against which Lee embarked upon her first full-length novel. She submitted the manuscript of *Watchman* to Tay Hohoff, an editor at publishers J. B. Lippincott & Co. Hohoff rejected the novel, but she had the insight to see that the flashbacks to Scout's childhood in the 1930s could become the heart of a compelling story told not in the third person, as in *Watchman*, but through the child's eyes. She asked Lee to rewrite the novel, setting it back in the 1930s, with a first-person viewpoint. In the course of two and a half years' hard work, revising, restructuring and rewriting the manuscript with advice from an experienced editor, Hohoff, (and probably from her friend Truman Capote) she found her voice – that of the eight-year-old girl, Scout (she's six when the story begins) – and turned a rather unsatisfactory novel into a masterpiece.

Both *Watchman* and *Mockingbird* have significant autobiographical elements, although Lee downplayed these. Atticus was based on her own father, a lawyer who served in the Alabama State Legislature and once defended two black men accused of murdering a shopkeeper (he was unsuccessful and both men, a father and son, were hanged). Maycomb is Monroeville in all but name, and the way Scout/Jean Louise views the town, both as a child and as a 26-year-old woman, is clearly based on Lee's recollections and perceptions. Dill (a central character in *Mockingbird* but barely mentioned in *Watchman*) was based on Capote, while the inspiration for the *Mockingbird* character Boo Radley was a man living in a nearby house who, like Boo, left objects in the trees for the two children to find and keep.

To Kill a Mockingbird

Published in 1960 to great popular and critical acclaim, *Mockingbird* won the Pulitzer Prize for Fiction and was made into the classic film starring Gregory Peck. The two principal protagonists are Scout, a tomboy with boundless energy and curiosity, and her father, Atticus, a hugely respected lawyer. He's an idealised father figure, characterised by integrity, humour and patience – a symbol of decency and justice who says 'equal rights for all; special privileges for none'. He's almost (but perhaps not quite) too perfect to be believable, and he's different from other Maycomb men: 'He did not do the things our schoolmates' fathers did: he never went hunting, he did not play poker or fish or drink or smoke. He sat in the living-room and read.'

Atticus takes on the hopeless case of a black man accused of rape – hopeless not because he's guilty, but because he's being tried by a white jury. He takes it on, he tells Scout, for a number of reasons.

> The main one is, if I didn't do it I couldn't hold up my head in town and I couldn't represent this county in the legislature, I couldn't even tell you or Jem not to do something again… Simply because we were licked a hundred years before we started is no reason for us not to try to win.

Published in 1960, when the civil rights movement was becoming ever stronger, *Mockingbird* had a huge impact.

Go Set a Watchman

Lee took the title of her original book from a passage in the Old Testament where the prophet Isaiah foretells the fall of Babylon: 'For thus hath the Lord said unto me, Go, set a watchman, let him declare what he seeth.' It's probable that she likened Monroeville to Babylon – 'the Babylon of immoral voices, the hypocrisy'.

The 26-year-old Jean Louise who returns to Maycomb at the start of the novel is every bit as feisty as the eight-year-old Scout: 'She was a person who, when confronted with an easy way out, always took the hard way.' She finds that both the town and the people she knew and loved have changed. There is a new distance between the races: 'Nobody in Maycomb goes to see Negroes any more,' says Aunt Alexandra. Atticus is very different from the hero of *Mockingbird*. Here he is a crotchety small-town apologist for racism who argues that the case for racial equality in the South is by no means as clear cut as campaigners in the North suppose. At the courthouse where her father defended a black man accused of rape (and, contrary to the story told in *Mockingbird*, secured an acquittal), Jean Louise now sees him chairing a meeting of white supremacists and introducing a speaker whose main interest 'was to uphold the Southern Way of Life and no niggers and no Supreme Court was going to tell him or anybody else what to do'. She's dismayed and revolted, as 'The only human being she had ever fully and wholeheartedly trusted had betrayed her... publicly, grossly and shamelessly.'

Jean Louise is quite fond of Henry ('Hank'), the Maycomb boyfriend she has known since childhood, but she's not really in love with him and she dreads the prospect of small-town life: 'I'd be churched to death, bridge-partied to death.' Like Atticus, he is opposed to civil rights for blacks. Jean Louise confronts, first, Hank ('I'm not going to marry you... you're a goddamned hypocrite.'), then her clever Uncle Jack, and, finally, Atticus. There's an enigmatic ending, with Atticus saying how proud he is of her: 'I certainly hoped a daughter of mine'd hold her ground for what she thinks is right – stand up to me first of all.' But he does not accept that she *is* right: 'I can take anything anybody calls me so long as it's not true.' I can't beat him, and I can't join him, concludes Jean Louise.

There are flashbacks to the childhood of Scout/Jean Louise: a mock Revival service conducted by her brother, Jem, during which Scout is 'baptised' in the river; a schoolboy's kiss which makes Scout believe she is pregnant; and a College dance which ends with her falsies fluttering in the breeze from the school's billboard. These flashbacks are something of a digression: they don't add much to the story or tell us much about the characters. But an inspired editor saw them as the starting point for a very different novel – a story set in the 1930s told in the first person through the eyes of the eight-year-old Scout.

Compare and contrast

Watchman is the more complex novel, but *Mockingbird* is – by some distance – the more powerful. We have an identical theme – racial inequality – but its treatment is very different. It's a strong, emotionally gripping subject, and at the time of *Mockingbird*'s publication in 1960 it was hugely topical – constantly in the news. In both books we have two strong, clearly drawn central characters – Atticus and Scout/Jean Louise. Their names are the same but, as we have seen, they are very different people.

In *Mockingbird* we have a strong supporting cast of memorable characters. There's Dill, a boy a year older than Scout, who spends his summers in Maycomb and becomes obsessed by the need to make the reclusive Boo Radley come out of his house. Boo is a constant presence, although we meet him in the flesh only at the very end of the story. Jem, Scout's loving brother, is a principled mini-Atticus. We also have some vivid minor characters, such as Sheriff Tate, Dolphus Raymond (who prefers the company of black people and likes to make people think that the cola he constantly sips is whiskey), Mr Cunningham ('basically a good man,' says Atticus, although he's been part of a lynching mob), nice Miss Maudie, morphine-addicted Mrs Dubose, and villainous, despicable Bob Ewell. Lee pokes gentle fun at Aunt Alexandra's Missionary Society: ladies of Maycomb who support efforts not only to spread their version of Christianity but also to combat poverty and injustice in Africa – but are blind to the very same problems on their own doorstep.

The supporting cast of *Watchman* is less impressive, but there are fine portrayals of Jean Louise's uncle, Dr Finch, and her Aunt Alexandra. The latter was 'the last of her kind: she had river-boat, boarding-school manners; let any moral come along and she would uphold it; she was a disapprover; she was an incurable gossip'. We have a nicely worked set piece – Aunt Alexandra's coffee morning, where Jean Louise struggles to make polite conversation with smug newlyweds talking only about their husbands, the Light Brigade (ladies in their early/mid-30s who 'devoted most of their time to the Amanuensis Club, bridge and getting one-up on each other in the matter of electrical appliances') and three Perennial Hopefuls ('jolly Maycomb girls of excellent character who had never made the grade'). An undercurrent of racial prejudice runs through much of the coffee morning conversation.

Watchman's third-person voice is conventional and uninvolving; it occasionally slips, rather confusingly, into the first or second person. The cleverness of *Mockingbird* lies in Lee's ability to retain an adult perspective while telling Scout's story in the voice of the child. *Mockingbird* is also a much pacier novel. The first mention of the Tom Robinson case which Atticus is to defend comes in Chapter 9, and as we follow the court case the pace gradually quickens. *Watchman* is less well-written, with no clear structure, and at times reads more like a series of autobiographical anecdotes than a purposeful novel. It culminates in the three discursive debates Jean Louise has, in turn, with Hank, Dr Finch and Atticus. This is where the manuscript would have particularly benefited from some judicious editing. Given that *Watchman*, Lee's first attempt at a novel, almost certainly had no input from an editor who advised her to set it aside and to concentrate on what was to become *Mockingbird*, it is understandable that the quality of the writing is not as good.

The greatest contrast between the two books is the character of Atticus. What should we make of his brutal metamorphosis from saintly lawyer to racist bigot? Should we go painstakingly through the *Mockingbird* text, searching for signs of his incipient racism? Or should we attribute his changed attitudes to the increase in racial tension in the South during the period between 1935, when *Mockingbird* is set, and the late 1950s of *Watchman?* Neither suggestion stands up to scrutiny. We must remember that *Watchman* was written before *Mockingbird*. The explanation for his changed character is surely very simple: that in the process of working on the manuscript, and turning what was essentially the first draft of a rather rambling first novel into the masterpiece that is *Mockingbird*, Harper Lee's conception of Atticus's character fundamentally changed. Perhaps her editor had suggested that a decent, morally impeccable Atticus would appeal much more to the American public?

Learning points

- Choose a strong, topical theme.
- Take on board any advice from an editor.
- Changing the viewpoint and timeframe may improve a novel.
- Autobiographical elements can sometimes strengthen a novel.
- Create clearly drawn, feisty protagonists and a strong cast of distinctive supporting characters.

ELMORE LEONARD
(1925–2013)

'If it sounds like writing, I rewrite it,' said Elmore Leonard, summing up his famous Ten Rules for Writing. His bestselling crime novels are notable for their razor-sharp street dialogue and character-based depiction of the American underworld. He was arguably the most cinematic novelist ever, with more than two dozen of his stories adapted for film or television. 'I've always seen my books as movies,' he once said.

How he began

He started to enter short-story competitions and to submit work to magazines when he was a student at the University of Detroit. Before graduating he worked as a copywriter for an advertising agency – a job he kept for several years – getting up at 5 a.m. to write for two hours before going to work. 'I'd come down in the dark into the living room – that Michigan cold – and I wouldn't even let myself heat the coffee water until I'd started writing,' he told *People* magazine. 'I'd write in longhand, one word after the other in pencil on a yellow pad, then rewrite on the typewriter. I'm so damned glad I did it. I studied hard, I worked hard, I learned what I could and couldn't do. I can't do description well, so now I don't do it at all.'

Leonard's first success came in 1951 with publication of the short story 'Trail of the Apaches'. He continued to write Westerns in the 1950s and early 1960s and had more than 30 short stories published. His first novel, *The Bounty Hunters*, was published in 1953, and this was followed by more Westerns; five of these, including *Hombre* (1961), were made into films. When the market for Westerns began to collapse he turned to writing thrillers, but it was another 20 years before he made the breakthrough to bestselling novelist with *Glitz* (1985).

Copywriting

Elmore Leonard was by no means the only famous writer to begin working life as a copywriter. If you want to become a writer, having a job that involves working with words every day of your life must be an advantage. There's a big difference between writing advertising copy (whether for a website or a printed publication) and writing a novel, but some of the skills are the same. In both, you need to choose the best word for your purpose and to use it effectively.

Glitz

The plot revolves around Vincent Mora, a Miami policeman. He's been shot by a mugger and is convalescing in Puerto Rico, where he is stalked by a villain he sent down seven and a half years ago. Teddy Magyk is a psychopath who kills prostitutes and rapes old ladies. Vincent meets a Puerto Rican call girl involved with some bad people and tries to dissuade her from taking a job they've offered her in Atlantic City:

> 'You're gonna get handed out, passed around. You're gonna have to learn how to smile.' 'I know how, Vincent. I smile when I'm not with you.' … 'You're gonna get treated like shit.' 'Oh, is that so? I'm tole a very important guy in business is going to flip over me.' Vincent said, 'It's too late, huh?' He stared at her and said, tired if not sad, 'Iris, you're the best-looking girl I've ever seen in my life.' 'Thank you, but is pronounce Eer-es.' 'And probably the dumbest.' 'Goodnight, Vincent.' 'Good-bye, Iris.'

Here, as we can see, Leonard's sharp dialogue is laced with a touch of humour. Iris accepts the job and the action moves to the glitzy casinos of Atlantic City, where Vincent gets involved with a motley array of gamblers, gangsters and women. There are murders and plot twists – and a satisfying conclusion. While Leonard's portrayal of the lowlife characters is often sympathetic, he paints a caustic picture of the Atlantic City gambling scene:

Two thousand [tour buses] a day came into the city, dropped the suckers off for six hours to lose their paychecks, their Social Security in the slots and haul them back up to Elizabeth, Newark, Jersey City, Philly, Allentown. Bring some more loads back tomorrow – like the Jews in the boxcars, only they kept these folks alive with bright lights and loud music and jackpot payoffs that sounded like fire alarms.

Get Shorty

Get Shorty (1990) is probably Leonard's best-known novel, due largely to the very successful film adaptation. It can be seen as an extended satire of Hollywood, drawing on Leonard's own repeated frustrations as a screenwriter. The main protagonist is ice-cool Chili Palmer, a tough guy not averse to violence. At the start of the book he's working for a loan shark.

Ernesto Palmer got the name Chili originally because he was hot-tempered as a kid growing up... Now he was Chili... because he had chilled down and didn't need the hot temper. All he had to do was turn his eyes dead when he looked at a slow pay, not say more than three words, and the guy would sell his wife's car to make the payment.

Chasing an unpaid debt leads Chili to Hollywood – and to a true story he's convinced would make a great film. He meets Harry Zimm, producer of *Slime Creatures* and Karen Flores, whose terrifying scream in that film made her a star. When Chili's offer of help in getting Harry's own idea for a new film off the ground is accepted, Karen says: 'This guy – what're you doing?' 'He's got some ideas, gonna help me out.' 'Harry, the guy's a crook.' 'So. This town he should fit right in.' There's a cast of arrogant actors, agents and producers – and lowlifes on the fringes of film-making who are involved in drug running. 'Rough business this movie business. I may have to go back to loan sharking for a rest,' says Chili.

How he wrote

After Elmore Leonard died in 2013, his son wrote:

> I remember when I was nine years old, going down the stairs to the basement to watch my father write. He sat at a small red desk in a cinder block room painted white. He wrote longhand on unlined yellow paper. His typewriter was on a metal stand next to the desk. Across the room was a red wicker waste basket that had half a dozen balls of crumpled yellow paper on the floor around it, scenes that didn't work, shots that didn't make it. In retrospect it looked like a prison cell, but my father didn't seem conscious of his surroundings, or of me standing at the bottom of the stairs; he was deep in concentration, midway through a Western called *Hombre* that would be made into a movie starring Paul Newman.

But it was not all plain sailing. After *Hombre* his next book, *The Big Bounce* (1969), was rejected 84 times before it eventually found a publisher. The story of an ex-con who falls into the clutches of a psychotic young seductress, the book found some devoted readers and for the first time placed Leonard in his natural milieu – the modern American underworld.

Leonard honed his dialogue-driven prose to a spare leanness, often taking liberties with grammar and letting conjunctions and punctuation drop away in the interests of speeding the story along. He cited Hemingway as an important influence (though he criticised his lack of humour), along with the prologue of John Steinbeck's *Sweet Thursday*, where a character says: 'I like a lot of talk in a book, and I don't like to have nobody tell me what the guy that's talking looks like. I want to figure out what he looks like from the way he talks. And another thing – I kind of like to figure out what he's thinking by what he says. I like some description too… I like to know what color a thing is, how it smells and maybe how it looks, and maybe how a guy feels about it – but not too much of that.'

> [*Sweet Thursday*] became the backbone of my tendrils for success and happiness in writing fiction: mainly don't describe too much, unless you really know what you're doing… From that time on, 1954, I concentrated on telling my stories in dialogue so I wouldn't have to describe the characters.

Leonard had a remarkable ear for American vernacular, picked up from the bars, police stations and courtrooms of Detroit. Asked to explain his facility with idiom, he said: 'There is no secret. I listen when people are talking. I listen when they're talking to each other, and I listen when they talk to me.' According to Julian Rathbone (writing in *The Independent*), Leonard created 'dialogue like broken glass, sharp and glittering, and a raft of lowlifes individualised in primary colours like hard-edged pop art'. 'I develop characters, and I'm not sure where they're going until I get to know them,' said Elmore. 'In fact, I seldom know before I'm halfway through what the thing is about.'

  His books are written in short, point-of-view chapters populated, as a 2008 *Washington Post* profile put it, by 'cops who aren't exactly good, crooks who aren't exactly bad, and women who have an eye for the in-between'. There's a good deal of violence, but it's described in a matter-of-fact way, as in this example from *Get Shorty*:

> Catlett said, 'I'm taking you out, Yayo,' and shot him in the chest, the gun going off loud – man, it was loud – but didn't buck as much as

Catlett expected. No, looking down at Yayo on the cement floor now among the oil stains, arms flung out, eyes stuck wide open, he'd put that hole right where he'd aimed.

From childhood Leonard lived in Detroit, where many of his stories are set, and in 2010 he set out his Ten Rules for Writing in the *Detroit Free Press*:

Never open a book with weather.

Avoid prologues.

Never use a verb other than 'said' to carry dialogue.

Never use an adverb to modify the verb 'said'... he admonished gravely.

Keep your exclamation points under control. You are allowed no more than two or three per 100,000 words of prose.

Never use the words 'suddenly' or 'all hell broke loose'.

Use regional dialect, patois, sparingly.

Avoid detailed descriptions of characters.

Don't go into great detail describing places and things.

Try to leave out the part that readers tend to skip.

Asked about his writing routine by Martin Amis (who greatly admired his work), Leonard said:

> I write every day when I'm writing, some Saturdays and Sundays, a few hours each day. Because I want to stay with it. If a day goes by and you haven't done anything, or a couple of days, it's difficult to get back into the rhythm of it. I usually start working around 9.30 a.m. and I work until 6 p.m.. I'm lucky to get what I consider four clean pages. They're clean until the next day, the next morning. The time flies by. I can't believe it. When I look at the clock and it's 3 p.m. and I think, 'Good, I've got three more hours.' And then I think, 'I must have the best job in the world.'

> **Learning points**
>
> - Don't try to be too literary.
> - Develop the story through sharp dialogue, laced with a touch of humour.
> - Keep descriptions of places and people to a minimum.
> - Taking liberties with grammar, conjunctions and punctuation can help the story to speed along.
> - Play to your strengths.

HILARY MANTEL
(1952–)

First get the history right; then fill in the gaps in a way that's plausible. That's Hilary Mantel's approach to historical fiction. With *Wolf Hall*, winner of the 2009 Man Booker Prize, she became the biggest-selling prize-winner ever, with 220,000 hardback copies sold in Britain alone. As if that was not impressive enough, she followed it with a second Man Booker success in 2012 with *Bring Up the Bodies,* the second in her trilogy of novels charting the rise and fall of Thomas Cromwell. The final volume, *The Mirror and the Light*, is expected to cover the last four years of his life.

Mantel's success did not come overnight. *Wolf Hall* was her ninth novel. Her first, *Every Day is Mother's Day,* inspired partly by her own experience as a social work assistant at a geriatric hospital, was published in 1985. It's a social comedy set in the 1970s, full of black humour. She has written contemporary fiction, an acclaimed memoir, *Giving Up the Ghost* (2003), and short stories: her collection of stories *The Assassination of Margaret Thatcher* (2014) was described as 'subversive, exhilarating, dark'. It caused a stir with its titled story about an intruder, an IRA assassin whom the narrator has mistaken for a plumber, who wants to use the window of her flat to take a shot at Mrs Thatcher.

It's a mistake to pigeon-hole Mantel as a historical novelist, but *Wolf Hall*, *Bring Up the Bodies* and *A Place of Greater Safety* (1992), about the French revolution, are the books for which she is best known. I'll focus on *Wolf Hall*, the book which catapulted her to fame. It chronicles the rise of Henry VIII's fixer, Thomas Cromwell, a man who oversaw the divorce proceedings against Catherine of Aragon, the break with Rome, the dissolution of the monasteries and Henry's marriage to Anne Boleyn. The story is very familiar, but Mantel tells it from an unfamiliar angle. She makes us see a set of people and historical events from an entirely different perspective.

Research

I feel research must be as good as I can possibly make it. Guesses should be made only where there are no facts to be had. They must be plausible. Where gaps occur, the way you fill them must offer a possible version. I owe these characters as much scholarship as I can contrive, and all my care to try to get them right.

Mantel spent five years researching and writing the book. To avoid contradicting history, she created a card catalogue, organised alphabetically by character, with each card containing notes showing where a particular historical figure was on relevant dates: 'You really need to know, where is the Duke of Suffolk at the moment? You can't have him in London if he's supposed to be somewhere else.' She had to make sure that her version of events matched the historical record.

Wolf Hall has 650 pages of meticulously researched period detail. Mantel uses striking imagery to bring the past vividly to life, and her portrayal of Henry VIII's court is convincing and compelling. Her language is refreshingly poetic and she has a flair for the arresting phrase: 'It's a morning of bone-chilling cold, the wind off the river like a knife in your face. We are breezing in to push our luck.' She excels at the small, telling detail. You can almost smell the rain-drenched wool cloaks and feel the sharp fibres of rushes under your feet. Her Tudor England is one of blood and filth, with Catholics and Protestants alike burning and torturing in the name of God.

Arresting phrases

Hilary Mantel has a flair for original, arresting phrases. By attaching a striking phrase to an individual, she illuminates character; and an arresting visual image makes the reader inhabit the place she's writing about. Whatever you're writing, it's worthwhile thinking carefully about the image you want to create, and the impression you want to leave with the reader – and then choosing the most apt and arresting phrase you can invent to represent that image and reinforce that impression.

Inhabiting the character

Mantel was drawn to Cromwell because of his extraordinary rise from blacksmith's son (with a father who was often drunk and violent) to Earl of Essex. 'How is that done?' she asked herself. Her characterisation was informed by a will, written in the 1520s, in which Cromwell named members of his household and parcelled out his favourite possessions, and by a letter written around the same time to a friend, which gave a hugely detailed description of the course of Parliament and all the business it dealt with. The letter ended with a simple, deflationary line, paraphrased as 'And at the end of it, absolutely nothing changed'. This was evidently a man with a wry sense of humour. Mantel believes that because they were so often dictated, letters (even those like Cromwell's which deal purely with business affairs) can impart a sense of the rhythm and vocabulary of the originator's spoken voice.

Mantel takes us back into the sixteenth-century mind. She puts herself in Cromwell's shoes, and the voice rings true. Her constant use of the pronoun 'He' to denote Cromwell is a simple but effective way of making her readers feel that they are inside his head, seeing the world through his eyes. She combines absolute precision of historical detail with a compelling sense of drama and convincing characterisation.

Mantel makes Cromwell human and credible. While he's usually been portrayed, both in history books and in literary accounts (such as Robert Bolt's *A Man for All Seasons*), as Henry VIII's ruthless, unprincipled enforcer, Mantel's Cromwell is not a villain, but a hard-working, powerful and highly effective civil servant. As he shins up the greasy pole of the Tudor court, he uses his sharp legal brain and his many skills to fulfil his master's wishes and implement his policies. He's a persuader and a negotiator, who uses force only when subtler methods of persuasion have failed. As Chapuys, the Spanish Imperial Ambassador (and enemy of Cromwell) puts it: 'When the cardinal [Wolsey] came to a closed door he would flatter it – oh you beautiful yielding door! Then he would try tricking it open. And you [Cromwell] are just the same... in the last resort you just kick it in.'

Mantel's Cromwell is a man of many parts: 'He can draft a contract, train a falcon, draw a map, stop a street fight, furnish a house and fix a jury.' 'He can chat away in a mixture of French, Tuscan and Putney, price a lady's brocades and furs on sight, or conjure up the perfect set of Venetian crystal-handled forks' to get himself into the good books of the mercurial Anne Boleyn. He's also an adroit businessman who puts his father-in-law's failing business back on its feet.

How she writes

> The only way I know how to make a book is to construct it like a collage: a bit of dialogue here, a scrap of narrative, an isolated description of a common object, an elaborate running metaphor which threads between the sequences and holds different narrative lines together.

She uses ring-binders for her notes because hard-spined notebooks 'drive the narrative in one direction; the relentless linearity oppresses you and seals off your narrative options early. Often what you need is not to delete what you've written, but just to swap it around a bit.'

She suspects that people who ask 'How many words do you do per day?' imagine that prose 'unwinds in a flowing, ceaseless stream of… unrevised narrative… as if the difference between good and bad writers is that the good ones have no need to do it again'. She believes that 'Almost the opposite is true; the better you are, the more ambitious and exploratory, the more often you will go astray on the way to getting it even approximately halfway right.' A brisk critic of anything muddled, pretentious or trite, she does not show her work to anyone until she has revised, rewritten and polished it.

She advises aspiring writers to read Dorothea Brande's *Becoming a Writer* and to write not for a perceived audience or market, but simply the kind of book that they themselves would like to read.

Learning points

- Research meticulously, establishing the facts and constructing a historically accurate timeline of events.
- Use your imagination to fill in the gaps, writing in the most direct and vigorous way you can.

- Bear in mind that letters, which were often dictated, can give you a sense of the writer's vocabulary and spoken voice.
- Description works best when coloured by the viewpoint of a character who is new to a place, to things around them or to a situation.
- Swapping text around, rather than changing it or deleting it, can often improve the narrative.

ANDY McNAB
(1959–)

Bravo Two Zero is the highest selling war book of all time. Published in 1993, shortly after Andy McNab (real name Steven Billy Mitchell) left the Special Air Service (SAS), it catapulted him to instant fame. He had spent ten years in the SAS before he turned himself into a bestselling author.

Bravo Two Zero

The book which made McNab's name is an account of an eight-man SAS patrol dropped behind enemy lines in Iraq during the first Gulf War of 1990–1991. Their mission was to cut the underground (fibre-optic cable) communication link between Baghdad and north-west Iraq and to find and destroy mobile Scud missile launchers. The action begins on 22 January 1991, when a Chinook helicopter takes them from a remote airfield in Saudi Arabia deep into enemy territory. The area where they are dropped turns out to be swarming with Iraqi troops and the patrol's radio communications prove to be ineffective. McNab's description of the situation is straightforward and powerful:

Of course you're afraid – anyone who says they're not are either lying or need to see a shrink. You want to make the biggest hole possible to hide in – you'd get your spoon out and start digging if that would help. But then the training takes over… you psych yourself up, check all your pouches are closed, your pockets don't open and your magazines are on tight… The Bergens were binned – we couldn't move quickly enough with them. Our belt kits carried what we couldn't do without – water and ammo. We could hear contacts in the distance. Whoever they were firing at it wasn't us.

It's not long before a boy goat-herder stumbles across the patrol and their whereabouts is compromised. There's a firefight as the patrol is forced to split up and run for their lives. Three are killed, four – including McNab – are captured and one manages to escape into neighbouring Syria. The book records the patrol's superhuman endurance on night marches over the desert in extreme conditions, with an ice-cold wind and driving snow – with the lights of enemy vehicles not far away. McNab is just four kilometres from the Syrian border when he is captured. The remainder of *Bravo Two Zero* – about half of the total narrative – records what happens to McNab in captivity. He's held for six weeks and subjected to horrendous torture. Released when the war ends, he needs several months of medical treatment and rehabilitation before he can return to active service.

There are question marks about the veracity of *Bravo Two Zero*. McNab's account and that of his patrol comrade Chris Ryan (real name Colin Armstrong), who escaped to Syria, are contradictory on many points. Moreover, the explorer, Arabist and former SAS reservist Michael Asher, who visited Syria with a Channel 4 film crew in 2000 and interviewed many eyewitnesses, concluded that there was no evidence that the Bravo Two Zero patrol accounted for a single enemy casualty. This was corroborated by the 22 SAS regimental sergeant major at the time of the first Gulf War who, based on the debriefing given to the regiment, said that the book's claim to be 'the true story of an SAS patrol in action' was unfounded.

From a writer's perspective, however, the truth or otherwise of *Bravo Two Zero* is beside the point. What matters is that it is a cracking war story. There's an enormous amount of technical detail about guns, military equipment and the day-to-day routines of an SAS patrol in action (to understand what was going on, I found that I often needed to refer to the glossary of military abbreviations, acronyms and SAS slang). This nitty-gritty detail gives the book its realism and authenticity. The narrative is driven along by the author's instinct for survival, and the reader keeps reading because they want to know how McNab will get through his many physical and mental ordeals. There's a lot of military slang, expletives and the kind of death-related humour that, I can easily believe, is the only thing that keeps soldiers going when things are as bad as they can get. When *Bravo Two Zero* was filmed in 1998 (with Sean Bean in the starring role), McNab wrote the screenplay.

Bravo Two Zero was followed by McNab's autobiography, *Immediate Action* (1995), which was at the top of the bestseller lists for 18 weeks. It largely chronicles his life after enlistment in the Royal Green Jackets, with particular focus on the intensive training exercises he went through and the time he spent in Northern Ireland. When it came to the SAS, he liked the fact that what his superiors were interested in was the end result – not how it was achieved. He was left alone to do his job in his own way, and that had a strong appeal. *Immediate Action* has the same detailed descriptions of weaponry and the same feeling of authenticity as his first book; but perhaps its most appealing feature is the brutal honesty with which the author shows us some of the more disagreeable and unpleasant aspects (dishonesty, extreme egocentricity) of his own teenage character.

> ### Fact and fiction
>
> Although it was categorised as non-fiction, the historical accuracy of the bestseller that made McNab's name is questionable. And looking at his fiction, we can see that this draws extensively on his own real-life experience of the SAS. This mixing of fact and fiction is nothing new. Many novelists have incorporated real events and experiences into their stories; and in many writers' autobiographies and memoirs it is not at all easy to distinguish fact from fiction. It is a mistake to imagine that everything in a novel has to be made up. Equally, it is for the non-fiction writer to decide to what extent (if at all) he or she wishes to embellish, or to be economical with, the truth – in which case it's usually important to make it clear that what you are presenting is your own version of what happened.

How he began

Andy McNab had an inauspicious start in life. Found in a carrier bag abandoned on the steps of Guy's Hospital in Southwark, he was brought up by his adoptive family in Peckham. He attended nine different schools over seven years and he became a petty criminal. In 1976 he was arrested for burglary and put in juvenile detention. While there he was visited by an army recruitment team and offered early release if he joined up.

He was 16 years old when he went straight from juvenile detention to the army. He has said that the army turned his life around, opening his eyes and making him realise that there were opportunities available if he was prepared to take them. He moved to the SAS in 1984 after passing the entry test (known as 'selection') at his second attempt. By the time of the first Gulf War, when he was put in charge of the Bravo Two Zero patrol, he was a sergeant and had been awarded the Military Medal.

Andy McNab was 17 years old, but with the reading age of an 11-year-old, when he read his first book: 'I can vividly remember the feeling of pride and achievement I felt from reading my very first book,' he said. 'It was a Janet and John series and was meant for primary school children but I didn't care. I'd read it, a whole book, and I was hooked!' He later said, 'I'm a perfect example of how reading became so important in my life and really changed my life.'

Fiction

McNab drew extensively on his SAS experience for his first novel, *Remote Control* (1998). Its hero, Nick Stone, is an ex-SAS man who finds himself enmeshed in a complex web linking British and US Intelligence, Columbian drug cartels and the IRA. With the exception of one little girl, the entire family of his friend is wiped out. Who did it, and why? That's the question Stone sets himself to answer. Although the book is a novel, the amount of real information McNab gives about the SAS's operating methods resulted in an injunction to prevent publication. Before publication was allowed to go ahead, the book was vetted by the Ministry of Defence (MoD) and McNab signed a legally binding agreement to submit all subsequent books for MoD vetting. He has said that as a writer he has not found the vetting process to be a major problem. MoD officials typically go through the book highlighting paragraphs they're unhappy with and he changes the text accordingly.

He has written 17 further Nick Stone stories, all of them characterised by their violent action, fast pace and authentic SAS detail. In the latest of these thrillers, *Detonator* (2015), an assassin's bullet on an isolated Alpine pass and a high-level Russian conflict propels him into a brutal mission; as the body count increases, he becomes one of Europe's most hunted men. McNab has also written three thrillers about ex-SAS trooper turned MI5 operative Tom Buckingham, and he has co-written the Boy Soldier series of books for children. He has also written four Quick Reads – most recently, *On the Rock* (2016), about an attempted terrorist attack in Gibraltar. Quick Reads are short new books by bestselling authors promoted by The Reading Agency charity, which says: 'They are perfect for regular readers wanting a fast and satisfying read, but they are also ideal for adults who are discovering reading for pleasure for the first time.'

In recent years McNab has visited the Army Foundation College in Harrogate, talking to new recruits about his war experiences and encouraging them to engage with the idea of reading and writing. He has written three YA books – the Liam Scott New Recruit series – based partly on the experiences and anecdotes of new recruits at Harrogate. When planning this series he invited them to think about their own army experiences, both good and bad, to write it all down, and to send it to him so that he could put it into the books. And that is what happened: 'I may have written these books and created the characters,' he said. 'But plenty of the material comes from those young lads up in Harrogate. These are their books too, I hope they are as proud of them as I am.'

What sets McNab apart from most other thriller writers is the amount of authentic detail his books contain. As *The Sunday Times* has put it, 'McNab's greatest asset is that the heart of his fiction is not fiction; other thriller writers do their research, but he has actually been there.'

Learning points

- Real-life experiences can provide good subject matter for fiction.
- Technical, nitty-gritty detail conveys realism and authenticity.
- Military slang, together with expletives and death-related humour, makes the characters come alive.
- Every book needs a driving force to compel the reader to continue reading. In *Bravo Two Zero* the reader needs to find out how the hero will survive his physical and mental ordeals.
- Anyone can become a writer if they give themselves the chance; you don't have to have a literary background.

MICHAEL MORPURGO
(1943–)

'The most solid, classical of children's authors' is how Anthony Horowitz has described him, with 'books… [that] have a strong social conscience and an honesty that makes them universal'. One of our best-loved children's authors, Michael Morpurgo has written more than 130 books. I'll concentrate on just three of them.

Beginnings

As a four-year-old, Morpurgo loved listening to his mother reading to him. He believes that the stories and poems she read then sowed the seed that gave him a love for the music of words. But unlike most well-known writers, he did not enjoy either reading or writing when he was a child. Any love of reading was wiped out when he went to prep school, where pupils, forced to stand up to read, were 'taught by fear'. His step-father gave him a copy of *Oliver Twist*, but he preferred to read comics and the books of Enid Blyton. The first book he read and enjoyed was *Treasure Island*. Interest in literature was reawakened at university:

> I remember at King's College my old professor sitting on a desk in a dusty room and reading us Sir Gawain and the Green Knight. He read it as if he loved it. And a little echo came into my head because the last person who had read to me like that was mother.

After leaving school Michael Morpurgo went to Sandhurst, but soon decided that the Army was not for him. Instead, he studied English and French at King's College London. His first job was teaching at a primary school in Kent and he remained a teacher for eight years. Every day he had to read the children a story. He soon realised that they were bored by the book he was reading and started to tell his own stories. These sparked their interest and he could see that there was magic in it for them; he realised there was magic in it for him too. So he began not as a writer, but as an oral storyteller. He progressed from storyteller to writer with his first book, *It Never Rained: Five Stories*, published in 1974. He later said that 'I was lucky. I happened to write some short stories that a publisher was looking for at that moment.'

In 1976, after moving to a farm in Devon, he and his wife Clare established the charity Farms for City Children. Forty years on, the charity has three farms and every year 3,000 city children and 400 teachers spend a week engaged in real, active farm work. Morpurgo's book *Didn't We Have a Lovely Time!* (2016) is a story told from the viewpoint of a schoolteacher who has taken children from London to spend a week on the farm. Living on a farm, Morpurgo is surrounded by animals. One of the recurring themes in his books is the connectivity between humans and animals. 'The more I am with them, the more I feel connected to them,' he says. 'What interests me most is… how we relate to them and how they relate to us.'

Connectivity with animals

Morpurgo's observations and experience of how animals live and react to humans, and how children react to animals, have fed into his writing. Many children are fascinated by animals. If you want to write for children, an animal story could be a good starting point. But the story will need to avoid sentimentality and to be based on the real physiognomy and behaviour of animals.

Influences and inspirations

Morpurgo's writing was inspired by Ted Hughes's *Poetry in the Making*, Paul Gallico's *The Snow Goose* and Ernest Hemingway's *The Old Man and the Sea*. Ted Hughes was a strong influence and 'a great inspiration'. Living and fishing nearby in Devon, he became a friend, neighbour and mentor, often reading Morpurgo's stories either before or after publication. It was a conversation between Hughes and Morpurgo that led to the inauguration in 1998 of the Children's Laureate, a post Morpurgo himself occupied from 2003–2005. Ted Hughes's *The Iron Man* is a favourite book; others he especially admires are Robert Louis Stevenson's *Treasure Island* and Rudyard Kipling's *Just So Stories*.

War Horse

War Horse (1982) is about Albert, a farmer, and Joey, a young horse – and how the bond between them survives the atrocities of World War One. There were three major inspirations for Michael Morpurgo's best-known work, which was brought to a wider public by the stage play and the Steven Spielberg film. Many years ago he met a World War One veteran, Wilfred Ellis, who drank in his local pub at Iddesleigh. He had been in the Devon Yeomanry, working with horses, and told him what it had been like to be a young soldier; he showed him his trenching tool and some old photographs. He met another villager, Captain Budgett, who had been in the cavalry in World War One, and a third, Albert Weeks, who remembered the Army coming to the village to buy horses. Hearing at first hand about the horror of war and the horses' involvement in it made such a strong impact on him that Morpurgo began to think about how the story of the war and the universal suffering it brought might be told from the viewpoint of a horse.

The second inspiration was a boy who spent a week at the Morpurgo farm. Speaking about this on Radio 4 in 2010, he said:

> One of the kids who came to the farm was from Birmingham, a boy called Billy. The teachers warned me that he had a stammer and told me not to ask him direct questions because it would terrify him

if he had to be made to speak because he doesn't speak... I came in the last evening into the yard behind this big Victorian house where they all live, and there he was, Billy, standing in his slippers by the stable door and the lantern above his head, talking. Talking, talking, talking, to the horse. And the horse, Hebe, had her head just over the top of the stable, and she was listening; that's what I noticed, that the ears were going, and I knew she knew that she had to stay there whilst this went on, because this kid wanted to talk, and the horse wanted to listen – this was a two way thing... the words were simply flowing. All the fear had gone, and there was something about the intimacy of this relationship, the trust building up between boy and horse, that I found enormously moving, and I thought: Well yes, you could write a story about the First World War through the eyes of a horse, and yes, the horse didn't understand every word, but she knew it was important for her to stand there and be there for this child.

The third inspiration for the book was an old oil painting that Morpurgo's wife had been left: 'It was a very frightening and alarming painting, not the sort you'd want to hang on a wall. It showed horses during the First World War charging into barbed wire fences. It haunted me.' The painting was by F. W. Reed, dated 1917, and showed a British cavalry charge on German lines.

The Butterfly Lion

The Butterfly Lion (1996) is the story of Bertie's love for an orphaned white lion cub he has rescued from the African veld; the cub's sale to a French circus; and Bertie's reunion with the grown lion when serving as an officer in France during World War One. The lion comes back to England with Bertie and lives happily in the parkland that surrounds his big house. When the lion dies, Bertie and his wife carve a lion into the chalk hill opposite their house, and whenever the sun shines after rain in summer Adonis Blue butterflies come out to drink on the chalk lion.

Inspiration for *The Butterfly Lion* came from the chalk white horse near Westbury in Wiltshire; a chance meeting with Virginia McKenna; a book about a pride of white lions; the true story of a World War One soldier who rescued some circus animals from death in France; and seven-year-old Michael Morpurgo's short-lived attempt to run away from boarding school (he got two miles down the road before he was picked up by a little old lady who fed him buns and then took him back to school). It's fascinating – and instructive – to see how Morpurgo skilfully weaves these true-life elements into a fictional story.

Private Peaceful

Private Peaceful (2003) was inspired by the name on a gravestone at Ypres and a letter dated 1916 on display at the In Flanders Fields Museum in Ypres. Written by a British officer, it was just six lines long: 'We regret to inform you that your son, Private X, was shot at dawn for cowardice. Yours sincerely.' This short letter got Morpurgo thinking about how the recipient, the soldier's mother in Manchester, must have felt, and then about the life and times of a young soldier in World War One. He discovered that some 300 men were shot for cowardice on the British side (and many more on the French and the German sides), many of them having already been identified as suffering from shellshock (in 2006 they were all given posthumous pardons).

The story's narrator is Thomas Peaceful ('Tommo'), younger brother of Charlie who has married Molly, the girl they both fell in love with at school. Tommo sits alone at night in the trenches during World War One, looking back over his childhood in the country. The first half of the book gives us a picture of rural life just before the outbreak of war, but this is no rural idyll: it's a raw, class-ridden society. We are then exposed to the horrors and brutality of war, as the clock ticks towards (though we don't know it until the book's final pages) the moment of Charlie's execution. He has been unjustly condemned to death for cowardice. The story ends with Charlie's execution and Tommo's promise to look after Charlie and Molly's new baby. With its vivid portrayal of innocence, comradeship, brutality and courage, *Private Peaceful* is a powerful, poignant novel.

How and why he writes

I write about what I care about, what I love, what makes me angry, what makes me sad. Sadness is upsetting, and so is disappointment when things don't work out as you would have liked them to, but the truth is that's part of life and living as I see it. Fiction should reflect that, and should not wrap things up in a pink ribbon simply because it is for the young. Young and old, we have to come to terms with the world as it is, not as we'd like it to be… I write to make me think, and I hope to make others think too. I think reading can help us work things out for ourselves… Almost all my stories have some reality as their inspiration, either my own experience or someone else's, or historical fact.

'For me, the greater part of writing is daydreaming, dreaming the dream of my story until it hatches out – the writing down of it I always find hard.' Michael's wife Clare is an indispensable sounding board for his writing. He always talks the story idea through with her before putting it down on paper. The most important part of the process, he says, is doing the research, weaving the story together and finding the right voice. His World War One research, for example, involved not only examining lots of written material (e.g. letters, poems, stories left behind by those who fought), but also talking individually to around a hundred people.

He writes his stories in exercise books; he does not work at a desk, but in bed, propped up with pillows, and he can only write in a silent room. Editing and rewriting is the part of the process which he does not enjoy. When he has completed a story he reads it aloud to himself – then to his grandchildren. The actual writing may take two or three months, and the editing and rewriting a further month. So the whole process of producing a new book usually takes upwards of six months.

Learning points

- Exploring the relationship between humans and animals can make compelling fiction.
- By writing about something you care about, you will create a book that your readers are likely to care about.
- A story can be inspired by historical fact or by your own or someone else's real-life experience.
- Read the story aloud to yourself; listen to the rhythm of the words and make sure that they are easy on the ear.
- Test your story on an audience of children (perhaps in your local library or school). Chances are, if they find it boring or incomprehensible, they'll tell you.

GEORGE ORWELL
(1903–1950)

For anyone who wants to write clear and concise English, there are few better models than Orwell. He is best known for two extraordinary novels, *Animal Farm* (1945) and *Nineteen Eighty-Four* (1949). Big Brother, Room 101, Doublethink, Newspeak – all Orwell's inventions – have entered our consciousness and become part of popular culture.

But Orwell also wrote an enormous amount of non-fiction, and he was probably a better journalist and essayist than he was a novelist. The range of his subject matter, his intelligence, and the clarity and vitality of his language are astounding.

If you're new to him, begin not with his novels, but with some of his essays, journalism and letters. Don't think of him as a purely political writer. Pieces like 'A Nice Cup of Tea' and 'In Defence of English Cooking', his long essay 'The English People', his many book reviews and his 'As I Please' columns in *Tribune* (the left-wing weekly) are more of a testimony to his fierce independence of thought, his sense of Englishness and his craftsmanship as a writer, than to his strong political views.

Orwell saw humbug and insincerity as the great enemies of clear language. His striking piece 'The Shooting of an Elephant', based on an incident in Burma while he was serving there as a young man in the Imperial Indian Police, illustrates his honesty and his willingness to put himself under the microscope: he confesses to killing the elephant for no other reason than to avoid looking a fool.

Orwell had a lot to say about the writing of good English and he encapsulated his views in six elementary rules. These have stood the test of time and are still a pretty good template for any writer:

(1) Never use a metaphor, simile or other figure of speech which you are used to seeing in print

The use of hackneyed similes, metaphors and other phrases is a symptom of lazy writing. It's much less trouble to describe the cliffs of Dover as 'snow-white' than to think of a more original and arresting descriptor. Does the hero of your detective story 'go fishing in troubled waters' or 'leave no stone unturned'? Metaphors like these are so stale that they are almost devoid of meaning. Much better to invent your own, fresh similes and metaphors.

(2) Never use a long word where a short one will do

The English language has two main derivations – Latin and Anglo-Saxon. Usually the word derived from Latin is longer; the word of Anglo-Saxon origin is invariably shorter – and sometimes more concrete too. Writers are occasionally tempted to use Latinate words because they believe this will impress their readers. This may be less prevalent today than it was in Orwell's time, but it persists, especially in academic and business writing.

'Concrete words are better than abstract ones,' wrote Orwell, 'and the shortest way of saying anything is always the best.' Few writers would choose the Latinate 'precipitation' in preference to the Anglo-Saxon 'rain'; but you might be tempted to use 'demonstrate' rather than 'show', or 'endeavour' when 'try' would do the job perfectly well – and take up less space. Occasionally a long word derived from Latin may be the only one that perfectly expresses your meaning. If that's the case, use it.

(3) If it is possible to cut a word out, always cut it out

However good a sentence is, you can often find a word or two that can be cut out without any loss of meaning. Far from weakening the prose, cutting out an adverb or an adjective that you don't really need can strengthen it. It's often possible, too, to sharpen a sentence by replacing a phrase with a crisp word or two. Don't write 'in my own personal opinion', but 'I think'. Instead of 'at the present time', just say 'now'. And avoid clumsy phrases: you can replace 'due to the fact that' with 'because', and 'the manner in which' with 'how'. Whenever I have completed a piece of writing I always try to put it away for a few days and then look at it again with fresh eyes. I have never, ever done that without finding at least one word or phrase that can be cut – and there are often more than one.

(4) Never use the passive where you can use the active

The passive voice is impersonal and indirect. It has traditionally been used by institutions (government, banks, commercial organisations, etc.)

when communicating with members of the public: 'Interest at 1 per cent per month will be chargeable...' instead of the more personal and direct 'We will charge you interest at 1 per cent per month...'; or 'The form should be returned to...' instead of 'Please return the form to...'.

The passive can make a sentence less clear, less interesting and more long-winded. It can also lead to the use of verbs as nouns. This practice, known as nominalisation, is common in official, technical and scientific writing: 'The conclusion of the report was that...' rather than the simpler 'The report concluded...'; or 'A decision on future strategy will be taken by the Board' instead of 'The Board will decide future strategy.'

Sometimes, however, we need to be less blunt or less direct. When that's the case, the passive can be very useful. And if we want to emphasise the object rather than the subject of a sentence, the passive is the way to do it. Newspaper sub-editors often use this technique to write eye-catching headlines: 'Top athlete [is] banned by Olympic Committee following drug tests.'

(5) Never use a foreign phrase, a scientific word or a jargon word if you can think of an everyday English equivalent

Writers need to interest and entertain their readers. To do that, they have to make sure that every word they write is comprehensible, and the best guarantee of that is to use plain language – simple, concrete words. If you use words your readers are unlikely to understand – obscure technical terms, foreign phrases, jargon that may be perfectly comprehensible to those in the know but is double Dutch to the outside world – you're putting up an unnecessary barrier. Writing is difficult enough as it is. Why make things even harder for yourself?

(6) Break any of these rules rather than write anything outright barbarous

One could stick religiously to every one of Orwell's first five rules and still end up with a badly constructed sentence that grates on the ear. So don't hesitate to break a rule if the alternative is to write something that looks (or sounds) contrived or ugly.

Listen to the words

Of Orwell's six famous rules for writers, the sixth is arguably the most significant. It's important to listen to the rhythm of the words. If (despite perfect vocabulary, grammar, punctuation and so on) they grate on the ear, something is wrong. A writer, like a composer of music, needs to hear the creation in his or her head. Does it sing? Does it sound right? Once it's been written down, reading it aloud will usually expose anything that is ugly.

'Good prose,' said Orwell, 'is like a window-pane.' He believed that before putting pen to paper a writer should ask himself four key questions:

(1) What am I trying to say?
(2) What words will express it?
(3) What image or idiom will make it clearer?
(4) Is this image fresh enough to have an effect?

He railed against writers who, instead of choosing words for the sake of their meaning and inventing images to make the meaning clearer, saved themselves the trouble of thinking by using ready-made phrases and stale idioms.
 Orwell wrote:

Probably, it is better to put off using words as long as possible and get one's meaning as clear as one can through pictures or sensations. Afterwards one can choose – not simply accept – the phrases that will best cover the meaning, and then switch round and decide what impression one's words are likely to make on another person.

I think that's pretty good advice. Putting yourself in the shoes of the reader is one of the keys to effective writing.

In his non-fiction writing Orwell has a conversational tone which, together with the use of rhetoric, gives the impression that he is speaking directly to the reader. His use of italics for emphasis is a good example of this: 'Kipling *is* a jingo imperialist'; 'It is quite possible that man's major problems will *never* be solved.' This device enables him to get his meaning across directly; without it, he would have to use a more artificial and literary sentence to bring out the emphasis.

Here I've focused on Orwell as a writer of non-fiction. No one who reads any of his substantial output – essays, journalism, letters, *Down and Out in Paris and London* (1933), *The Road to Wigan Pier* (1937), *Homage to Catalonia* (1938) – can fail to be impressed by the immediacy and vigour of the writing. His merits as a writer of fiction (he wrote six novels) are more open to argument, but, as Orwell said, 'Ultimately, there is no test of literary merit except survival.' By that yardstick *Animal Farm* and *Nineteen Eighty-Four* are surely two of the greatest English novels of the twentieth century. Has anyone written a better opening line than the first sentence of *Nineteen Eighty-Four*? 'It was a bright cold day in April, and the clocks were striking thirteen.'

Learning points

- Insincerity and humbug are the enemies of clear language.
- Use a conversational tone to speak directly to the reader.
- Use short, concrete words – and delete words you don't need.
- Invent your own fresh similes and metaphors.
- Put yourself in the shoes of the reader.

BEATRIX POTTER
(1866–1943)

'You may go into the fields or down the lane, but don't go into Mr. McGregor's garden: your Father had an accident there; he was put into a pie by Mrs. McGregor.'

But Peter is a naughty rabbit who does not do as he is told, and he does not follow Mrs Rabbit's instructions. His behaviour mirrors that of a naughty child. No wonder *The Tale of Peter Rabbit* (1902) was such a success. Beatrix Potter went on to write and illustrate a further 23 bestselling books of animal tales.

Artist and naturalist

From an early age Potter was fascinated by natural history, science and art. Born in 1866 into a well-to-do, upper middle-class Victorian household, she was brought up by nannies and governesses; but on the third floor of the family house in Bolton Gardens, Kensington, she and her brother were allowed to keep a menagerie, which included, at various times, rabbits, a green frog, lizards, newts, bats, snails, guinea pigs, a canary, a budgerigar, a duck, a tortoise and a hedgehog. She observed these animals closely and drew them endlessly.

Her interest in natural history was also stimulated by long holidays spent at Dalguise House, Dunkeld, the family's second home in Perthshire, and at Camfield Place, her grandparents' home in Hertfordshire. From an early age she observed what was around her and loved to draw and paint. Her earliest sketchbook, 'Dalguise 1875', includes a careful watercolour study of caterpillars, as well as scenes depicting what she observed around her: a farmer with a cow, a bridge over the river, the house at the foot of the mountain. Another sketchbook of the same period shows rabbits on ice skates, wearing jackets, hats and scarves. By 1880 she was drawing serious, anatomically perfect, studies of rabbits.

From an early age Potter demonstrated an exceptional gift for drawing and painting, encouraged between the ages of 12 and 17 by the tutelage of her art teacher, Miss Cameron. Close observation of animals was the basis of her artistic realism. Millais, the famous painter who was a friend of her father's, said: 'Plenty of people can draw... but you have observation.'

How she began

Before the age of eight, two books made a particular impression on Potter: Edward Lear's *Book of Nonsense* and Lewis Carroll's *Alice's Adventures in Wonderland*. She was also entranced by books read to her by her Scottish nurse at Dalguise. These were full of folklore, rhyme, adventure and fantasy (she especially liked fantasy). Her favourites included *Aesop's Fables, Grimm's Fairy Tales*, the *Fairy Tales* of Hans Christian Andersen, Charles Kingsley's *The Water Babies* and the Waverley novels of Sir Walter Scott.

At the age of 14, inspired by her admiration of James Boswell and Samuel Pepys, Potter began to keep a diary. This was her literary apprenticeship, as she experimented and imitated the styles of admired writers such as Edward Lear, Lewis Carroll, Jane Austen and her special heroine, Fanny Burney.

Her first published illustrations, at the age of 24, were animal designs, based on one of her pet rabbits, used in Christmas and New Year cards. Three years later, on 4 September 1893, she wrote a picture letter to Noel Moore (son of one of her governesses), who was sick in bed, about a disobedient young rabbit called Peter; and she followed this up, the next day, with a picture letter to Noel's younger brother, five-year-old Eric, about a frog called Jeremy Fisher.

In 1894 she sold nine frog drawings to a publisher of fine art prints who had bought a few of her earlier drawings. At this time she was absorbed in mycology, the study of fungi, and wrote a scientific paper on the subject. Between 1892 and 1896 she produced fantasy illustrations of favourite stories and rhymes, including *Cinderella, Alice's Adventures in Wonderland* and Edward Lear's *The Owl and the Pussycat*. She also produced drawings for *Sleeping Beauty* and *Puss in Boots*, and illustrations for stories from *The Arabian Nights* and *Aesop's Fables*. Most significant of all, perhaps, were eight illustrations of Joel Chandler Harris's *Nights with Uncle Remus*; his stories about Brer Rabbit were to influence her own writing.

Her picture letters to the Moore children were pivotal in her development both as illustrator and writer. We can see how she handled the transition between natural science and fantasy, and developed her art of illustrated storytelling. She built on Harris's sense of the absurd and his technique of embellishing the ordinary, but incorporated her own observations and experiences. She knew that the Moore children were interested in nature and in how things worked, and that they liked a story with adventure and humour. These were to be the main ingredients of her books, the best of which were based on her picture letters.

In January 1900 Annie Moore, Potter's former governess, suggested that some of her picture letters could be made into interesting books for little children. Potter borrowed them back so that she could make copies and consider which one would be most suitable for a book. She decided upon her very first picture letter – the Peter Rabbit story of 1893. She added new text and new black and white illustrations, and sent it to at least six publishers. They all rejected it.

Among the publishers who rejected the book was Frederick Warne & Co, which said that it was 'absolutely necessary that the pictures should be coloured throughout'. Potter thereupon decided to self-publish. She adopted the small-size picture-book format of Helen Bannerman's *Little Black Sambo*, believing that this size was ideal for small children, who could handle the book easily – and that it would sell. Potter sent Warne a copy of her privately printed edition and – at last accepting the publisher's views – included more coloured illustrations. She insisted on a low price and on the small-size format. Warne agreed, and the book was published in October 1902, priced 1s 6d.

Animal tales

With *The Tale of Peter Rabbit* an immediate success, Warne was keen for Potter to produce more books in the same style. By Christmas 1902 she had proposed at least three new books – *Squirrel Nutkin, Mr Jeremy Fisher* and *The Tailor of Gloucester*. Before these stories were submitted for publication, she tried them out on children she knew. Around the time of *Nutkin*'s publication, she also began sending little letters to some of her young friends – anecdotes about her animal characters or conversations between them. One early, charming example is from Squirrel Nutkin to Old Brown (the owl): 'Dear Sir, I should esteem it a favour if you will let me have back my tail, as I miss it very much. I would pay postage. Yrs truly Squirrel Nutkin. An answer will oblige.'

In 1905, at the age of 39, she purchased Hill Top Farm at Sawrey, a small village near Hawkshead in the Lake District. This was followed by a remarkable outburst of creativity: over the next eight years she produced 13 stories set in Hill Top Farm and the surrounding countryside, and these included much of her best work. *The Tale of Jemima Puddle-Duck* (1908), written for the children of her farm manager, was inspired by his wife's habit of giving ducks eggs to Hill Top hens to incubate, as well as by her own amusement at her farmyard ducks. The children and their mother appear in the story, as do some Hill Top animals, including the collie, Kep. *The Roly-Poly Pudding* (1908) was inspired by an invasion of rats at Hill Top and Potter's ongoing battles against them; it incorporates details of the house and its furnishings.

The Tale of Mr Tod (1912) is a longer, darker and more violent story, and she was particularly proud of her opening paragraph:

I am quite tired of making goody goody books about nice people. I will make a story about two disagreeable people, called Tommy Brock and Mr. Tod.

At the insistence of her publisher, however, she had to drop 'goody goody', and to substitute 'well-behaved' for 'nice'. Tommy Brock is a badger and Mr Tod a fox. *The Tale of Pigling Bland* (1913), which came directly out of her farming experiences, has several biographical touches and Potter herself appears in the story. It was stimulated partly by the little black pig she bought soon after her arrival at the farm.

In 1914 she sent her publisher the text of another story, *Kitty-in-Boots*, but she had done only one illustration for this when 'interruptions' – World War One, marriage, illness – prevented her from completing it. The story was lost sight of until, remarkably, it was discovered, handwritten in school notebooks, a hundred years later in the Victoria and Albert Museum archive. Featuring some of the characters from earlier books, including Mr Tod, Mrs Tiggy-Winkle and an older, slower and portlier Peter Rabbit, it was published in 2016 by her original publisher, Frederick Warne and Co. with illustrations by Quentin Blake.

The previous year, 1913, she had tried to capture some of the qualities of ordinary folk life, and experimented using local dialect, in a short story, 'Fairy Clogs', published in *Country Life* magazine. Four years later a collection of nursery rhymes she had written and illustrated was published: *Appley Dapply's Nursery Rhymes* (1917), which she had first proposed to Warne following the release of *Peter Rabbit* in 1902, helped to stave off the company's ruin following a financial scandal. The following year the most autobiographical of all her stories, *The Tale of Johnny Town-Mouse*, was published. This story, put together during the war years, showed her deep understanding of animal nature – and reflected her own happiness as a 'country-mouse'. By this time, however, her eyesight was beginning to fail and the drawings, though charming, are not up to the standard of her best work.

Later life

In 1923 Beatrix Potter became a significant Lake District landowner with her purchase of the 2,000-acre Troutbeck Park Farm. The previous year had seen the publication of *Cecily Parsley's Nursery Rhymes*, a satirical collection full of local colour (it included a caricature of one of her husband's golfing partners, Dr Parsons). Thereafter, the breeding of Herdwick sheep, together with the restoration and preservation of the surrounding Lake District landscape, largely replaced her interest in writing and illustrating books for children.

A meeting with an American publisher, who visited her in Sawrey, resulted in some stories and one book, *The Fairy Caravan* (1929), being published in the US. Her last illustrated animal book for children was *The Tale of Little Pig Robinson* (1930). Unlike her earlier books, this had more fantasy than reality and did not have the same impact. However, she was particularly pleased with one of the drawings. She wrote to the book's American publisher, saying: 'I think Pig Robinson looking into a shop window is the best black and white I ever did.' But by this time she was at the end of her career as writer and illustrator. 'I am "written out" for story books, and my eyes are tired for painting,' she wrote in 1934.

How she worked

Beatrix Potter had an intuitive sense about what children liked. In *The Tale of Peter Rabbit*, Peter's reckless bravado, deciding to do something (going into Mr McGregor's garden) which has been expressly forbidden, is recognisable not only as something a 'very naughty' young rabbit might well do, but also as the behaviour of a naughty child. That seamless harmony between animal and human nature is at the heart of Beatrix Potter's books, and goes a long way towards explaining their enduring popularity.

Potter's starting point was the physiognomy and natural behaviour of animals: she studied their behaviours, and built their characters around those. Her portraits of animals are never sentimental. She recognised that nature had a hard edge and could be cruel, and she knew that violence could be popular with children. So mice are always in danger from cats and owls, little frogs can be gobbled up by big fish, and rabbits are on the lookout for gardeners. She appreciated nature, but respected its ruthlessness. With her lifelong interest in artistic realism, her drawings of animals were set in real backgrounds: the gardens, houses, and landscapes which she knew and lived in.

Potter's straightforward, humorous tone is perfectly pitched to capture the interest and sympathy of her young readers. She paid great attention to her choice of language: rhythm, cadence and the sound of the word were very important. And she always took enormous trouble over the beginnings and endings of her books. She usually wrote out the story in a paper-covered exercise book and then pasted her drawings into a dummy book. She was always extremely particular about the look of the finished product.

Potter never wrote down to children, as we can see from the first sentence of *The Tailor of Gloucester*:

> In the time of swords and periwigs and full-skirted coats with flowered lappets – when gentlemen wore ruffles, and gold-laced waistcoats of paduasoy and taffeta – there lived a tailor in Gloucester.

That vocabulary, in a children's book, seems quite extraordinary, though we must remember that this book was written for children a little older (perhaps 11 or 12) than her earlier readers. 'This is my own favourite amongst my little books,' she wrote on a presentation copy, and her opinion never wavered.

Animal and human behaviour

Peter Rabbit appeals to children because he behaves pretty much like a naughty child. If you want to create believable animal characters that appeal to children, you need to do two things. First, make sure your animals not only have the physiognomy of real animals but also behave like real animals. Second, give them human characteristics that children can recognise and relate to. Children don't always do what their parents tell them to do. So when Peter disobeys his mother's instructions and goes into Mr McGregor's garden, they are immediately on his side. It's exactly the kind of thing a naughty child might do.

Learning points

- Keep a diary. The immediacy and authenticity can produce lively writing which you may later be able to draw on; and a regular diary entry (or, these days, a blog) can be used, rather like barre exercises for ballet dancers, to prepare yourself for a session of serious creative writing.
- Build the character of animals around their observed behaviour.
- Take great trouble over the choice of language, and over the beginning and ending of the story.
- Don't patronise or write down to children; it's important to speak to them on equal terms.

IAN RANKIN
(1960–)

If J. K. Rowling is Scotland's most famous contemporary author, Ian Rankin cannot be far behind. Britain's bestselling crime writer accounts for one in ten of all crime books sold, and his work has been translated into 25 languages. How does he do it, and what can a budding writer learn from him?

Black and Blue (1997), the eighth book featuring Inspector John Rebus, was the novel that catapulted Rankin into the bestseller lists. The previous books had been well reviewed, but sales were modest. By now he had served his apprenticeship and he knew what made Rebus tick. He decided to write in the staccato style of James Ellroy and to fill Rebus's world with real crimes and real villains.

An Ian Rankin book can be difficult to put down. A gripping plot, intricate and well-paced, hooks the reader and keeps him or her turning the pages, and Rankin weaves the disparate strands together with great skill. The denouement is often as unexpected as it is inevitable.

But suspenseful plotting is what we expect from any decent crime novel. The real key to Rankin's popularity and his status as our pre-eminent crime writer lies elsewhere – with his strong sense of place, persuasive characters and authentic dialogue. These are the ingredients – alongside the dry wit and the economy of language – that lift Rankin and his Detective Inspector John Rebus several notches above run-of-the-mill crime fiction.

Place

Think of Rebus and you think of Edinburgh. He belongs to the city, just as Morse does to Oxford and Maigret to Paris. The city is not simply the backdrop to Rankin's novels. Rebus *is* Edinburgh: he reflects its personality. This is not the smart Scottish capital of the tourist brochures, with its Georgian houses, expensive shops, upmarket tearooms, its Castle and its Festival. With Rebus, Rankin gets beneath the skin of the city and shows its murky underbelly – the parts the tourists do not see. He gives you the sounds, the smells, the taste of the city, and you can almost feel the rain on your skin. Rebus's Edinburgh is one of grimy backstreets and down-at-heel pubs, narrow passageways and graffiti-ridden housing estates, drunks and junkies and prostitutes. It's a city with a dark history: the city of Deacon Brodie, city councillor by day and burglar by night, and of Burke and Hare, who sold the corpses of their victims for dissection at the city's Medical College. No wonder Rankin has been dubbed the king of 'tartan noir'.

Rankin crams his books with the names of real streets and real buildings. Here's an example from *Exit Music* (2007):

> He kept walking, reaching Forrest Road. Instead of heading straight on in the direction of The Mound, he took a fork at Greyfriars Bobby and descended into the Grassmarket. Plenty of pubs still open, and people loitering outside the homeless hostels… Smokers were standing in clusters outside the Beehive and Last Drop pubs. The fish 'n' chip shop had a queue. A gust of fat-frying hit Rebus as he walked past and he breathed deeply, savouring it. At one time, the Grassmarket had boasted a gallows, dozens upon dozens of Covenanters dying there.

This brings the reader face to face with Edinburgh's street life and gives the writing an air of real authenticity.

Rebus's flat in Arden Street (where Rankin was living when he got the idea for his first Rebus story, *Knots and Crosses*, 1987) and the Oxford Bar, his favourite watering hole, now feature on literary tours of Edinburgh alongside buildings associated with Sir Walter Scott and Robert Louis Stevenson. Rankin's portrayal of the city has been compared with Dickens's London, Chandler's Los Angeles and Balzac's Paris. The sense of place is overwhelming.

Character

Rebus (defined in the dictionary as an enigmatic picture-puzzle) is a complex, flawed character. Cynical, world-weary, hard-nosed and hard-drinking, he is a tough guy in the tradition of Raymond Chandler's Philip Marlowe and James Ellroy's *L.A. Confidential*. With a none-too-happy childhood, a psychologically damaging spell in the SAS and a broken marriage all behind him, he's a man with 'attitude' and a bleak view of the world. In *Knots and Crosses* he has no compunction about stealing bread rolls and milk as he arrives home in the early morning. Snatches of his pre-police past are woven into the narrative in the form of memories of his early years in Fife. Rankin grew up in Fife and many of the memories he gives Rebus are his own.

Unlike most writers, Rankin does not plan his characters: he has said that Rebus arrived virtually fully formed on the page. Rebus's sidekick Siobhan was originally conceived as a minor role, but became so interesting that he decided to develop her into a major character. Rankin has the knack of creating vivid, realistic characters with a minimum of description, typically using dialogue and music (such as Rebus's enthusiasm for rock) to delineate character, and often delving into their psyche to give added depth.

Rebus is an outsider, a maverick who mistrusts team work and goes out of his way to get up the nose of suspects and superiors alike: that's how he gets fun out of life. He seems to derive as much satisfaction from antagonising those around him as he does from solving the crime puzzle. For Rebus, the job is everything: 'He loathed his free time, dreaded Sundays off' (*Let it Bleed*, 1995). By losing himself in his investigations he can avoid thinking about his own failings. As Rankin has put it, 'He is a good cop because he is a bad social human being.' But he softens Rebus's character by giving him a dry sense of humour: 'Why in God's name would Cafferty want a Russian poet killed?' asks a police colleague in *Exit Music*. 'Maybe he gets annoyed when verses don't rhyme,' says Rebus.

For all his cynicism and hard-boiled toughness, there is something brittle and vulnerable about Rebus. Perhaps that is why readers all over the world have warmed to him. He is not all black or white: he's a mixture of good and bad and he keeps most of his feelings and emotions hidden from those around him. Aren't most of us like that?

Dialogue

Rankin has a sharp ear for realistic dialogue, and he uses this to develop character, to provide information and to drive the plot along. One writer Rankin admires is Elmore Leonard, of whom he has said: 'He pares everything down to the bone. There are very few adjectives and adverbs and these books are driven by dialogue.'

In *Black and Blue* Rankin grabs the reader's attention with his first line: 'Tell me again why you killed them.' Dialogue takes up a good chunk of the first chapter, and by the end of it anyone coming to Rebus for the first time has a pretty good idea of his character. Reading dialogue aloud to yourself is, Rankin believes, the only way a writer can learn how to write realistic dialogue: 'If it sounds natural, it probably is natural.'

Realistic dialogue

Revealing and developing character by means of spot-on realistic dialogue is one key to Rankin's success. He also uses dialogue both to provide information and to drive the plot along. To write realistic dialogue that sounds authentic, you need to listen really carefully to the way people speak – the words, vernacular phrases, intonation and so on. People from different geographical areas, professions and social classes speak very differently. An ear for the way people really speak will help you to create believable characters. And sharp dialogue with a touch of humour makes a book easy to read.

Crime writer?

Rankin's many fans may be surprised to learn that he does not really see himself as a crime writer. 'I'm writing commentaries on Scotland's present, its foibles and psychoses,' he has said, and the breadth and vigour of his social portraiture has been compared with that of Dickens. Crime keeps the reader turning the pages, but Rankin's books touch on some big themes. *The Naming of the Dead* (2006), for example, is set against the background of the 2005 G8 summit at Gleneagles, which focused on poverty in Africa. Rebus is predictably dismissive of the ability of rock stars, concerts, marches or protests to change politicians' minds or alter world events. At the core of this book, says Rankin, is one question: can the individual make a difference?

Writing advice

'To become a writer you have to believe in yourself and in your work,' says Rankin. 'You'll face rejections (my first novel has never been published).' He believes that short stories are an excellent apprenticeship and 'a fantastic discipline for any writer', and he has three pieces of advice about the writing of these:

(1) Cut the slack: Write something down, then start taking out a word or a phrase. Does the passage still make sense? You'll be surprised how much you can take out, and at the end it's usually better.

(2) Grab the reader's attention: The opening sentence is the most important… You've got to grab the reader from the very start… They need to be compelled to go to the second sentence, then the third.

(3) Think outside the box: Short stories are a great laboratory… It's all about experimenting with different voices, perspectives and time frames… You can write short stories set in the future or in the past… you need a central character who is coming up against a situation they've never had to deal with before.

He cut his own teeth on short stories, winning a Radio Forth contest with a tale based on an incident from his own family history, and in 1983 'The Game', about a factory closure in Fife, won second prize in the Sinclair/Scotsman Short Story Competition (the winner was Iain Crichton Smith).

Rankin advises anyone who wants to write to read a lot: 'You'll copy your favourites, which will help you find your own voice eventually.' His own favourites include Muriel Spark, Elmore Leonard, Raymond Chandler, Lawrence Block, Anthony Burgess and Robert Louis Stevenson. He acknowledges the influence of Stevenson's *Dr Jekyll and Mr Hyde*, with its theme of good and evil – dark and light – embodied simultaneously in one man.

> I owe a great debt to Robert Louis Stevenson and to the city of his birth. In a way they both changed my life. Without Edinburgh's split nature Stevenson might never have dreamt up Dr Jekyll and Mr Hyde, and without Dr Jekyll and Mr Hyde I might never have come up with my own alter ego, Detective Inspector John Rebus.

Learning points

- The names of real streets and buildings, together with thumbnail descriptions of the sights, sounds and smells, can create a strong sense of place.
- Use dialogue and music to delineate character.
- Dry humour can be used to soften the character of a tough guy.
- Cut out words you don't need.
- Grab the reader with your first sentence.

RUTH RENDELL
(1930–2015)

She wrote more than 70 crime novels, but her writing career had an inauspicious beginning. Ruth Rendell resigned from the *Chigwell Times* after committing one of journalism's cardinal sins – sending in a report on an event that she had not attended. It was the annual dinner of the local tennis club and she had missed the death, in mid-flow, of the after-dinner speaker.

Rendell wrote two unpublished novels before she was offered a £75 publishing deal for *From Doon with Death* (1964), her first Inspector Wexford story. There are three strands to her crime novels: the Inspector Wexford police procedurals; stand-alone novels, dating from her second book, *To Fear a Painted Devil* (1965); and the psychological crime novels, written as Barbara Vine, which began with *A Dark-Adapted Eye* (1986).

Wexford

Inspector Wexford is Rendell's best-known creation, due largely to the successful TV adaptations starring George Baker (48 episodes were broadcast between 1987 and 2000). She said that Wexford was of no particular importance when she put him into her first murder mystery: 'I had to have an investigating officer so I just picked one from my reading of detective fiction.' 'In subsequent books,' she said, 'he became a more liberal, more literate, more understanding, more tolerant, more endearing person, and that has worked because people love him.' He was modelled loosely on Rendell's father, a teacher. Wexford's liberalism is counterbalanced by the conservatism of his deputy, Mike Burden.

Rendell wrote 24 Wexford novels. 'I don't get sick of him because he's me,' she once said in an interview. 'He doesn't look like me, of course, but the way he thinks and his principles and ideas and what he likes doing, that's me. He likes to read what I like to read.' Rendell liked to read poetry and she enjoyed walking around London. So does Wexford.

Wexford is a civilised man, tolerant and compassionate. He's by no means infallible and he occasionally succumbs to the same social conventions which he exposes as harmful. His success in case-solving is often based on his ability to discern emotions and motivations in people that others may overlook. He's as keen to understand the mindset of the murderer as he is to discover his (or her) identity – a characteristic he shares with Simenon's famous detective, Maigret.

Over the years Wexford's investigations have brought him up against all kinds of emotive issues – feminism, racism, the environment, labour exploitation, domestic violence, female circumcision, immigration, paedophilia. Murders and other crimes are invariably linked, either directly or indirectly, to social injustice.

Stand-alone crime novels

Rendell's second book, *To Fear a Painted Devil*, was a crime thriller without Wexford and for the next 20 years she alternated her Wexford series with stand-alone novels. These are more directly concerned with social and political issues than the Wexford books and connections between crime and social and economic disadvantage are more explicit: crimes are the result of social exclusion and the indifference of the bourgeoisie for those who live on the margins of society.

There is less reliance on suspense and the main focus is the motivation of the murderer. In fact, the identities of the murderers and victims are sometimes revealed at an early stage, as in the striking first sentence of *A Judgement in Stone* (1977): 'Eunice Parchman killed the Coverdale family because she could not read and write.'

In these books she explores the darker impulses of her protagonists and gets the reader to identify with characters, invariably alienated from society, as diverse as a failed writer (*The Face of Trespass* – 1974), a compulsive strangler (*A Demon in My View* – 1976), an illiterate housekeeper (*A Judgement in Stone* – 1977) and a teenager who sells his soul to the devil (*The Killing Doll* – 1984).

Barbara Vine

In 1986 she published, under the pseudonym of Barbara Vine, her first psychological novel, *A Dark-Adapted Eye*. The Barbara Vine novels have deeper psychological characterisation and a more sustained social critique than the stand-alone Rendell books.

In *The Blood Doctor* (2002) the theme of family inheritance is seen both from the medical standpoint of haemophilia and from the political one of the 1999 reform of the House of Lords. In *The Minotaur* (2005) an outsider in 1960s rural England, who is thrown into the unfamiliar world of a family apparently suffering from mental illnesses, exposes the partiality and inaccuracy of the medical diagnosis.

The Birthday Present (2008) has two contrasting narrators, the well-off accountant Rob Delgado and (through her diary entries) Jane Atherton, a lonely and self-obsessed woman in her 30s. The story, played out against a background of political upheavals and scandals and IRA bombings of the early 1990s, is the fall from grace of Rob's brother-in-law, Ivor Tesham, a hubris-driven politician with an inability to care for anything other than himself and his career. Jane's self-absorption is a convincing mixture of self-pity, jealousy and resentment. The story revolves around Tesham, but Jane is the book's strongest, most memorable creation.

Rendell often used Vine to write about the evolution of morality:

> I try to reflect the society I live in as it changes. There were two strands of injustice, simply unjustified nastiness in society, over a very long period of time. The first was the horrible stigma of

illegitimacy, and the suffering of women, usually young girls, who had illegitimate children.

The other, she said, was homosexuality. *The Child's Child* (2012) is driven by two children who are born out of wedlock.

How she wrote

Discipline and order were ingrained in Rendell's daily routine. She got up at six o'clock, had a vigorous workout followed by a light breakfast, and then wrote from 8.30 until 11 a.m. or noon. She wrote every weekday morning and was still publishing a book a year when she died at the age of 85.

She did not plan or write down the plot, but simply spoke the narrative in her head. Explaining her writing method, she said:

> I have found that if I stop to write down a plan for the story, it all goes away. So I just write it as it comes and then go over it with great care… A lot of people think it's very easy for me – it just flows out of me. Well it doesn't. I don't find writing easy. That is because I do take great care, I rewrite a lot. If anything is sort of clumsy and not possible to read aloud to oneself, which I think one should do… it doesn't work.

'I really do literally put myself into a character's shoes,' she said. 'I try, and I think I succeed, in making my readers feel sorry for my psychopaths, because I do. I think, why would anybody do that, what is it in her background, what is it in their lives that makes them do it. It's that people do these things almost by accident, or because of anger, their rage, their madness – and then probably regret it.' Her novels typically deal with those on the periphery of society – the loners and the lonely, the mentally ill, the addicts. She steers clear of moral judgments, but draws attention to people's haphazard approach to morality. In *The Monster in the Box* (2009) she writes:

Not for the first time, Wexford marvelled at people's selective morality. Presumably, it was all right for Yasmin to help her son conceal the body of a man he had killed and attempt to deceive the police by taking part in a plan to hide that dead man's car, while all wrong to rent out her property to a cohabiting couple.

Rendell saw suspense and the ability to make the reader keep turning pages, wanting to know what happens next, as the essence of crime writing. She explained exactly what she meant in an interview in *The Guardian*: 'A good suspense writer,' she said, [must have] 'a sort of withholding.' She gave as an example of this the character of Jane Fairfax in Jane Austen's *Emma*: 'We know there's something strange about her, but it's not until very far on that we realise that all the time she's been engaged to Frank Churchill. … There's nothing clumsy about it, nothing appears to be contrived, and it's done by withholding… Some new writers will tell you everything in the first chapter… so there's nothing to wonder about. I do think it should be part of any story, if it is told well, whether or not it is detective fiction. The reader has got to be thinking, what does it mean? Why did they do that?'

Withholding

Don't give the reader too much information too soon. Withholding key details can help to maintain suspense. Readers will want to know more; they will search for explanations and wonder what will happen next. By raising doubts and putting questions into the readers' minds – questions which are answered only much later, as the narrative unfolds – you can get them thinking about the meaning and the implications of what is on the page. If the writing is suspenseful enough, the reader will be curious enough to keep reading.

> **Learning points**
>
> - You can give a character your own principles, ideas, likes and dislikes.
> - Get inside the head of your main protagonists and put yourself into their shoes.
> - Don't give your readers too much information too soon: keep them wondering and asking questions.
> - Crime writing can be used to explore all kinds of serious issues.
> - Understanding the murderer's mindset and discerning the motivation can be the key to solving the crime.

J. K. ROWLING

(1965–)

J. K. Rowling's first book, *Harry Potter and the Philosopher's Stone*, was published in 1997 with an initial print run of just 1,000 copies. The manuscript had been turned down by more than a dozen publishers before it was accepted by Bloomsbury.

Ten years later, on 20 July 2007, thousands of Harry Potter fans – children and adults alike – were queuing outside bookshops all over the country. At midnight the doors were opened and sales of the seventh and final book, *Harry Potter and the Deathly Hallows*, broke all records, selling an astonishing 11 million copies on its first day of release in the UK and the United States. The Harry Potter books have been translated into 67 languages and worldwide sales exceed 400 million. Only the Bible and Mao Zedong's *Little Red Book* are ahead of it.

How does Rowling do it? What is it about Harry Potter that has struck a chord with millions of young (and not so young) readers all over the world? They are rollicking, good-against-evil adventure stories that keep us turning the pages. But you could say the same about scores of other books. Neither wizards nor boarding schools are original subjects, and J. K. Rowling is not even the first author to combine the two. So what's her secret?

Let's begin by looking at some of the key elements: an action-packed plot, inventive wizardry, the setting of an English boarding school, convincing characters and humour.

Themes and plotting

The struggle between good and evil is at the heart of Harry Potter and we can readily identify two of the most familiar themes in all storytelling, 'overcoming the monster' and 'the quest' (both are in Christopher Booker's masterly *The Seven Basic Plots*).

Rowling's plotting is intricate, and her tight, pacey writing and adroit twists keep us glued to the page. In the penultimate story, *Harry Potter and the Half-Blood Prince* (2005), the smallest details of the previous books start to come together and to make sense at last. The excitement is maintained, but in this and the final book the narrative becomes much darker and more complex. Death is a central theme – Voldemort's obsession with conquering death, and the way in which Harry comes to terms with the death of his parents.

Inventive wizardry

Few of Rowling's magical beings or creatures are original, but we are bowled over by a cast that includes giants, ghosts, poltergeists, trolls, goblins, ghouls, elves, dragons, centaurs, werewolves and a phoenix. Standard magical props are given a new twist, with wands made from phoenix tail feathers and broomsticks that are constantly upgraded (like a teenager's mobile phone). There are portraits that move and talk, staircases that change direction, the brilliant game of Quidditch, and – perhaps most inventively of all – bizarre spells with results that are often outlandish.

Setting

Hogwarts School of Witchcraft and Wizardry, set in a Gothic castle on a rocky crag, alongside a deep lake and a forbidden forest, is full of mystery and danger; yet, with its four-poster beds and its huge platters of food, it is strangely safe and comforting.

For all its peculiarities Hogwarts is in many respects a very familiar institution. Thomas Hughes's *Tom Brown's Schooldays* (1857) was the first in a long line of hugely popular stories set in boys' and girls' boarding schools. Familiar features include a strong sporting ethos, competition between school houses, a hero or heroine (sustained by a small group of friends) confronted by an adversary, and a supporting cast of prefects and eccentric teachers.

The richly imagined magical world of Hogwarts, Hogsmeade and Diagon Alley contrasts with an everyday world we can all recognise (well-known London streets, a village with a pub and a church). The Weasleys' home, The Burrow, seems much like any large, happy, rather disorganised family household, while number four, Privet Drive epitomises the Dursleys' mundane, lacklustre lives and their obsession with conformity.

Characters

When first we meet Harry he is an orphan who sleeps in the cupboard under the stairs and his appalling treatment at the hands of the Dursleys immediately arouses our sympathy. He is an ordinary, academically average, old-fashioned sort of boy – cheerful, kind, good at games and rather moral. Honest and brave, he is not afraid to stand up for what he believes is right. But he is by no means perfect. Sometimes he gets things wrong, and he can misjudge people and fly off the handle.

Ron, trying to live up to the successes of his elder brothers, and Hermione, the brainy, rule-abiding swot who Rowling has said is a caricature of herself, are also recognisable characters who change and grow as the stories progress. Hagrid, Albus Dumbledore and Snape are foremost among a supporting cast of vividly drawn characters who stick in the mind.

Harry and his friends are typical teenagers, sharing homework and messy rooms, rushing to classes and sports practices – and, as they get older, flirting. The dialogue is not always convincing, but these are believable characters. Despite all the supernatural goings-on, Rowling keeps the emotions, fears and triumphs of her characters on a human scale.

Humour

The spry sense of humour that permeates Harry Potter is one of the keys to the books' appeal. We have, among much else, eccentric pointy-hatted wizards, Bertie Bott's Every-Flavour Beans, chocolate frogs and toads, OWLs (Ordinary Wizarding Level exams), the wacky inventions of Fred and George, Hagrid jinxing Dudley so that a pig's tail grows from his behind, blast-ended skrewts, absurd passwords and a three-headed monster of a dog called Fluffy so vicious that a note or two on Hermione's flute sends it to sleep.

As the series progresses and the books get darker, there is less slapstick and fewer pratfalls, but even in *Harry Potter and the Deathly Hallows* there is room for schoolboy humour: 'How do you feel?' George Weasley is asked after the Death Eaters remove one of his ears, leaving him with a hole in the head. 'Saint-like... You see... I'm holy. Holey, Fred, geddit?'

And there are still magic spells that don't quite work:

'Accio glasses' [commands Harry, pointing his wand at the cluttered desk where he has left his glasses]. There was something immensely satisfying about seeing them zoom towards him, at least until they poked him in the eye.

'Slick,' snorted Ron.

Satire and moral values

Rowling pokes fun at the tabloid press, with her depiction of Rita Skeeter and the *The Daily Prophet,* and even indulges in a little political satire:

"'Scrimgeour [Minister of Magic] doesn't want to admit that You-Know-Who is as powerful as he is."

"Yeah, why tell the public the truth?" said Harry.'

There is also social commentary, with Hermione's earnest campaign for better working conditions for house-elves, and the anger Harry shows at Lupin's averred intention (later reversed) to abandon his wife and unborn child.

In *Harry Potter and the Philosopher's Stone* it is the personal qualities shown by Harry, Ron and Hermione – courage, skill and logical thinking – that win Gryffindor the House Cup, and in *Harry Potter and the Goblet of Fire* (2000) Dumbledore stresses 'choice between what is right and what is easy'. On the other side of the coin, the baseness of Voldemort and his Death Eaters is shown in their quest for racial purity and their persecution of those who do not buy into this doctrine – reminiscent of the Nazis' and other genocides.

Influences and antecedents

I haven't got the faintest idea where my ideas come from, or how my imagination works. I've taken horrible liberties with folklore and mythology, but I'm quite unashamed about that, because British folklore and British mythology is a totally bastard mythology... we've been invaded by people, appropriated their gods, taken their mythical creatures, and soldered them all together to make... one of the richest folklores in the world... So I feel no compunction about borrowing from that freely, but adding a few things of my own.

Influences acknowledged by Rowling include 'The Iliad', the Bible, Shakespeare, Jane Austen, C. S. Lewis, E. Nesbit and Dorothy L. Sayers. Critics and academics have pointed to others – most obviously, J. R. R. Tolkien's *The Lord of the Rings*, with clear similarities between Rowling's Voldemort and Tolkien's Sauron and other elements such as Dementors/Nazgûl and Wormtail/Wormtongue. Books about young wizards or witches who receive magical education include Jill Murphy's *The Worst Witch* series (1974) (set in a school remarkably similar to Hogwarts), Diana Wynne Jones's *Charmed Life* (1977), Ursula K. Le Guin's *A Wizard of Earthsea* (1968) and Jane Yolen's *Wizard's Hall* (1991).

Every writer borrows from and builds on what has gone before. Rowling takes ideas from literature, mythology, folklore and religion, and produces a melange that is all her own.

Multiple sources

Rowling has acknowledged many different sources of inspiration. Mythology and folklore are two of the most obvious, but she has also drawn on many other literary (and other) traditions. Whatever kind of book you are writing, it's worthwhile casting your net as widely as possible in seeking raw material that can inspire you – and which you can draw on in producing your own stuff. By adding in your own personal experience and way of looking at things, you will produce work that builds on what has gone before, and yet is unique.

Secrets of Harry Potter's success

For me, three factors are at the heart of Rowling's phenomenal Harry Potter success. The first is her decision to let Harry and his friends grow up in parallel with her target audience: this made it easy for those who had been with Harry Potter from the beginning to continue to identify with him. Second is the sheer verve and scope of writing that contains elements of many different genres. The third is her brilliant mixing of the magical and the everyday worlds – with both humour and humanity.

Robert Galbraith

After Rowling's first non-Harry Potter book, *The Casual Vacancy*, became one of the bestsellers of 2012, she made her debut as a crime writer with *The Cuckoo's Calling* (2013) published under the pseudonym of Robert Galbraith. *The Cuckoo's Calling* was acclaimed by writers and critics as 'a stellar debut', but when it became known that Robert Galbraith was J. K. Rowling, sales of the book went through the roof, increasing by 4,000 per cent. It was followed by *The Silkworm* (2014) and *Career of Evil* (2015), each of them featuring private investigator Cormoran Strike.

For her first two crime novels she had already undertaken lengthy research into amputation, forensics and the decomposition of bodies, but *Career of Evil* was planned more meticulously than any book she had ever written, using colour-coded spreadsheets. Each book is a carefully plotted whodunnit, with lots of convincingly portrayed characters, who are often damaged and/or unpleasant, and a satisfying denouement. Cormoran Strike himself is a memorable creation. A former Royal Military Police investigator who lost half of his leg while serving in Afghanistan, he is tall, ungainly and slightly raddled. His relationship with his clever young woman assistant, Robin Ellacott, which develops and changes as the series progresses, is at the heart of these books. Rowling plans to write several more Cormoran Strikes.

> **Learning points**
>
> - The struggle between good and evil is an old but very potent theme.
> - Borrow from, and build on, what has gone before. For example, familiar magical beings, creatures and objects can be made fresh by giving them a new characteristic or twist.
> - Suspense can be maintained by a skilful mix of safety and danger. Note the contrast between the mysterious Gothic setting of Hogwarts and the comfort and safety of an institution run on traditional boarding-school lines.
> - Pacey writing and humour will keep the reader turning the pages.

SALMAN RUSHDIE
(1947–)

New writers are often advised to begin by imitating a writer they admire. This is how you can serve your apprenticeship, learn your craft and eventually find your own voice. But what if the writer you admire is Salman Rushdie?

With his weaving together of themes from Indian and Western culture, his fictionalised historical perspectives, his mixing of fantasy and reality, and the dazzling pyrotechnics of his prose, Rushdie is surely a unique talent, impossible to imitate. But, as we shall see, there is a great deal that any writer or would-be writer can learn from him.

In 1993 *Midnight's Children* was judged the best novel to have won the Man Booker Prize for Fiction in the award's 25-year history, and for almost 30 years Rushdie has been a major (and often controversial) force in world literature.

Magic realism

Rushdie's stories often challenge historical truth and suggest alternative realities. 'The point from which fiction begins,' he has said, is 'the acceptance that all that is solid has melted into the air, that reality and morality are not givens but imperfect human constructs.'

Rushdie says:

> Literature is where I go to explore the highest and the lowest places in human society and in the human spirit, where I hope to find not absolute truth but the truth of the tale, of the imagination and of the heart.

Magic realism is the term generally used to describe Rushdie's work. First applied to literature of Latin America, the genre incorporates fantastical events in an otherwise realistic narrative, typically drawing on fables, myths and folklore while at the same time maintaining a strong contemporary social relevance. 'Sometimes,' says Rushdie in *Midnight's Children*, 'legends make reality and become more useful than the facts.' 'I am only telling a sort of modern fairy-tale,' he says in *Shame*, where his unlikely hero, Omar Khayyam Shakil, 'made the surprisingly adult resolution to escape from the unpalatable reality of dreams into the slightly more acceptable illusions of his everyday working life.'

The Tin Drum of Günter Grass and *One Hundred Years of Solitude* by Gabriel García Márquez are among other well-known works usually described as magic realism. But the term itself is controversial. Terry Pratchett said that magic realism 'is like a polite way of saying you write fantasy', while Gene Wolfe (the American science-fiction and fantasy writer) has described magic realism as 'fantasy written by people who speak Spanish'.

Most critics, however, draw a distinction between fantasy and magic realism. The key difference is between writing which involves the creation of new worlds and writing which suggests the magical in our world and, crucially, blurs the distinction between fantasy and reality. Illogical situations are set within a framework of reality, characters are given supernatural powers, and there is an equal acceptance of the ordinary and the extraordinary.

Midnight's Children

Midnight's Children 'sounds like a continent finding its voice', said one critic, and the life of its protagonist and narrator, Saleem Sinai, can be seen as a metaphor for India's post-colonial history. The children of the novel's title are the 1,001 children (reduced to 581 by the age of ten) born, like Saleem, during the hour following the stroke of midnight, 15 August 1947, the instant of India's independence. Each of these children has a special gift, for example: the ability to fly; to remember everything ever seen or heard; to step into a mirror and re-emerge through any reflective surface anywhere in the country; to increase or reduce in size at will; to travel in time and prophesy the future; to inflict physical wounds by using sharp words. Saleem has 'the greatest talent of all – the ability to look into the hearts and minds of men', a telepathic gift which enables him to discover the truth about his own identity.

Midnight's Children begins with Saleem's grandfather's return to Kashmir in 1915 as a newly qualified doctor, but the heart of the book is Saleem's upbringing as the supposed son of a wealthy Muslim family, and the course his life then takes as it mirrors the post-colonial history of India. 'In this world without quiet corners there can be no easy escapes from history, from hullabaloo, from terrible, unquiet fuss,' Rushdie has said, and there can be no better illustration of that than the vast historical sweep (by no means limited to the twentieth-century timeframe of Saleem's story) of *Midnight's Children*.

Themes and style

The interweaving of themes from Islam and Hinduism and Western culture is one of the hallmarks of Rushdie's writing: 'Once upon a time,' he says in *Midnight's Children*, 'there were Radna and Krishna, and Rama and Sita, and Laila and Majnu; also (because we are not unaffected by the West) Romeo and Juliet, and Spencer Tracy and Katharine Hepburn.'

Rushdie's prose can take your breath away with its exuberance and its stunning display of puns and alliteration, juxtaposition, wordplay and rhyme. Two small examples: (1) the catchy little Gujarati rhyme he gives Saleem: '"Soo ché? Saru ché! Danda lé ké maru ché!" (How are you? – I am well! – I'll take a stick and thrash you to hell!)'; (2) the memorable nicknames he invents for Saleem's grandmother and sister – Reverend Mother, Brass Monkey – which capture their characters and stick vividly in the mind.

Midnight's Children, published in 1981, is widely regarded as Rushdie's masterpiece, but he has written nine other novels and some of them must be mentioned here. His often overlooked first novel, *Grimus* (1975), is important because it introduced many of the themes – displacement, unsettled identity, cultural hybridity – which were to be developed in his later books. His third novel, *Shame* (1983), which was shortlisted for the Man Booker Prize, is a thinly veiled satirical history of Pakistan played out through a family drama involving a military dictator and his mentally disabled, ultimately murderous daughter. One of the characters (Talvar Ulhaq) has the gift of clairvoyance, while the stillborn son of another (Bilquis Hyder) is given a whole life history:

… being stone dead was a handicap which the boy managed… to surmount. Within… weeks, the tragically cadaverous infant had 'topped' in school and at college, had fought bravely in war, had married the wealthiest beauty in town and risen to a high position in the government. He was dashing, popular, handsome, and the fact of his being a corpse now seemed of no more consequence than would a slight limp or a minor speech impediment.

The Satanic Verses (1988) is a satire on the state of migration in the UK and an exploration of good and evil, religious faith and fanatical belief. The novel caused a furore and earned Rushdie notoriety among Muslims on account of its unfavourable depiction of the Prophet Mohammed and its fictional reworking of Islamic history. Rushdie has also written short stories, children's books, non-fiction, essays and criticism; but his fame and reputation rest on his craft and flair as a novelist.

Learning from Rushdie

If we look at Rushdie's novels, we can identify four key elements: cultural hybridity, historical breadth, innovative prose and, finally, that distinctive combination of fantasy and reality. (Incidentally, each of these can be found in other writers, but the way in which they coalesce in Rushdie's writing – and especially in *Midnight's Children* – is surely unique.)

So why not take one of those four elements – the key characteristics of Rushdie's writing – and use that as a basis for developing your own writing? Perhaps you want to have a go at combining fantasy with reality? Or maybe you're attracted by the sweep of Rushdie's historical perspective? Or the way in which he weaves together elements from different cultures? Or perhaps you're captivated by the sheer exuberance and originality of the prose? Any one (or any combination) of these could provide the starting point you need.

If none of those characteristics sparks your imagination, there is one thing you can still learn from him. And to my mind it's the most important – most exhilarating – of all: that in writing, *anything* is possible. That, Rushdie has said, is what he himself learned from writers like James

Joyce and Günter Grass: that boundaries are arbitrary limits imposed by man and that you can rewrite any set of conventions, however firmly entrenched. So don't be afraid to experiment. Trial and error will help you to discover what works for *you*.

Stretch your wings and fly. You don't have to be constrained by conventional ideas about writing. You can mix fact and fiction, past and present (and future), probable and improbable – even possible and impossible. You can go *anywhere*. That is surely the key learning point; that is what we can all learn from Rushdie.

Anything is possible

A writer can write whatever he or she likes. You do not have to be constrained by precedent or convention (and, unlike a playwright or a film-maker, there are no budgetary constraints). There are no limits to what you can do – what you write about and how you write it. You can experiment to your heart's content. Isn't that an exciting, exhilarating thought?

Learning points

- Fantasy plus reality equals magic realism.
- Don't be limited by narrow genre definitions – just write what you feel compelled to write.
- You can juxtapose phenomena of wildly different cultures and different historical periods.
- Catch the reader's eye with dazzling, innovative prose.

C. J. SANSOM

(1952-)

'There is nothing I like better than a good crime story,' C. J. Sansom said in an interview. 'It can be a great way of exploring character and also of showing all aspects of society from top to bottom.' He succeeded in doing just that with *Dissolution* (2003), his debut historical novel which became an immediate bestseller. There are beggars in gutters, conspiracies at court and a political system based on birth rather than merit.

The hero is Matthew Shardlake, a hunchbacked lawyer. The protagonists of most successful crime novels – whether they are police officers, private investigators, forensic scientists, or lawyers – come to us with some kind of flaw. It's often inside the head – the result, typically, of an unhappy childhood, a failed relationship or a bad life experience that has destroyed faith in human nature and turned a good man or woman into a hard-bitten cynic, always expecting the worst.

Shardlake's flaw is not inside the head, but in his external appearance. In an age when people were judged more often than not by their physical appearance, his hunched back is a serious disadvantage. It's a handicap he has overcome through resourcefulness, intelligence and sheer hard work. In Sansom's series of crime mysteries (six so far) he is pressed into service, in turn, by Thomas Cromwell, Archbishop Cranmer and Catherine Parr (Henry VIII's last queen), as he cuts through the murk of Tudor England to solve a succession of gruesome murders.

Why the Tudors?

Sansom fixed on Tudor England because of his fascination with the period:

> It's the moment at which the medieval certainties that had endured for centuries were turned upside down. It was a time of extraordinary

ferment… the more I read about it, the more I realised how like the twentieth century it was in its anxiety and uncertainty, even though people thought so differently then. If I were to talk to someone from the sixteenth century they'd think I was mad, and probably heretical. That's what's so interesting about writing about the period… the mindset of people living at a time when so many daily realities, and religion and ideology, were quite different from ours.

The theme for his first novel came to him easily: 'I'd always thought the dissolution of the monasteries would make a great setting for a murder mystery.' Henry VIII has proclaimed himself Supreme Head of the Church. Under the orders of Thomas Cromwell, Henry's number one fixer, a team of commissioners is sent out to investigate the monasteries. There can be only one outcome: they are to be dissolved. But at Scarnsea, a monastery on the Sussex coast, Cromwell's commissioner has been found dead, his head severed from his body. Cromwell sends Shardlake, a long-time supporter of reform, to uncover the truth behind a succession of sinister happenings. His investigation forces him to question everything he hears – and everything he believes.

Over the years there have been many different interpretations of Cromwell's character. 'He's been controversial ever since he had his head cut off,' says Sansom. 'Some think he was the blackest of villains; others that he was a great, positive reformer. I'm somewhere in the middle, but I do believe he had a dark side.'

Dissolution, set in the bitter winter of 1537, is a classic closed-setting mystery. For much of the book the monastery is cut off from the world by the weather, with the suspects locked inside. By the final pages, the snow has melted and the monastery's walls have come down too. The retreating ice reveals boggy marshland with old paths which cannot be relied upon – a metaphor, perhaps, for the treacherous political terrain Shardlake has to negotiate.

Why a lawyer?

Sansom has explained why he made his Tudor hero a lawyer. He practised law himself and has said: 'I find legal practice endlessly interesting.' It's a cardinal rule for any writer: write about what you know and about things in which you are passionately interested. Secondly, the law provides an element of continuity: it existed then and it exists now. Today's laws are radically different from those that existed in Tudor times but, as Sansom has pointed out, 'some basic structures of English law – the adversarial common law system, many of the rules of evidence, the process of bringing a civil (less so with a criminal) action to trial – have continued down the centuries'. It provides an element of continuity to which the reader can relate. Sansom's third reason for making his principal protagonist a lawyer is perhaps the most obvious: the profession gives Shardlake an entrée into an endless range of crimes and into the lives of an infinitely varied cast of characters.

The Tudor Morse?

Plaudits for *Dissolution* came from P. D. James, who said, 'the sights, the voices, the very smell of this turbulent age seem to rise from the page'; and from Colin Dexter, the creator of Morse, who called it 'extraordinarily impressive'. Shardlake has been dubbed 'the Tudor Morse'. He shares Morse's intelligent, thoughtful character, as well as his bad luck with women, but the comparison should not be pushed too far. Like Morse, Shardlake brings a rational, sceptical mind to bear on his investigations, but the milieu in which he operates is very different. Tudor England was rife with ignorance, superstition and religious zealotry. As he struggles to reconcile his intellectual support for Cromwell's reformation with revulsion at many of the acts perpetrated in its name, he becomes less certain in his faith.

Like many fictional investigators, Shardlake has a prickly sidekick. His apprentice assistant in *Dissolution*, Mark, absconds to Europe and is replaced in *Dark Fire* (2004), the second of Sansom's Tudor crime novels, by Jack Barak, whose background and personality is very different from Shardlake's. Not averse to sexual innuendo or a spot of violence, Barak has plenty of rough edges and, especially during the early days of working together, they quarrel a good deal. He speaks his mind and stands up to Shardlake. Their relationship deepens as they go from initial mistrust, through danger and on to mutual respect and real friendship. For my money Barak's a great character – perhaps the most engaging Sansom has created.

Winter in Madrid

After completing *Dissolution* Sansom ignored the advice authors are often given to stick to one genre. *Winter in Madrid* (2006) is a very different type of novel. It's a wartime thriller about a damaged ex-public schoolboy (Harry), recovering from the horrors of Dunkirk, who is recruited to spy for British Intelligence on a former school friend (Sandy), now a dodgy businessman trying to make his fortune in Franco's Spain.

Sansom deploys a fractured time scheme, moving between past and present, and uses three viewpoint characters (Harry, Bernie and Barbara). We are back in the public school where Harry and Sandy first meet, then in murky 1940s Madrid, where betrayal is the order of the day. With the other viewpoint characters too, we are catapulted from present to past and back again. With believable characters, authentic-sounding dialogue and convincing evocations of time and place, Sansom deftly draws the disparate strands together as *Winter in Madrid* reaches its conclusion. The novel has drawn comparisons with Ernest Hemingway and Graham Greene. Writing in *The Guardian*, Laura Wilson called it 'a tense, literate page-turner, full of twists, authentic detail and real pathos'.

The Shardlake series

After the success of *Dissolution* and the clamour for another Shardlake, Macmillan took the decision to publish *Dark Fire* ahead of *Winter in*

Madrid; it won the 2005 Crime Writers' Association Historical Dagger. Set in 1540, the hottest summer of the century, amid the muck and clamour of London's streets, the story involves torture, child murder, treachery and death by fire – and culminates in the execution of Cromwell. Shardlake has two parallel quests: to find the 'dark fire' of the title (a kind of petroleum-based WMD) and to uncover the truth about the apparent murder of a child for which a young girl is about to be put to death. Sansom provides pace by linking both stories within a matching timeframe: 12 days for Shardlake to find the dark fire and the same 12 days to find the truth of the murder before the girl's stay of execution runs out.

Sovereign (2006), Sansom's third Shardlake novel, covers Henry VIII's progress to the North. There is a Yorkshire plot to overthrow Henry and fears of another Northern rebellion. The objective is to overrule the North and tie it firmly to Tudor England. *Revelation* was published in 2008, but of all his Shardlake novels, *Heartstone* (2010), the fifth in the series, is Sansom's personal favourite. It brings the Tudor barrister to within two years of Henry's death. The novel covers events in the summer of 1545, when Henry dragged England into a futile war with France. The fleet is massing at Portsmouth, soldiers are being pressed into service and taxes are being raised to fund another military campaign. Against this background Shardlake is commissioned by an old servant of Queen Catherine Parr (Henry's final, surviving wife) to travel to Portsmouth to investigate 'monstrous wrongs' inflicted upon a young ward at court.

Sansom's novels are crammed with period detail. His research is rigorous but far from easy:

> With Tudor times, information is sparse: things have single or contradictory sources. But where there are established facts, I do everything I can to insert the story around them. I put a lot of effort into the historical note: if there's anything I've changed, for plot reasons, I say so there.

Dominium

Sansom's writing took a new turn with the publication of his counter-factual novel *Dominium* (2012), which imagines a 1950s Britain that surrendered to Nazi Germany after Dunkirk. Lord Halifax, rather than Churchill, succeeded Chamberlain as Prime Minister and the country is run by a puppet government that includes Lord Beaverbrook and Oswald Mosley. Churchill leads the Resistance, Jews are being deported and David Fitzgerald is a civil servant who has agreed to spy for – or against – his country. It's a richly imagined, page-turning thriller as David and a disparate group of resistance activists struggle to survive in Nazi-controlled London in the Great Smog.

How he began writing

After studying history at Birmingham University Sansom left with a PhD, but soon abandoned academia to retrain as a lawyer. Once qualified, he frequently represented the underdog in legal aid cases – experience he put to good in the Shardlake novels. Passionate about his work as a lawyer, he had, however, always wanted to write. As a lawyer he did a little writing and went to writing groups, but did not have the energy to tackle a novel. The opportunity came in 2000, when his father's death left him with a small inheritance. He decided to take a year off to have a shot at a novel. The rest, as they say, is history.

Sansom writes in the morning, spends the afternoon going over and revising what he has written, and then has the evening to himself. His advice to aspiring writers is to keep at it: 'First and foremost, bottom on seat and keep practising.' Quite often those who succeed (in writing as in many other spheres of activity) have no more talent than their peers. What makes the difference, more often than not, is determination and perseverance. Sansom's second piece of advice is to positively seek constructive criticism, which he believes every writer needs. He also says that novelists should keep a distance between themselves and their subject and avoid writing autobiographically.

Seek criticism

Every writer needs constructive criticism. It's incredibly difficult to be objective about your own work. Putting a piece of writing aside and looking at it again a week or two later helps (you're bound to find something that can be improved), but you also need objective comment and criticism. If you're an established writer, you'll probably get that from your agent or your editor. If you're an aspiring writer, you'll have to look elsewhere. You might be able to get it from a writing group, especially if its members read the kind of stuff you write and are prepared to give honest and constructive feedback. Online groups for writers and social media are other options.

Learning points

- A crime story can show all aspects of society, from top to bottom.
- Write about things you know about or in which you are passionately interested.
- A time limit within which a solution has to be found (such as the 12 days of *Dark Fire)* maintains the suspense.
- A fractured time scheme, moving between past and present, can be an effective device.
- Keep at it: if you want to become a successful writer, determination and perseverance are essential.

Dr SEUSS
(1904–1991)

'Learning to read is fun with Dr Seuss,' says the blurb on the back cover of *The Cat in the Hat* (1957). It was the first of his Beginner Books, and who could disagree? The combination of silly rhymes, crazy stories and lively drawings that leap off the page is irresistible.

How he began

His real name was Theodor Seuss Geisel (I'll stick to Seuss). Born in 1904, he attended Dartmouth College, New Hampshire, and then Lincoln College, Oxford, where he studied English literature. He left Oxford without a degree and returned to the United States in 1927, having decided to give up thoughts of becoming an English teacher in order to pursue drawing as a career. His first nationally published cartoon appeared in 1927 and later that year he obtained a job as writer and illustrator for the humour magazine *Judge*, where he began to use the pseudonym 'Dr Seuss' (he added the 'Dr' because his father had wanted him to practise medicine; almost 30 years later, in 1956, Dartmouth College awarded him an honorary doctorate). Over the next ten years he became a well-known cartoonist and illustrator and established a successful career in advertising.

In 1936 Seuss was returning from a European holiday with his wife when he was captivated by the rhythm of the ship's engines. This inspired the signature lines of his first children's book: 'And that is a story that no one can beat / And to think that I saw it on Mulberry Street.' It's a fantasy a boy dreams up on his way home from school after his father has told him: 'Marco, keep your eyelids up / And see what you can see.' He imagines a progressively more elaborate parade of animals, people and vehicles marching along a road, Mulberry Street. But when Marco gets home and his father asks what he has seen, he turns red with embarrassment and tells him the truth: all he saw was a horse and cart.

The manuscript of *And to Think That I Saw It on Mulberry Street* (1937) was rejected by more than two dozen publishers. Among the reasons given were the lack of demand for fantasy and for children's books in verse, and the absence of any clear moral message. Seuss is said to have reacted angrily: 'What's wrong with kids having fun reading without being preached at?' His wife thought the cartoon-like drawings and a story which could have been interpreted as encouraging daydreaming and lying to one's parents might also have explained the book's rejections.

Luck played an important part in *Mulberry Street*'s eventual acceptance. Seuss was walking down Madison Avenue in New York when he happened to run into an old Dartmouth College classmate who had recently become juvenile editor at the publishing house Vanguard Press. He was introduced to Vanguard's President, who agreed to publish the book provided the title (originally *And That is a Story that No One Can Beat*) was changed. 'If I had been walking down the other side of Madison Avenue, I'd be in the dry-cleaning business today,' Seuss said later, acknowledging his stroke of luck.

The book was very well received. There was a one-sentence review in *The New Yorker* which Seuss could still quote near the end of his life: 'They say it's for children, but better get a copy yourself and marvel at the good Dr Seuss' impossible pictures and the moral tale of the little boy who exaggerated not wisely but too well.' *The New York Times* said it was 'highly original and entertaining' and 'a masterly interpretation of the mind of a child in the act of creating one of those stories with which children often amuse themselves and bolster up their self-respect'.

Most critics preferred Seuss's later books, and the author himself had reservations about *Mulberry Street*: 'I think I was a little aloof, too outside there. It was written from the point of view of my mind, not the mind of a child.' He wrote four more books, including *The 500 Hats of Bartholomew Cubbins* (1938), before the United States entered World War Two and he became a political cartoonist for the New York newspaper *PM*, drawing over 400 cartoons in two years (many of these denounced Hitler and Mussolini and criticised non-interventionists). In 1942 he began to draw posters for the Treasury Department and the War Production Board and the following year he joined the US Army as a Captain and was put in charge of the Animation Department of the Army's Motion Picture Unit.

The Cat in the Hat

'Bring back a book children can't put down' was the challenge Seuss faced in 1954, after a report on illiteracy had concluded that children in the US were not learning to read because their books were boring. Seuss was given a list of 348 words which had been identified as words that every six-year-old should be able to recognise. He was asked to reduce the list to 250 and to produce a book using only those words.

Nine months later Seuss had written *The Cat in the Hat*, using just 236 words. Frustrated by the difficulty of writing a story with such a limited vocabulary, he eventually decided that he would go through the list of words he'd been given and pick out the first two that rhymed – and write a story based on those. Of course, the words he found were cat and hat. The book was an immediate critical and financial success. A groundbreaking, hugely popular alternative to traditional primers (such as the Dick and Jane books), it sold over a million copies within three years of publication. It was the first in a series of early readers for Random House which sold more than 30 million copies in the US by 1970.

The starting point of *The Cat in the Hat* will be familiar to anyone who has young children. How often have you heard them say: 'I'm bored. What can I do?' Two children, brother and sister, are at home on a wet day. And they are bored: 'Too wet to go out / And too cold to play ball. / So we sat in the house. / We did nothing at all... / And we did not like it. / Not one little bit.'

The children are startled by the sudden arrival of a cat. Its appearance is striking – it's wearing a red and white striped hat and a red bow tie – and it's anthropomorphic. The cat entertains them by performing various tricks, which the children's pet goldfish finds understandably worrying, and then brings in a big red box containing two identical creatures – Thing One and Thing Two. These have blue hair and red suits, and they bring with them kites which they fly indoors, creating lots of mess and mayhem. The boy eventually catches the Things, and the cat puts them back in the box. Just before the children's mother arrives home the cat returns, riding a fantastical multi-purpose machine that picks everything up and cleans the house, leaving it spick and span. The cat departs in the nick of time: 'Then our mother came in / And she said to us two, / "Did you have any fun? / Tell me what did you do?"' And the children don't know what to say: 'Should we tell her about it? / Now, what SHOULD we do? / Well... / What would you do / If your mother asked you?' Isn't that a nice question? To my mind it makes a brilliant ending to the story.

How he wrote

Seuss was a perfectionist. He wrote the words of *And to Think That I Saw It on Mulberry Street* out in pencil on yellow paper and then went through it, discussing every page with his wife. He spent at least six months on the book, questioning every single word and writing draft after draft. In all he wrote 46 books for young children. They may be very short, with simple vocabulary and straightforward storylines, but that does not mean that they were easy to write. Far from it. It was not unusual for him to discard 95 per cent of his material until he'd settled on a theme, and he routinely spent up to a year on a single book.

Seuss used a simple rhyming scheme of two unstressed syllables followed by one stressed syllable – four times in each line. The technical name for this is anapaestic tetrameter. Its regularity emphasises the breezy, melodic feel of the rhythm, though the initial unstressed beat of a line is quite often omitted. It's a rhyming scheme commonly used in comic verse, though not exclusively (Lord Byron's *Don Juan* contains much anapaestic tetrameter).

Be a perfectionist

When choosing a theme for a new book Seuss routinely discarded the vast majority of the material he had assembled. Once he had decided on the theme and written a first draft, he put every page under the microscope and went through it meticulously, questioning every single word. He wrote draft after draft, and spent between six months and a year on each book. Whether you are writing a short children's book or a blockbuster novel, you need to take the same care over the choice and use of words. Select the most apt word you can find – and make sure that not a single word is wasted.

Green Eggs and Ham

In 1960, Bennett Cerf, founder of Random House, bet Dr Seuss $50 that he would not be able to write an entertaining early reader using only 50 different words. Seuss won the bet with *Green Eggs and Ham*. It has sold more than 200 million copies, making it the fourth bestselling English language book for children of all time. These are the 50 words he used: a, am, and, anywhere, are, be, boat, box, car, could, dark, do, eat, eggs, fox, goat, good, green, ham, here, house, I, if, in, let, like, may, me, mouse, not, on, or, rain, Sam, say, see, so, thank, that, the, them, there, they, train, tree, try, will, with, would, you.

The story is narrated by a character known as 'Sam-I-Am', who pesters an unnamed character to sample a dish of green eggs and ham. He refuses, responding throughout the story: 'I do not like green eggs and ham. I do not like them, Sam-I-Am.' He's asked to sample them in various locations and with a variety of animals, but still refuses. Finally, he gives in and tries them. He discovers that he certainly does like them, and happily responds: 'I do so like green eggs and ham. Thank you. Thank you, Sam-I-Am.'

The power of constraints

Seuss's success with his $50 bet – having to write a story using just 50 words – shows the power of setting constraints. It's a useful lesson for any writer. Setting clear limits for yourself can often deliver better results than working without constraints on a blank, open-ended canvas. It may seem counter-intuitive, but setting tight constraints for your writing – whether that's the number and/or type of words you can use, the deadline by which you must complete a piece of writing, or some other challenging constraint – can help you not only to develop good writing habits but also to become more creative. Constraints don't allow you to procrastinate: they force you to get some words down on paper or screen. And if you're a writer, that's the name of the game.

Learning points

- To write children's books you need to get inside the mind of a child.
- Don't imagine that books with simple vocabulary and straightforward storylines are easy to write; they take a great deal of time and effort, and they demand real craft and artistry.
- Setting clear limits and writing within tight constraints can help you both to develop good writing habits and to stimulate creativity.
- Take infinite care and put every page of your manuscript under the microscope.

GEORGES SIMENON
(1903–1989)

In 1931 Georges Simenon scribbled some notes on the back of an old yellow envelope. Those notes were the starting point for *Pietr-le-Letton*, the first Maigret novel, and the yellow envelope was to become a ritual which Simenon stuck to for the rest of his life.

Maigret had made his first appearance a couple of years earlier in a short story written for a detective magazine. Simenon left school at 15, but he read widely, and was especially impressed by the works of Nikolai Gogol and Fyodor Dostoyevsky. He began work as a journalist in his native Liège (Belgium), but it was not long before he was writing short stories.

The yellow envelope

It would be misleading to describe Simenon's back-of-the-envelope notes as a plot outline, because they give you no idea of the story. His method was to begin by deciding on the setting and creating his characters. These were the first – and, for Simenon, by far the most important – building blocks. The yellow-envelope notes typically gave the title of the book (which he sometimes later changed), a few biographical details of the main character(s) and a sketch of the proposed setting (for example: a street plan showing key locations such as a café, a bar, a shop, someone's flat, a metro station).

After the yellow envelope, Simenon spent two days writing some preparatory notes. But these notes, too, did not give any indication of plot. There were two elements. The first consisted of fleshing out the biographical and geographical details. The second was the invention of some serious but everyday incident which would provide a starting point for the story: for example, a serious illness, a death, a separation, the discovery of some past misdemeanour, a family rupture. Often this event pushes someone to act in a way which is out of character, but has its roots in the past.

'I need to know all the character's family up to the grandfather and grandmother, although I rarely use these,' said Simenon. 'I need to know all the past... their childhood, which school they went to, how they dressed when they were 18. I need a plan of their house, their telephone number, their address, all the ins and outs, if they have brothers or sisters in law, if these are people who regularly call on one another.' Once the main characters (given names taken from a telephone directory) had been fleshed out, Simenon concerned himself with the topography. This involved studying maps, street plans and train timetables, and checking on specific details. He avoided historical research: the action often takes place at the time he is writing.

Only then, when he had a clear idea of his characters and his setting, did Simenon think about how to begin his story – and this always stemmed directly from the character he had created:

> Given this man, the place where he finds himself, where he lives, the climate in which he lives, given his profession, his work, his family – given all that, what can happen to him that pushes him to the limit?

So it's a matter of inventing some event that suddenly changes the life of the character. This event is the novel's starting point and it often takes up the first chapter of the book.

How Simenon wrote

Once he had his main character, his setting and an event that put the character under extreme pressure, Simenon began writing – without knowing how the story would develop or how it would end. When writing a novel he lived almost like a monk, not seeing or speaking to anyone or taking telephone calls. He wrote without interruption, quickly and intensely, from 6.30 to 9 a.m. every day, one chapter per day. The morning spent at the typewriter was usually preceded by a manuscript version written the previous evening (Simenon started each novel armed with four dozen new, freshly sharpened pencils). Sometimes the two versions were virtually identical and sometimes they were different.

As I tap out this piece on my laptop, I have a pile of half a dozen Maigrets beside me. Each one of them has precisely eight chapters, and most of them have 184–186 pages. For me the short length and limited vocabulary is one of the attractions (I can read them in French without having to look up more than the occasional word).

Three-quarters of Simenon's 75 Maigret novels were written in eight days, and at his peak he was producing between four and six of them a year. During these periods of intense writing he is said to have been in an almost trance-like state. Once the novel was finished, he put it away for a variable period of up to a month before undertaking a final revision, which took him just two or three days. He called this 'la toilette du style', and it meant cutting out adjectives, adverbs and any unnecessary or overblown sentences. Simenon said that the most useful piece of advice he was ever given was from an editor who told him that his early stories were 'too literary, always too literary'.

Maigret is Simenon's most famous creation, but his reputation rests equally on his non-Maigret novels (The Stain on the Snow (1948) is generally regarded as one of the best) and his autobiographical writing, notably Mémoires Intimes (1981). The writer, critic and philosopher André Gide considered him one of the twentieth century's greatest writers, 'a novelist of genius'. His output was staggering. During his 86 years he wrote 192 novels, 158 short stories and several autobiographical works under his own name – and almost as many again under innumerable pseudonyms.

A piece about Simenon has to end with Maigret. How can we explain his enduring popularity?

Maigret's character

The character of Maigret gives us part of the answer. As the blurb on one of the books in front of me puts it, he is '*parfois bougon, mais combien sympathique*' (sometimes grumpy, but so nice). He's a man of few words. When someone asks 'What do you think about it?' his invariable response is 'I don't think anything'. And if he's asked whether he thinks a suspect is guilty or innocent, his standard reply is 'I don't know'.

A man of simple tastes, most at ease in the lower middle-class environment he knows, Maigret is distrustful of the rich and powerful, and often feels uncomfortable in their company. He hates pretentiousness and condescension. He treats his inspectors (Lucas, Janvier, Torrence, Lapointe) as a second family. He likes his wife's simple, traditional French cooking (*blanquette de veau* is his favourite), and when he can't get home for lunch, or when he's conducting a long interrogation, he orders beer and sandwiches from the Brasserie Dauphine. He likes a drink and in the course of an investigation he gets through a fair number (usually beer or white wine, but he may have a cognac). Once a month he and his wife invite their friends Dr and Mrs Pardon to dinner, and once a month the invitation is reciprocated. Once a week they go to the cinema. His only real passion is his work.

The pipe-smoking Maigret is not a Poirot or a Sherlock Holmes, endowed with exceptional intelligence or powers of analysis. He's a quietly spoken observer of human nature, and his method of detection is very different from theirs. He begins by immersing himself in the environment where the crime has been committed and soaking up the atmosphere. He observes the people around him, without knowing in which direction the investigation will go. After a while he begins to identify and classify his observations and feelings. This often leads to an initial hypothesis, which he may seek to test in some way. A hesitation or a set-back may follow, with the investigation sometimes going backwards. Finally, the scenario becomes clear and Maigret gets his man (or woman).

Perhaps Maigret's most attractive quality is his humanity. There is no moral condemnation. He does not judge his criminals; he tries to understand them. Unlike, say, Agatha Christie, Simenon is not primarily interested in the identification of the murderer, or in providing a surprise solution to the crime. What interests him is the motivation: the psychology of the criminal.

A nice character

Maigret's personality provides part of the explanation for his enduring popularity. A man of few words and simple tastes, he likes a drink and enjoys his wife's traditional cooking. He tries to understand, rather than judge, his criminals. He hates pretension and he's always distrustful of the rich and the powerful. A vividly drawn character with good, simple qualities, and tastes that readers may share, can make an appealing protagonist, particularly if he sides with the man in the street against the Establishment, as Maigret often does.

Place and description

Simenon never gave a story a setting he himself did not know. Many of the Maigret novels give us a wonderfully evocative portrait of post-war Paris. He's a master of atmosphere and mood, often created by allusions to the time of year and weather, as shown in these two examples:

That morning, after a wet spring, the heat had suddenly come, and Maigret had worked with the windows open, in shirt-sleeves.

Although it was already 25th March, it was the first real day of spring, much clearer as there had been one last shower during the night, accompanied by the distant rumble of thunder. For the first time that year Maigret had left his overcoat in his office cupboard and from time to time the breeze caught his unbuttoned jacket.

The scenes are sketched with spare descriptive detail. Avoiding anything abstract or poetic, Simenon uses concrete, everyday words to paint a vivid picture in just one or two short, simple sentences.

> **Learning points**
>
> - Begin a story by deciding on the setting and creating your characters.
> - Invent a serious but everyday incident that pushes the protagonist to act out of character and in an extreme way.
> - Cut out superfluous adjectives, adverbs and unnecessary or overblown phrases.
> - Paint a vivid picture with concrete, everyday words and short, simple sentences.

MARTIN CRUZ SMITH
(1942–)

Gorky Park (1981) was the international bestseller that catapulted him to fame. From the gripping opening scene – three corpses found frozen in the snow in Gorky Park, faces and fingers missing – it's a riveting page-turner. Its publication coincided with Ronald Reagan's 'Evil Empire' speech. At that time it was a huge risk to write an American novel with a Russian hero – but it paid off. 'The US at last has a domestic Le Carré,' claimed *Time Magazine*, while *The New York Times* said: 'Cruz Smith writes extraordinarily well in a genre not usually considered literature...

[He] is not merely our best writer of suspense, but one of our best writers, period.'

Influences and beginnings

As a teenager Smith was captivated by the works of Evelyn Waugh, George Orwell and Aldous Huxley:

> Orwell and Huxley were commenting on the world in a way that made a terrific impact on a 14-year-old kid who cared about things like that. I remember being absolutely stunned by the candour of Orwell.

He took a creative writing course at the University of Pennsylvania and then earned money for a trip to Europe by selling ice cream. On returning to the States he worked for the Press Association before joining the tabloid *Philadelphia Daily News*. He then moved to New York to work for Magazine Management (editing and writing much of the content of *For Men Only*), a publishing company which was a forcing house for commercial writing talent. Among those who worked there were Mario Puzo and the American novelist and journalist John Bowers, who described the house style: 'We wasted no words getting someone through a door; we couldn't fool around with Henry Jamesian language. We learned how to hold a reader's attention, to move people and emotions quickly, something which often gives beginning writers a hard time.'

Smith's time at Magazine Management taught him to write fast, lively stories with resonant, easily understood characters. He left in 1969, when he was sacked for refusing to introduce more sexual content to the magazine. Now married, he moved to Portugal and wrote what he subsequently described as 'a terrible, terrible book that has never been published' – about a young man taking a morally questionable job as a speechwriter for the soon-to-be-disgraced American vice-president Spiro Agnew. Back in the US, he wrote his first published novel, *The Indians Won* (1970), a faux-documentary thriller set in a world where the middle of America was still Indian territory. He then embarked on a series of crime books featuring Roman Grey, a Gypsy with an eye for art and antiques. *Canto for a Gypsy* (1972) was his first book to be published in Europe. 'They were nice books in their own way,' he later said, 'but they were still very traditional in that it was a slightly exotic detective and they really operated within the parameters of a television movie.'

Gorky Park

He started work on what was to become *Gorky Park* in 1972, almost ten years before it was published. Having discovered the work of the Swedes Per Wahlöö and Maj Sjöwall, who jointly wrote socially and politically aware crime fiction, he had the idea of writing 'something big and different about Russia'. But his publisher was far from convinced, and there was a long-running dispute. During this time, while continuing to work intermittently on *Gorky Park*, he wrote a large number of formulaic crime stories, mysteries and westerns under pseudonyms that included Simon Quinn and Jake Logan.

Known to his friends as 'Bill', in 1977 he changed his middle name from William to 'Cruz' (his maternal grandmother's name) after discovering other authors writing as Martin Smith. *Nightwing* (1977), a thriller about vampire bats, was his first big commercial success. The paperback rights were sold for $400,000, and it was later made into a film. This financial security enabled him to hold out for the $1 million he eventually got for *Gorky Park*.

Gorky Park's depiction of contemporary Soviet life was so alarmingly accurate that the book was soon banned in the Soviet Union. What is so extraordinary is that Smith's descriptions of the city and its people were based on just five days he spent there in 1973, when he took a two-week Intourist holiday in the Soviet Union. He speaks no Russian, but managed to escape from the escorted visits to do his own thing: walking around the city; taking trams, buses and taxis; and sketching some of the buildings. On his return to the States he checked out the accuracy of his facts and impressions with Russians (émigrés and defectors) who were living in New York. He also studied English versions of some Soviet law books and read about the process of recreating human faces from skulls – a technique used in *Gorky Park* to identify the female victim discovered under the snow.

Smith's Moscow, with its meticulous attention to detail, is an all-pervasive presence in the book. He has said:

> *Gorky Park* may have been one of the first books to take a backdrop and make it into a character. It took me forever to write because of my need to get things right. You've got to knock down the issue of 'Does this guy know what he's talking about or not?'

Well, he certainly does. I lived and worked in the Soviet capital for two and a half years when Brezhnev was in power, and I can vouch for the authenticity of Smith's Moscow.

Smith's ability to evoke atmosphere is one of *Gorky Park*'s strengths. Another is the character of its hero, Arkady Renko. In some ways he's a classic good cop, who inevitably collides with his superiors and those in power. But there's much more to him than that. The son of a sadistic Soviet general (now retired) and a mother who committed suicide, he's a troubled, tobacco-addicted, persistent Chief Investigator, at once cynical and romantic, who both loves and loathes his country. After a privileged start in life as the son of a Hero of the Soviet Union, he has bucked the system and fallen from grace because of his refusal to sweep inconvenient truths under the carpet. He's an ambivalent, multi-layered – and hugely appealing – character.

At one stage in the book the disgraced investigator is 'treated' for supposed mental illness, and the 'doctor' gives him a chilling diagnosis:

> You have unreal expectations... You... are... suffering from the pathoheterodoxy syndrome. You overestimate your personal powers. You feel isolated from society. You swing from excitement to sadness. You mistrust the people who most want to help you. You resent authority even when you represent it. You think you are the exception to every rule. You underestimate the collective intelligence. What is right is wrong and what is wrong is right.

Convincing characterisation is one of Smith's trademarks. In the country house outside Moscow where this 'treatment' is taking place, Renko is thrown into close contact with the KGB's Major Pribluda. Early in the book Pribluda is portrayed as a stock villain who has no compunction about killing: he seems to regard it as a simple matter of obeying orders and doing his job. But when he is faced with having to make a real moral decision – whether or not to shoot Renko – he becomes more interesting – and more real. In the next Renko novel, *Polar Star* (1989), Pribluda, now promoted to Colonel, turns out to be the good guy who has rescued Renko from internment in Moscow's Serbsky Institute of Forensic Psychiatry.

William Kirwill, the NYPD detective who eventually becomes Renko's friend, is another convincingly drawn character. Here's how Smith describes Renko's discovery of Kirwill's body:

> Kirwill was waiting at the next curve. He faced them, one arm high, before a large tree, an elm. Ray stopped the car a meter in front of him. Kirwill didn't move, his eyes boring into the car and through it. Snow had settled deeply on his shoulders and hat and in the cuff of his upraised hand. ... Snow obscured the two pink holes over his breast. His face was totally white. Now Arkady saw the ropes around his waist

and wrist that tied him to the tree. … Kirwill's eyes were paler than ever, the irises collapsed. He had an expression of weariness, as if he had been condemned to carry a tree on his back all his life.

Not surprisingly, *Gorky Park* did not go down well with the Soviet authorities. When the book was banned, Smith was referred to as 'anti-Soviet scum'. However, by the time he returned to Moscow in the late 1980s, things had changed. He was treated well and the book was finally being published there.

Visit the setting

When he wrote *Gorky Park* Smith had spent just five days in Moscow. A short visit to an unknown country may provide enough material for the setting of a novel. But you'll need to do your homework, filling in the gaps with research both before and after your visit. Importantly, you'll need to make a real effort to get away from the tourists. To write about a place convincingly, you need to see things at first hand – not only the nice bits, but also the nastier side of things. You need to meet people and hear what they have to say, and what they really think, about the place. Get under the surface of the publicity brochures and find out what life there is really like.

From Cold War to Putin

Smith has written eight Arkady Renko novels, mirroring the historic upheavals that have taken place in Russia over more than 30 years. They act as a political and social timeline, taking us from the Cold War-rooted Soviet Union of Brezhnev, through Gorbachev's *perestroika* and *glasnost*, Yeltsin's failed push towards democracy and the Wild-West entrepreneurship that followed the collapse of the Soviet Union, to the hard-line control of the Putin regime.

There's a good example of Smith's ability to reflect the changing political environment in *Polar Star*. Volovoi, the Communist Party's official representative on board the factory ship, is trying to prevent any further investigation into the death of Zina Patiashvili, whose body has been hauled on board along with tons of fish:

> 'A death is a tragedy,' Volovoi said, 'but an investigation is a political decision. Any further on-board investigation would be a mistake. On this I must speak for the Party.'... 'Well,' the fleet engineer said, as if he had just thought of something. His voice had a timbre like a woodwind with a cracked reed, and he talked directly to Volovoi. 'In the past, comrade, everything you say would have been correct. It seems to me, however, that the situation has changed. We have a new leadership that has called for more initiative and a more candid examination of our mistakes. Captain Marchuk is symbolic of this new, forthright leadership.'

Tatiana

'It was the sort of day that didn't give a damn.' It's the kind of sentence that Raymond Chandler could have written. In fact, it's the first sentence of *Tatiana* (2013), the eighth Arkady Renko novel. Published after he went public with the news that he had been suffering from Parkinson's disease since 1995, it was dictated to his wife Emily. The opening is as gripping as we've come to expect. A translator in possession of a notebook full of strange symbols is killed on a desolate beach near the seaport city of Kaliningrad. The killer is a psychopathic butcher who trawls the beach in a van with a smiling plastic pig on its roof.

The stimulus for *Tatiana* was Anna Politkovskaya, the journalist who defied the Russian authorities to file critical reports on the war in Chechnya and was murdered in Moscow in 2006. Did Tatiana Petrovna jump or was she pushed? That's the question Renko has to answer. There's not much room for doubt: a journalist with a sense of mission and a belief in the possibility of a more civilised Russia, Tatiana is an unlikely candidate for suicide. But not all is as it seems. There's a twist to the story before Renko can find out exactly what happened, who did it and – more importantly – why.

Tatiana has a collection of believable characters from all levels of Russian society – artists, poets, thugs, bureaucrats, burnt-out police officers and losers living on the edge of society. Like other Arkady Renko novels, it depicts the frustrating, often absurd nature of daily life in a fractured and fascinating country.

Learning points

- A fast, lively story with resonant characters will hold the reader's attention.
- If a setting is created with real knowledge, and meticulous attention to detail, it can become a character in its own right.
- An ambivalent protagonist with lots of contradictions in his make-up can make the reader want to find out more and more about his character – and, therefore, to keep on reading.
- A novel can be used to explore periods of historical change or political turmoil.

ROBERT LOUIS STEVENSON
(1850–1894)

Human beings are not all black or white. We all have bits of good in us, and some bits that are not so good. *Strange Case of Dr Jekyll and Mr Hyde*, a novella of less than 30,000 words, takes this simple idea and pushes it to frightening extremes. Stevenson's story not only embodies good and evil – dark and light – simultaneously in one man; it also changes his physical appearance – and his personality.

Jekyll and Hyde, published in 1886, established Stevenson's reputation, but he already had a substantial body of work behind him including, most notably, *Treasure Island* (1883), his first full-length work of fiction. *Kidnapped*, also published in 1886, was another popular success.

Stevenson (or RLS, as he was known for much of his life) was a constant, restless traveller. He spent time, especially, in France, the United States and the Pacific Islands. He travelled partly out of temperament and inclination, and partly in pursuit of better health. Throughout his life he was dogged by serious illness, including tuberculosis. He died (not from TB but from a stroke) at the age of 44. In his short life he was a prolific short-story writer, travel writer, essayist and poet, but is probably best remembered for his novels. Let's focus on the three I've mentioned.

Treasure Island

Treasure Island has three distinctive characteristics: first, a gripping, swashbuckling plot that carries the reader along. The elements are pure romance, and they are hardly original: a boy, a treasure map, pirates, a deserted island and a frantic chase to find hidden gold.

Second is the creation of a unique and extraordinarily memorable character – Long John Silver, a fictional pirate who is probably more real to most people than any pirate read about in a history book. His shifting, duplicitous character and the abrupt changes in his manner and behaviour – from pleasant-tempered landlord and obliging sea-cook to bloodthirsty mutineer – are convincingly done, and the unlikely friendship and mutual respect between Silver and the cabin boy Jim Hawkins (the first-person narrator for most of the book) seem entirely credible. Jim himself develops from naïve child to a capable young man who soon learns to size up the character of his shipmates.

Finally, although *Treasure Island* is an exciting, swashbuckling yarn, there is a striking lack of sentimentality. The pirates have a barbarous past, with plenty of dastardly deeds and dead men behind them, and their conduct is brutal. The pirates' song, first heard from tyrannical Captain Flint at the Admiral Benbow, tells us what kind of behaviour we can expect: 'Fifteen men on the dead man's chest / Yo-ho-ho, and a bottle of rum! / Drink and the devil had done for the rest / Yo-ho-ho, and a bottle of rum!' Stevenson makes no attempt to romanticise the pirates, and the world that surrounds Jim is (with the sole exception of Dr Livesey) one of greed and self-interest.

Stevenson modelled the vegetation of Treasure Island on the Monterey coastline in California, where he spent several months in 1879. Long John Silver was based on the poet and critic W. E. Henley, who had suffered from tuberculosis of the bone and, with his left leg amputated below the knee, walked with the help of a crutch. 'The idea of the maimed man, ruling and dreaded by the sound, was entirely taken from you,' Stevenson told Henley, but the character of Silver may also owe something to Jules Simoneau, a 58-year-old expatriate Frenchman who ran a hostelry in Monterey and became a close friend of Stevenson's.

Jekyll and Hyde

The idea for *Jekyll and Hyde* came to Stevenson in a dream, but he acknowledged that it was inspired by the true story of Deacon Brodie's double life in Edinburgh – respected city councillor by day and burglar by night. Although Stevenson's story is set in London, it may also have been informed by Edinburgh's division into a warren-like Old Town and a respectable New Town. Like the Scottish capital, Victorian London was full of juxtapositions of class and privilege, and Stevenson makes good use of these. Dr Lanyon's Mayfair exists cheek by jowl with Hyde's Soho. In the nineteenth century Gothic fiction often explored the contradictions of Victorian society and the dividing line between civilisation and barbarism.

Jekyll and Hyde is a Gothic melodrama; but it is much more than that. It explores the idea of dualism (two parts, usually opposites, within one whole). Jekyll talks about 'the profound duplicity of life' and says that 'man is not truly one, but truly two'. Jekyll's respectability and Hyde's corruption exist simultaneously in the same body. Hyde is the evil side of Jekyll and the vices he indulges – and Stevenson is careful never to specify what these are – are desires he has repressed in order to conform to the middle-class standards of respectability expected of an eminent physician. The Jekyll/Hyde persona can also be seen as a way of exposing the hypocrisy of a society which did not always practise the moral values it preached.

Kidnapped

Kidnapped has a very simple plot: a boy sets out in the world to seek his fortune; on his travels he gets into danger and undergoes hardship; and eventually he returns, now a man, to claim his inheritance. Its enduring popularity can be explained partly by its being a 'rattling good yarn'. But there are plenty of those around, and few have endured as well as *Kidnapped*. So we need to look for other explanations. Perhaps the best clue lies in its authenticity. The historical and topographical background is described with great care and factual accuracy, and some of the scenes have the immediacy of a documentary. The characters, too, have an air of real authenticity (explained in part by Stevenson's familiarity with the Scottish character). We have the contrasting, but equally convincing, characters and perspectives of David Balfour (his first-person narrator), representing Lowland Scotland (law-abiding, prudent, Presbyterian), and the Highland Jacobite Alan Breck (feudal, romantic). Unlike *Treasure Island*, *Kidnapped* is rooted in realism.

Writing apprenticeship

Describing his writing apprenticeship, Stevenson said:

Nobody had ever such pains to learn a trade as I had; but I slogged at it, day in, day out; and I frankly believe (thanks to my dire industry) I have done more with smaller gifts than almost any man of letters in the world... Whenever I read a book or passage that particularly pleased me... in which there was either some conspicuous force or some happy distinction in style, I must sit down at once and set myself to ape that quality. I was unsuccessful... but... I got some practice in rhythm, in harmony, in construction and the coordination of parts. I have thus played the sedulous ape to Hazlitt, to Lamb, to Wordsworth, to Sir Thomas Browne, to Defoe, to Hawthorne, to Montaigne, to Baudelaire, and to Obermann.

Study, practice, impersonation: 'that,' said Stevenson, 'like it or not, is the way to learn.' The words he used to describe his debt to other writers – 'playing the sedulous ape' – have entered the lexicon of literary *bons mots*.

So those are two things writers can learn from Stevenson: the value of sticking at it 'day in, day out' and the benefit to be derived from copying the style (not the content) of a writer whose work you like. After all, that's how artists usually learn their craft – by imitating works of art which they admire.

Quantity means quality

Stevenson learned to write effectively by imitating passages of admired writers that he found particularly pleasing. By study and hard work he made the most of what he described as his 'smaller gifts'. Those who succeed in any activity or walk of life often have no more talent than their peers, but are more prepared to put in the hard graft. To become a successful writer, you need to put in the hours; there is no short cut. The good news is that writing is one of the few activities where quantity is guaranteed to mean quality. The more you write, the better you'll get.

Critical opinion and public popularity

Stevenson was a celebrated, much-praised writer in his own lifetime. After about 1914 his reputation went into a steep decline from which it has only recently recovered. For much of the twentieth century he was neglected, dismissed as a second-rate writer (excluded, for example, from the 1973 *Oxford Anthology of English Literature*) and remembered, if at all, only as a writer of children's books and horror stories.

More recently, however, Stevenson's ability to depict a simple series of actions in the freshest and most engaging way, together with the rhythm and flow of his sentences, have been recognised and appreciated afresh. Critics have pointed approvingly to 'the clean light clarity of his style', 'miraculously simple and unadorned', and have praised the 'verbal exactitude and economy' of his writing and 'the moral nucleus' of his stories.

Many critics now place Stevenson alongside writers such as Joseph Conrad and Henry James, and today he ranks among the 30 most translated authors in the world. He spent his last years in Samoa, where he adopted the native name Tusitala. It means 'a teller of tales'. That's not a bad epitaph for someone who was, above all, a great storyteller.

Learning points

- Study and imitate the writing styles of authors you admire.
- A gripping, action-packed, fast-paced plot forces the reader to keep turning the pages.
- Strong characters that leap off the page attract our interest, whether they are good or bad.
- A simple theme (such as *Jekyll and Hyde*'s good versus evil or *Treasure Island*'s search for gold) can be hugely compelling.
- Accurate topographical description and authentic historical background can give a story a feeling of realism and immediacy.

EVELYN WAUGH
(1903–1966)

'I expect you'll become a schoolmaster, sir. That's what most of the gentlemen does, sir, that gets sent down for indecent behaviour.' These words are from *Decline and Fall* (1928), Evelyn Waugh's first published novel. It draws on his undergraduate years at Oxford as well as the short time he subsequently spent as a teacher (he was not sent down from Oxford, but he led a dissolute life there and left with a third-class degree). 'Write what you know' is the advice routinely given to new writers, and there are few better exemplars than Evelyn Waugh. To a large extent his 17 novels fictionalise the main events of his life.

Early satirical novels

In 1925 Waugh spent six months teaching at a prep school in North Wales, experience reflected in the first chapter of *Decline and Fall*. The hero considers an advertisement for a teaching position in Wales:

> *Augustus Fagan, Esquire, Ph.D., Llanabba Castle, N. Wales, requires immediately junior assistant to teach Classics and English to University Standard with subsidiary Mathematics, German and French. Experience essential; first-class games essential...*
>
> 'Might have been made for you,' said Mr Levy.
>
> 'But I don't know a word of German, I've had no experience, I've got no testimonials, and I can't play cricket.'
>
> 'It doesn't do to be too modest,' said Mr Levy. 'It's wonderful what one can teach when one tries.'

Decline and Fall and *Vile Bodies* (1930) satirise the hedonism and amorality of the Bright Young People who dominated fashionable

London society in the 1920s. The incessant round of mad party-going depicted in *Vile Bodies* draws on the intense social life which Waugh led intermittently between 1924 and 1927. The novel demonstrates Waugh's aptitude for exposing false attitudes as well as his keen appreciation of the ridiculous, and there are some good comic lines: 'All this fuss about sleeping together. For physical pleasure I'd sooner go to my dentist any day,' says the principal female character. The most amusing scene, in which Agatha Runcible unwittingly gatecrashes 10 Downing Street, is based on a real incident. Two young women friends of Waugh, who had gone to a party and left their latch key behind, turned up in distress very late at night at the home of Prime Minister Stanley Baldwin.

Both *Decline and Fall* and *Vile Bodies* satirise the smart, upper-crust London society to which Waugh aspired. The world he depicts is one of frivolity and futility. Although many of the characters are two-dimensional and unbelievable, these novels have stood the test of time, largely due to Waugh's gift for writing dialogue that is both clever and very funny.

By contrast, William Boot, the hero of *Scoop* (1938), is a believable comic character. He may be naïve and eccentric, but he is principled and well-meaning – and the reader cares about him. An obscure nature correspondent with a distinctly OTT writing style ('feather-footed through the plashy fen passes the questing vole'), he is plucked from the country-house obscurity he loves and sent as war correspondent to the African Republic of Ishmaelia. It's a case of mistaken identity by Lord Copper, the domineering newspaper magnate, owner of Fleet Street's *Daily Beast*, who prides himself on his flair for discovering ace reporters. With his *folie de grandeur,* Copper was thought to be based partly on the *Daily Mail*'s Lord Rothermere and partly on the *Daily Express*'s Lord Beaverbrook, while his habit of giving ridiculous orders to underlings may have owed something to the ageing Lord Northcliffe. Today's readers may see him as the megalomaniac forerunner of Robert Maxwell, Conrad Black and Rupert Murdoch. Lord Copper is a man to whom his employees never dare to say 'no'. They limit their side of any conversation to expressions of assent. When he is right, they say, 'Definitely, Lord Copper.' When he is wrong, it's, 'Up to a point, Lord Copper.'

In *Scoop*, a satire on journalism and foreign correspondents, Waugh drew on his experience as a temporary war correspondent for the *Daily Mail* in Abyssinia. Boot is said to have been based partly on Bill Deedes, who as a young man covered the Abyssinian war for the *Morning Post* and went on to become an eminent journalist and politician. However, the truth is probably more complicated. Deedes himself wrote that: 'Waugh like most good novelists drew on more than one person for each of his characters. He drew on me for my excessive baggage – and perhaps for my naivety.' Another model was almost certainly William Beach Thomas, a quietly successful countryside columnist, who became a hopeless *Daily Mail* war correspondent. He described Britain's first battle day on the Somme (19,000 British dead): 'All went well.' Thomas and his fellow correspondents dished up the false reports that army intelligence gave them.

Brideshead

Brideshead Revisited – The Sacred and Profane Memories of Captain Charles Ryder (1945) marked a departure from Waugh's previous satirical style. It was written at Chagford in Devon during a six-month period of leave from Waugh's war service as an Army officer. He notes in his diary: 'Up at 8.30… and at work before 10… by dinner time I had finished 1,300 words all of which were written twice and many three times before I got the time sequence and the transitions satisfactory.' Then later: 'Working steadily; much rewriting; 1,500–2,000 words a day. Today an arduous revision, rescription and reordering.' Waugh wrote by hand and sent each chapter off to be typed as it was completed. He then revised the typed manuscript again. He began work on *Brideshead* on 1 February 1944 and on 16 April he notes in his diary, 'I have completed the revision, with many changes, of the first two books of the novel.' He finished the last chapter on 6 June.

Brideshead was probably based on Madresfield Court in Worcestershire, the family seat of William Lygon, the Seventh Earl Beauchamp, where Waugh was a frequent visitor. Hugh Lygon, the Earl's second son, was a friend of Waugh's at Oxford and almost certainly the basis for Sebastian Flyte. Earl Beauchamp himself is generally regarded as the model for Brideshead's exiled Lord Marchmain.

Bridehead enjoyed immense popularity on both sides of the Atlantic. With its selection as American Book of the Month, sales in the US dwarfed those in Britain. In 1981 the novel was given a new lease of life by Granada's hugely successful television adaptation (starring Anthony Andrews and Jeremy Irons), which introduced a new generation of readers to Waugh.

It's the first of Waugh's novels in which his Catholic religion and his right-wing politics come clearly into focus. At the beginning and the end of the book he also introduces, through the character of the junior officer Hooper, a theme that was to persist in his post-war fiction: the rise of mediocrity in the Age of the Common Man.

Brideshead divided (and continues to divide) the critics. Some regarded it as overwritten, disliked the perceived snobbery and deference to aristocracy, and felt that Waugh had lost the ironic detachment of his earlier novels. Many others rated it very highly – and for some, it was his masterpiece.

Diaries, non-fiction and style

Waugh is best known for his novels, but he was a prolific writer whose work included short stories and an enormous amount of non-fiction – travel writing (based particularly on his many trips overseas in the 1930s), biography, journalism, essays, reviews and autobiography. He was a keen letter-writer, and he kept diaries almost continuously from the age of seven until a year before his death in 1966.

In an article for the *Daily Mail* (28 July 1930) he commended the practice of keeping a diary:

> It is not necessary to be in touch with famous people in order to write a valuable diary... Nobody wants to read other people's reflections on life and religion and politics, but the routine of their day, properly recorded, is always interesting and will become more so as conditions change with the years.

Keep a diary

A regular diary (or, these days, a blog) can help to get your mind and body prepared for the task of writing. Putting into words (either on paper or on a computer screen) something you have done or felt in the recent past – importantly, without much thought or reflection – may produce a piece of writing that is more immediate, more lively and more authentic than something you have thought about and worked on over a longer period.

Waugh's diaries (serialised in *The Observer* prior to their publication in book form in 1976) testify to his cantankerous character, and some entries support a view of him as snobbish, intolerant, and contemptuous of those he regarded as his inferiors. His comments on friends and acquaintances are candid, entertaining and occasionally malicious. On joining a new Army unit he observes: 'There was no Officer who would have been worth making a corporal... Colonel X was insane... Officer Y a dipsomaniac.' Randolph Churchill, who asked Waugh to join his military mission to Croatia (Yugoslavia) in the second half of 1944, is 'a flabby bully who rejoices in blustering and shouting down anyone weaker than himself and starts squealing as soon as he meets anyone as strong… a bore – with no intellectual invention or agility… no independence of character.' Waugh noted later: 'How boring it was to be obliged to tell Randolph everything twice – once when he was drunk and once when sober.'

An attractive feature of Waugh's diaries is that he is as hard on himself as he is on others. He concludes his diatribe against Randolph with this realistic assessment: 'He is not a good companion for a long period, but the conclusion is always the same – that no-one else would have chosen me, nor would anyone else have accepted him.' Two people who were not easy for others to get on with.

More importantly for any writer, the diaries reveal Waugh's astonishing capacity for meticulous observation of the world around him. They clearly provided much raw material for both his fiction and his non-fiction. They also show his ferocious intelligence, his acute sense of the ridiculous and his keen eye for caricature.

Waugh is widely regarded as a master of style. In the view of critic Clive James 'Nobody ever wrote a more unaffectedly elegant English'; while Graham Greene (in a letter to *The Times*) saw him as 'the greatest novelist of my generation'. His novels, said *Time Magazine*, 'will continue to survive as long as there are readers who can savour what critic V. S. Pritchett calls "the beauty of his malice".'

Learning points

- Write what you know: you can fictionalise your own life.
- Draw on people you know to create composite fictional characters.
- A comic character needs to be believable.
- Constantly observe the world around you.
- The absurdities of modern life provide plenty of raw material for satire.

BIBLIOGRAPHY
OF PRIMARY SOURCES

This bibliography lists, alphabetically by author, the publications from which illustrative passages are quoted. It gives the date of first publication and, in the case of modern texts, the place and publisher of first publication in the UK and US, together with imprints of paperback editions (pb) available in the UK and US at the time of compilation (April 2017).

Austen, Jane *Sense and Sensibility*. 1811. UK and US pb Penguin.

Pride and Prejudice. 1813. UK and US pb Penguin.

Emma. 1815. UK and US pb Penguin.

Ballard, J. G. *The Drowned World*. London, Gollancz, 1962. New York, Berkley, 1962. UK pb Fourth Estate; US pb Liveright.

Empire of the Sun. London, Gollancz, 1984. New York, Simon & Schuster, 1984. UK pb Fourth Estate; US pb Simon & Schuster.

Miracles of Life. London, Fourth Estate, 2008. New York, Liveright, 2008. UK pb Fourth Estate; US pb HarperCollins.

Bennett, Alan *Writing Home*. London, Faber & Faber, 1994. New York, Random House, 1994. UK pb Faber & Faber; US pb Picador.

The History Boys. London, Faber & Faber, 2004. New York, Farrar, Straus & Giroux, 2006. UK pb Faber & Faber; US pb Farrar, Straus & Giroux

Untold Stories. London, Faber & Faber, 2005. New York, Picador, 2007. UK pb Faber & Faber; US pb Picador.

Keeping On Keeping On. London, Faber & Faber, 2016.

Brontë, Charlotte *Jane Eyre*. 1847. UK and US pb Penguin.

Brontë, Emily *Wuthering Heights*. 1847. UK and US pb Penguin.

Brown, Dan *The Da Vinci Code*. New York, Doubleday, 2003. London, Bantam Press, 2003. UK pb Corgi Adult; US pb Doubleday.

Bryson, Bill *The Lost Continent: Travels in Small-Town America*. London, Secker & Warburg, 1989. New York, Harper & Row, 1989. UK pb Secker & Warburg; US pb HarperCollins.

Neither Here Nor There: Travels in Europe. London, Secker & Warburg, 1991. New York, William Morrow, 1992. UK pb Black Swan; US pb Harper Perennial.

Notes from a Small Island. London, Doubleday, 1995. New York, William Morrow, 1995. UK pb Black Swan; US pb HarperCollins.

The Road to Little Dribbling: More Notes from a Small Island. London, Doubleday, 2015. New York, Doubleday, 2015. UK pb Black Swan; US pb Anchor Books.

Notes from a Big Country. London, Doubleday, 1998. New York, Broadway Books, 1999 (*I'm a Stranger Here Myself*). UK pb Black Swan; US pb Bantam Doubleday Dell.

Burgess, Anthony *A Clockwork Orange*. London, William Heinemann, 1962. New York, W. W. Norton & Company, 1963. UK pb Penguin; US pb W. W. Norton & Company.

Le Carré, John *The Constant Gardener*. London, Hodder & Stoughton, 2001. New York, Scribner, 2000. UK pb Hodder & Stoughton; US pb Scribner.

The Pigeon Tunnel: Stories from My Life. London, Viking, 2016. New York, Penguin, 2016. UK and US pb Penguin.

Tinker Tailor Soldier Spy. London, Hodder & Stoughton, 1974. New York, Alfred A. Knopft, 1974. UK pb Sceptre, Hodder & Stoughton; US pb Scribner.

Carroll, Lewis *Alice's Adventures in Wonderland*. 1865. UK pb William Collins; US pb Dover Publications.

Through the Looking Glass, and What Alice Found There. 1871. UK pb Macmillan; US pb Random House.

Chandler, Raymond *The Big Sleep*. London, Hamish Hamilton, 1939. New York, Alfred A. Knopf, 1939. UK pb Penguin; US pb Vintage Crime/Black Lizard.

Farewell, My Lovely. New York, Alfred A. Knopf, 1940. London, Hamish Hamilton, 1940. UK pb Penguin; US pb Vintage Crime/Black Lizard.

The Long Good-Bye. London, Hamish Hamilton, 1953. Boston, Houghton Mifflin, 1953. UK pb Penguin; US pb Vintage Crime/Black Lizard.

Chevalier, Tracy *Girl with a Pearl Earring*. London, HarperCollins, 1999. New York, Dutton, 1999. UK pb HarperCollins; US pb Penguin.

Child, Lee *Killing Floor*. New York, Putnam, 1997. London, Bantam Press, 1998. UK pb Bantam; US pb Berkley.

Christie, Agatha *Appointment with Death*. London, Collins Crime Club, 1938. US, Dodd, Mead and Company, 1938. UK pb HarperCollins; US pb William Morrow.

Cat Among the Pigeons. London, Collins Crime Club, 1959. New York, Dodd, Mead & Company, 1959. UK pb HarperCollins; US pb William Morrow.

Coben, Harlan *Deal Breaker*. New York, Dell, 1995. London, Orion, 2001. UK pb Orion; US pb Dell.

Dahl, Roald *James and the Giant Peach*. New York, Alfred A. Knopf, 1961. London, George Allen & Unwin, 1967. US and UK pb Puffin.

Charlie and the Chocolate Factory. New York, Alfred A. Knopf, 1964. London, George Allen & Unwin, 1967. US and UK pb Puffin.

The BFG. London, Jonathan Cape, 1982. New York, Farrar, Straus & Giroux, 1982. UK and US pb Puffin.

Ellroy, James *L.A. Confidential*. New York, The Mysterious Press, 1990. London, Mysterious Press, 1990. US pb Grand Central Publishing; UK pb Windmill Books.

Farrell, J. G. *The Siege of Krishnapur*. London, Weidenfeld & Nicolson, 1973. New York, Harcourt Brace & Company, 1974. UK pb Orion; US pb NYRB Classics.

Fielding, Helen *Bridget Jones's Diary*. London, Picador, 1996. US, Viking, 1998. UK pb Picador; US pb Penguin.

Fleming, Ian *Thunderball*. UK, Jonathan Cape, 1961. New York, Viking, 1961. UK pb Vintage; US pb Thomas & Mercer.

Dr. No. London, Jonathan Cape, 1958. New York, Macmillan, 1958 *(Doctor No)*. UK pb Vintage; US pb Thomas & Mercer.

Ford, Madox Ford *The Good Soldier: A Tale of Passion*. 1915. UK pb Collins; US pb Penguin.

Parade's End. 1924–1928. UK pb Wordsworth; US pb Vintage.

Grahame, Kenneth *The Wind in the Willows*. 1908. UK and US pb Penguin.

Greene, Graham *Brighton Rock*. London, William Heinemann, 1938. New York, Viking, 1938. UK pb Vintage; US pb Penguin.

The Third Man. London, William Heinemann, 1950. New York, Viking, 1950. UK pb Vintage; US pb Penguin.

Our Man in Havana. London, William Heinemann, 1958. New York, Viking, 1958. UK pb Vintage; US pb Penguin.

Grisham, John *A Painted House*. New York, Doubleday, 2001. London, Century, 2001. US pb Dell; UK pb Arrow Books.

Hardy, Thomas *The Return of the Native*. 1878. UK pb Wordsworth; US pb Penguin.

The Woodlanders. 1887. UK pb Wordsworth; US pb OUP.

Hemingway, Ernest *A Farewell to Arms*. London, Jonathan Cape, 1929. New York, Scribner, 1929. UK pb Vintage; US pb Scribner.

A Moveable Feast. London, Jonathan Cape, 1964. New York, Scribner, 1964. UK pb Arrow Books; US pb Scribner.

Herbert, James *The Rats*. London, New English Library, 1974. New York, Signet, 1975. UK pb Pan Books; US pb Pan Macmillan.

Ash. London, Pan Macmillan, 2012. New York, Tor Books, 2012. UK pb Pan Macmillan Books; US pb Tor Books.

Herriot, James *If Only They Could Talk*. London, Michael Joseph, 1970. New York, St. Martin's Press, 1972 *(All Creatures Great and Small)*. UK pb Pan Books; US pb St Martin's Griffin.

Let Sleeping Vets Lie. London, Michael Joseph, 1973. New York, St. Martin's Press, 1974 *(All Things Bright and Beautiful)*. UK pb Pan Books; US pb St Martin's Griffin.

Every Living Thing. London, Michael Joseph, 1992. New York, St. Martin's Press, 1992. UK pb Pan Books; US pb St. Martin's Griffin.

Huxley, Aldous *Brave New World*. London, Chatto & Windus, 1932. New York, Doubleday Doran, 1932. UK pb Vintage; US pb Harper Perennial.

Jacobson, Howard *Coming from Behind*. London, Chatto & Windus, 1983. New York, St. Martin's Press, 1984. UK and US pb Vintage.

King, Stephen *The Shining*. New York, Doubleday, 1977. London, New English Library, 1977. US pb Anchor; UK pb Hodder & Stoughton.

The Drawing of the Three. West Kingston, Donald M. Grant, 1987. London, Sphere Books, 1989. US pb Scribner; UK pb Hodder & Stoughton.

Lee, Harper *To Kill a Mockingbird*. Philadelphia & New York, J. B. Lippincott Co., 1960. London, William Heinemann, 1960. US pb Harper Perennial; UK pb Arrow Books.

Go Set a Watchman. New York, HarperCollins, 2015. London, William Heinemann, 2015. US pb Harper Perennial; UK pb Arrow Books.

Leonard, Elmore *Glitz*. New York, Arbor House, 1985. London, Viking, 1985. US pb William Morrow; UK pb Orion.

Get Shorty. New York, Delacorte Press, 1990. London, Viking, 1990. US pb William Morrow; UK pb Orion.

Mantel, Hilary *Wolf Hall*. London, Fourth Estate, 2009. New York, Henry Holt & Co, 2009. UK pb Fourth Estate; US pb Picador.

Orwell, George *The Collected Essays, Journalism and Letters of George Orwell*. London, Martin Secker & Warburg, 1968. US Harcourt, Brace & World, 1968. UK pb Penguin; US pb David R. Godine.

Nineteen Eighty-Four. London, Martin Secker & Warburg, 1949. New York, Harcourt, Brace & Company, 1949. UK pb Penguin; US pb Signet.

Potter, Beatrix *The Tale of Peter Rabbit*. 1902. UK pb Frederick Warne & Co.; US pb Penguin.

The Tailor of Gloucester. 1903. UK pb Frederick Warne & Co.; US pb Penguin.

Rankin, Ian *Exit Music*. London, Orion, 2007. Boston, Little, Brown and Company, 2008. UK pb Orion; US pb Back Bay Books.

Let it Bleed. London, Orion, 1995. New York, Simon & Schuster, 1996. UK pb Orion; US pb Minotaur Books.

Black & Blue. London, Orion, 1997. New York, St. Martin's Press, 1997. UK pb Orion; US pb Minotaur Books.

Rendell, Ruth *A Judgement in Stone*. London, Hutchinson, 1977. New York, Doubleday 1978. UK pb Arrow Books; US pb Vintage Crime/Black Lizard.

The Monster in the Box. London, Hutchinson, 2009. New York, Scribner, 2009. UK pb Arrow Books; US pb Scribner.

Rowling, J. K. *Harry Potter and the Deathly Hallows*. London, Bloomsbury, 2007. New York, Arthur A. Levine, 2007. UK pb Bloomsbury; US pb Arthur A. Levine.

Harry Potter and the Goblet of Fire. UK, Bloomsbury, 2000; US, Arthur A. Levine, 2000. UK pb Bloomsbury; US pb Scholastic.

Rushdie, Salman *Midnight's Children*. London, Jonathan Cape, 1981. US, Alfred A. Knopf, 1981. UK pb Vintage; US pb Random House.

Shame. UK, Jonathan Cape, 1983. New York, Alfred A. Knopf, 1983. UK pb Vintage; US pb Random House.

Sansom, C. J. *Heartstone*. London, Mantle Books, 2010. New York, Viking, 2011. UK pb Pan Books; US pb Penguin.

Seuss, Dr. *And To Think That I Saw It On Mulberry Street*. New York, Vanguard Press, 1937. London, HarperCollins, 1937. US and UK pb HarperCollins.

The Cat in the Hat. New York, Random House, 1957. London, HarperCollins, 1958. US pb Random House; UK pb HarperCollins.

Green Eggs and Ham. New York, Random House, 1960. London, HarperCollins, 1960. US pb Random House; UK pb HarperCollins.

Simenon, Georges *Maigret et le Clochard*. Paris, Presses de la Cité, 1963. London, Hamish Hamilton, 1973 (*Maigret and the Dosser*). New York, Harcourt Brace Jovanovich, 1973 (*Maigret and the Bum*). US pb Harcourt Brace Jovanovich.

Smith, Martin Cruz *Gorky Park*. New York, Random House, 1981. London, Collins, 1981. US pb Ballantine Books; UK pb Simon & Schuster.

Polar Star. New York, Random House, 1989. London, Macmillan, 1989. US pb Ballantine Books; UK pb Simon & Schuster.

Tatiana. New York and London, Simon & Schuster, 2013. US and UK pb Simon & Schuster.

Steinbeck, John *Sweet Thursday*. New York, Viking, 1954. US and UK pb Penguin.

Stevenson, Robert Louis *Treasure Island*. 1883. UK pb Alma Classics; US pb Dover Publications.

Strange Case of Dr Jekyll and Mr Hyde. 1886. UK and US pb Penguin.

Waugh, Evelyn *Decline and Fall*. London Chapman & Hall, 1928. New York, Doubleday, Doran & Co, 1929. UK pb Penguin; US pb Back Bay Books.

Vile Bodies. London, Chapman & Hall, 1930. New York, Jonathan Cape/Harrison Smith, 1930. UK pb Penguin; US pb Back Bay Books.

Scoop. London, Chapman & Hall, 1938. Boston, Little, Brown and Company, 1938. UK pb Penguin; US pb Back Bay Books.

The Diaries of Evelyn Waugh. London, Weidenfeld & Nicolson, 1976. Boston, Little, Brown and Company, 1976. UK pb Penguin; US pb Phoenix.

ACKNOWLEDGEMENTS

The articles on which this book is based were originally published (between September 2009 and April 2017) in *Writing Magazine*. I should like to thank the magazine's editor Jonathan Telfer for his longstanding and continuing commitment to the 'Beat the bestsellers' column.

At Summersdale I should particularly like to thank Claire Plimmer, who recognised the potential of this project and gave it her enthusiastic support, and my editors Robert Drew and Abbie Headon, who encouraged me with sound advice, helpful suggestions and, not least, good humour.